REA

ALLEN COUNTY PUBLIC LIBRARY

FRIENDS
OF

818
Stahl, J. D.
Mark Twain,
gender

D1482846

ALLEN COUNTY PUBLIC LIBRARY
FORT WAYNE, INDIANA 46802

You may return this book to any location of
the Allen County Public Library.

DEMCO

Mark Twain,
CULTURE AND GENDER

Samuel Clemens sitting for a sculpture portrait by Theresa
Fedorowna Ries, Vienna, Austria, 1897. Photograph by Scolik.
Picture Archives of the Austrian National Library, Vienna.

Mark Twain,

CULTURE AND

GENDER

ENVISIONING

AMERICA

THROUGH EUROPE

J. D. STAHL

THE UNIVERSITY OF GEORGIA PRESS

ATHENS AND LONDON

© 1994 by the University of Georgia Press
Athens, Georgia 30602
All rights reserved
Designed by Betty Palmer McDaniel
Set in 11.5 on 13 Garamond #3
by Tseng Information Systems, Inc.
Printed and bound by Thomson-Shore, Inc.
The paper in this book meets the guidelines for
permanence and durability of the Committee on
Production Guidelines for Book Longevity of the
Council on Library Resources.

Printed in the United States of America

98 97 96 95 94   C   5 4 3 2 1

Allen County Public Library
900 Webster Street
PO Box 2270
Fort Wayne. IN 46801 2270

Library of Congress Cataloging in Publication Data

Stahl, J. D. (John Daniel)
Mark Twain, culture and gender : envisioning
America through Europe / J. D. Stahl.
p.   cm.
Includes bibliographical references and index.
ISBN 0–8203–1559–1 (alk. paper)
1. Twain, Mark, 1835–1910—Knowledge—Europe.
2. National characteristics, American, in literature.
3. American literature—European influences.
4. Americans in literature.   5. Sex role in literature.
6. Europe in literature.   I. Title.
PS1342.E85S7   1994
818'.409—dc20   93-12347

British Library Cataloging in Publication Data available

To the memory of my mother
LOIS KRAYBILL STAHL

Contents

Preface

Every generation should produce its own literary history.
—SACVAN BERCOVITCH

My method in this book is to read Samuel Clemens's texts closely, examining what they reveal about his constructions of gender and culture. Much of the time I read Clemens's writing as if it were all on one level, whether it is a private journal entry, a published sketch, a travel book, or a novel. I assume that each form of writing says something about its author, though of course I pay attention to his tone, the characters through whom he states opinions, and the context of his writing. Nevertheless, I often read "against the grain" of traditional critical practice in the sense that I do not assume that different forms and contexts are necessarily to be interpreted separately and in different ways. I also pay attention to the conscious and possibly unconscious double meanings in Clemens's writings, especially the ironies, contradictions, and puns that reveal more than Clemens may have intended.

Discussion of the "unconscious" implications of a writer's work raises the controversial issue of the relation between an author's intentions and the significations of a text. E. D. Hirsch, in *Validity in Interpretation,* makes a sharp distinction between "meaning," which he defines as "that which is represented by a text . . . what the author meant by his use of a particular sign sequence . . . what the signs represent," and "significance," which, to him, "names a relationship between that meaning and a person, or a conception, or a situation, or indeed anything imaginable" (8).[1] Without delving into the

problematic issue of whether "meaning" can be separated her-
meneutically from "significance" as neatly as Hirsch seems to
think (and I am philosophically inclined to think that it cannot), I wish to state clearly at the outset that my study inves-
tigates "significance" as well as "meaning" in Hirsch's sense of
those terms. I do not, unlike some Mark Twain critics, such
as Everett Carter, for example, restrict myself to the pursuit
of "meaning" alone.[2] My aim is not to confirm a preconceived
theory of what Mark Twain's text says but rather to discover
what his fiction and nonfiction tell us that he himself may not
have been willing or able to state analytically or directly. I believe that the pursuit of "significance" is legitimate. I find some
confirmation of my purpose in Hirsch's emphatic acknowledgment that "it would be very foolish to say that symptomatic,
involuntary meanings are not a proper and legitimate concern of
criticism. In fact, they are one of the most interesting subjects
of critical inquiry," he adds (56).[3] As Gregory Ulmer has argued
in his interpretation of Derridean philosophy, "the meaning
effect may occur in the absence of, or against the grain of, any
intended communication in the restricted sense. . . . Writing
may serve as a vehicle for transporting a content of ideas, but
this aspect does not exhaust the event of sense" (25). In this process, however, I do consider myself bound to what the text says;
I am not attempting to "invent" a new text or a new author. I am
simply trying to see, without some of the preconceptions which
it is easy to bring to familiar—and unfamiliar—texts, what is
there in the texts that is not necessarily easy to see. In pursuit
of "significance," I seek to avoid the ahistorical procedure of
claiming authorial intentions that are anachronistic, but I do
believe in the validity of seeing more in what an author wrote
than he or she meant and of using modern critical and theoretical terminology to discuss it. I agree with Alfred Habegger,
who states, "My basic equation—character types are a symbolic
form of ideal gender roles" (x).

Mark Twain's predominant myth of gender is the all-pervasive search of the son for his father. But that myth has many ancillary narratives worthy of analysis for their own sake and in relation to his central story and its variations. In reading Twain's narratives and his comments about cultural and gender issues in letters, notebooks, and speeches, I seek to illuminate the familiar through a process of selective estrangement. By "Mark Twain" I refer to the public persona Samuel Clemens created, though I recognize that the lines of distinction between Clemens and Mark Twain often blur.

It is important to see that Samuel Clemens's psychological dilemmas, as they are manifested in his fictional representations, are both an evolving quest for cultural and personal authority and attempts to imagine resolutions to some of the contradictions between ideology, desire, and reality. What value we assign to his fictional creations will depend in large part on how we judge the nature of the goals behind his efforts of imagination. Of the many ways in which we can approach Mark Twain's works, I am particularly interested in this book in several interconnected themes.

What are the psychological inner workings of Mark Twain's characters, especially with regard to sexuality and gender? Among Twain's characters I include Mark Twain himself, who is both a semifictional character in Samuel Clemens's autobiographical writings and a narrative presence in the fiction by "Mark Twain." How do Twain's male characters think of themselves as male, and how do his female characters think of themselves as female or reveal themselves through their actions as culturally marked as female? How does Mark Twain envision his characters as masculine and feminine, and how do the storytellers within his stories conceive of gender, and why? Though I recognize the risks of applying speculative psychology to fictional or semifictional characters, I think there is also much to be gained by interrogating a text with such questions in mind, particularly when the critic pays close and accurate attention to the details and patterns of the text, as I believe I have done.

The discovery of the physical reality of the body beneath the comfortable surface of quotidian life is one of the ancillary narratives that run throughout Mark Twain's works. It seems to me that one of the features of Twain's genius is that, in spite of all his idealism, he seldom forgot that, as human beings, we inhabit startlingly real and particular bodies. Twain did not forget or ignore that we share the experience of physicality with the animals, and, like so many of the great satirists, he felt at times an intense revulsion against the flesh. However, he also took great comfort and pleasure in the body. The sudden awareness of physical being, sometimes grotesque and threatening, sometimes simple and comforting, recurs throughout Mark Twain's works as a counterpoint to flights of fancy, idealistic aspirations, and the dullness of habit. There is no doubt that Mark Twain was squeamish—or, to put it charitably, extremely cautious— about including the physicality of sex in his published works. Yet the evidence suggests that he was not squeamish in private and that he was neither prudish nor lacking sensuality. What then does his sense of decorum about sexual matters mean? It signifies more than a prevalent double standard of public versus private, I believe. Though the realities of sex are generally well hidden in Twain's work, there are not infrequently hints of sexual significance visible in the apparently nonsexual allusions to bodily being. Where does he let his sense of decorum slip, and where does it reveal more than he may have intended to reveal?

I have largely chosen to limit myself to Mark Twain's works set in Europe, a choice that perhaps requires some explanation. As an American who grew up in Europe, I began my studies of Twain with a fascination with his representative Americanness. I was interested in how Twain, as an archetypal American, perceived and portrayed Europe. As I investigated his uses of what

Henry Nash Smith has so aptly called "the matter of Europe,"
I began to see that the preoccupations with which Twain approached Europe were as much psychological as cultural. His
ways of representing himself vis-à-vis Europe not only had a
great deal to do with how he perceived himself as a *man*, they revealed a gendering imagination at work, using the materials of
European history and society as ways of exploring and defining
his understanding of masculinity and femininity. The "matter of
Europe" furnished Mark Twain with culturally potent images
of power, authority, and tradition. These images were plastic
material in his hands: he sculpted them with a freedom—or obsession—that revealed his own character and aspirations as well
as those of his culture and time. History is always a subjective
construct, but Mark Twain in his uses of European history was
frequently not even interested primarily in accurate representations of historical events, even when he claimed to be. Instead,
his shaping of characters and events borrowed from European
history served to express the conflicts and uncertainties of gender in America: what it meant to be a man in Victorian America;
what Twain thought it meant to be a woman; how men and
women did, could, or should relate to each other. Thus I found
that the European works are revealing embodiments of Twain's
explorations of gender and sexuality. In a sense, the distance
from what he was most familiar with, the exoticism of foreign
culture, was also what enabled Twain to pour into his European
writings some of his most intimate preoccupations.

One of those preoccupations, already mentioned, is the
archetypal son's search for a symbolic father, a theme that unites
many of his American works with the works set in Europe. The
father-son relationship, and the quest for father-son ties, are
at the center of many of his fictions. But the father figure is
rarely the physical father; rather, it is often a surrogate father
whose role in the son's life is defined frequently by social roles
founded in European society and history. Priests, kings, and

aristocrats provided Mark Twain with psychologically as well as socially significant types to express hopes for intimacy and social success in a kind of symbolic shorthand. Similarly, queens (especially Queen Elizabeth), aristocratic ladies, and servant women furnished Twain with female types who enact symbolic fears and desires in a kind of shadow play of the imagination in his fictional works and travel narratives.

One of the most significant and yet until recently relatively unexplored dimensions of Twain's writing is his use of popular and stereotypical images of masculinity and femininity. Alfred Habegger has written that "the United States, without the ballast of a landed aristocracy or a massive cultural inheritance, gave way to the pressures of industrialism in a most illuminating way: men were redefined in terms of business interests, women in terms of the home; and this separation in their spheres of activity tended to lead to separate goals, values, and ethical systems. Men respected men who were shrewd, aggressive, and self-seeking; while women, practicing the imitation of Christ, looked on love and nurture as the essential feminine traits" (23). Thus the "sentimental," idealistic, compassionate, and relational qualities became associated with "feminine," and the "tough-mindedness," competitiveness, practicality and mechanical skill of stock exchange and battlefield came to be thought of as characteristic of "masculine." These associations are part of the often unconscious vocabulary of characterization employed by Mark Twain, expressing, perpetuating, and in some cases subtly altering the gender images prevalent in his society. The symbolic vocabulary of European images that he drew on served him to express an American gender ideology that shared much in common with British and other contemporary ideas about gender but was also often distinctively American in content. The particular forms Twain gave to mother-daughter, father-daughter, and mother-son relationships (the latter two appear far less frequently than father-son and mother-daughter relationships) are conditioned by their

representation through symbolic modes derived from or projected into the European scene. For example, one of his most
frequent images of mother-daughter ties is a scene of execution
at the stake: the mother is about to be burned, and the daughter
is torn away by soldiers. Mother and daughter are in an agony
of grief. Though the scene could refer to New England witch
executions or to the parting of mothers and daughters at slave
auction, it is in fact most frequently located in the European
past. It is necessary to ask why so many of Mark Twain's women
are martyred and why so many of his central male characters
are essentially self-glorifying adolescents. The answers contain
clues not only to the nature of Mark Twain or Samuel Clemens
but to the shape of his culture, his nation, and his era and
ultimately to the issues that shape us as his readers.

I leave to other scholars and critics the question of the relative importance of the European writings in comparison with
"the matter of Hannibal" and the works rooted in the American
scene generally. It seems to me that one's answer to that question of comparative value depends largely on one's particular
cultural bias. Certainly Mark Twain's vivid vernacular representations of American landscapes, characters, speech forms,
habits, and values have served to define a major strand of American culture. American literary and cultural histories have employed Twain's Mississippi and Western writings as touchstones
for the development of distinctly American idioms and themes.
However, in the process, Twain's works with European historical and cultural affiliations have tended to be undervalued or
ignored completely. Twain was, in several senses, a citizen of
the world, a cosmopolitan, not only through his travels and his
extensive periods of living abroad but in his political views and
in his ability to reach an international public. I hope that my
work contributes to a fuller recognition of this dimension of
Mark Twain's achievement.

I wish to thank the friends and colleagues who generously
helped me in the writing of this book. Michael D. West's

firm, wise, and shrewd mentoring nurtured the confidence that made it possible to pursue this work in the first place. I also owe a special debt of gratitude to Tom Riggio, whose astute, skillful guidance was absolutely indispensable and exemplary. I have not forgotten—and will not forget—what Yasmin Azad, Charisse Gendron, Brian Striar, and Jack Wenke taught me during the earliest stages of my work on Twain. Thanks to Paul Machlis for his assistance during my first visit to the Mark Twain Papers at Berkeley. Courtney Clark and Kevin Scaggs, editorial assistants at the Mark Twain Papers, deserve a special thanks for their diligent search of the photo collection at the Mark Twain Project for illustrations. Thanks also to Rob Browning, photo editor at the Mark Twain Project, for his consulting help. I am indebted to Ruth Salvaggio, Minrose Gwin, and Fritz Oehlschlaeger for their early, stimulating conversations and advice. Uli Knoepflmacher offered me invaluable encouragement and insights. Walt VomLehn's and Jane Bradley's friendship and faith in me and in my work have helped and sustained me more than I can express. I am deeply grateful for the support of my father, stepmother, and sister. Len Hatfield, Ellen Brown, Bruce Ronda, and Margaret L. Shaw aided me tremendously with their close, critical readings. I wish to thank Hilbert Campbell and John C. Stubbs for their administrative decisions that gave me time to do research and write. I also want to acknowledge my enormous debt to the many excellent Twain scholars and critics whose work has influenced me and on whose scholarship I have built. Among them I wish particularly to name Henry Nash Smith, Howard Baetzhold, Louis J. Budd, James M. Cox, Judith Fetterley, Susan K. Harris, Justin Kaplan, Robert Regan, and Tom H. Towers. Robert H. Hirst of the Mark Twain Project at the University of California at Berkeley has been unstintingly generous and superbly well informed in aiding my work at many stages. Earlier versions of chapters 2 and 3 appeared in *Studies in American Fiction* and in *American Literature* respectively. Portions of chapters 4 and 6

were presented as papers at the 1989 Elmira Conference on
A Connecticut Yankee and at the special session led by Louis J.
Budd titled "Mark Twain on Language, Gender, and Fiction
Making" at the 1989 Modern Language Association Conference
in Washington, D.C.

Mark Twain,

CULTURE AND GENDER

Introduction
~~✲~~

What I set out to show in the following pages is how the relativity of European values, customs, and beliefs in comparison with Samuel Clemens's own American ideas, attitudes, and practices informed and permeated his envisioning of gender and vice versa. Clemens often employed differences between European and American cultural values to dramatize the verities of American gender definitions as he saw them. But cultural comparisons also had the effect of questioning and placing into new perspectives the fixities of his own culture. Clemens expressed some of his deepest and most enduring concerns with gender and sexuality through European metaphors. These concerns involved father-son relationships, legitimation through parentage, fascination with and anxiety about female political and sexual power, the victimization of "good" women, and, ultimately, the desire to bridge or even destroy the barriers between the sexes. European history and culture formed one of the major imaginative settings in which he enacted, in his writing, the themes of sexuality, morality, and identity. He used the romantic distance and malleability of European materials as means to give form to private anxieties, desires, fears, and aspirations. The European stage served Clemens as a platform for expressing his views on many issues. It helped him to develop the persona of Mark Twain in *The Innocents Abroad:* bold, humorous, mischievous. In *The Prince and the Pauper,* the European setting helped to dramatize political as well as psychological themes. *A Connecticut Yankee in King Arthur's Court* brings political discussion to the fore in very obvious ways. Less obviously, but no less significantly, that novel expresses the development of psychological themes as well. As his preoccupation with these psychological themes deepened in his final years, Samuel Clemens's understanding of gender and culture became more complex: the fascination with role-playing and the appropriation of symbols of authority from other cultural realms remained, but they reflected a more interior preoccupation, in his characters and in their author, and subtler, more paradoxical insights, obsessions, and fantasies.

The Duke and the Dauphin, charlatans and companions in crime, are probably the most famous pretenders to European nobility in American literature. In order to carry out their imaginative schemes for bilking the gullible, they avail themselves of roles from various realms of cultural authority: the clergy, medicine, South Seas missions, the London theater, and of course, eponymously, French royalty. As the last two realms suggest, European culture, subversively manipulated, was a major source of power for the two imposters. They illustrate Mark Twain's pervasive imaginative play with cultural symbols. Their energetic schemes for staging elaborate falsehoods culminate in impersonating a British relative of a deceased American who has left a substantial fortune behind. These exploitative men are compulsive actors whose roles include travesties of Hamlet and prancing about naked as "the Royal Nonesuch" but who also do not shrink from female impersonation, playing Juliet as well as Romeo. The Duke and the Dauphin move toward bestiality, and in their final humiliation, being ridden out of town on a rail, tarred and feathered, their alien plumage echoes and parodies their earlier voluntary and deceitful assumption of royal, foreign, and female roles and costumes. In the carnivalesque ritual of their humiliation and punishment, they are exposed naked again, but this time they have become pitiable in Huck Finn's compassionate gaze as he recognizes in their tormentors a general human tendency toward cruelty and, in them, victims who are simply human. Their punishment also oddly resembles the fate of many martyrs in Twain's

fiction—most of them female. In many of his works, virtuous women, usually in a fictionalized European setting, end
up being burned at the stake, emblems of pathetic, suffering
humanity. Frequently Twain's scenes of slavery and torture are
transposed from the American South into European settings,
and victimized women dramatize the oppression of men. All
of this role shifting and cultural transposition suggests not only
Twain's fascination with theatricality but a cultural commentary about the improvisation of social roles, including the roles
that define or delimit gender.

In the twentieth century, the idea that gender is to a significant extent a cultural construct has been gaining prominence.[1]
As a result, what have traditionally been seen as masculine and
feminine roles in Western society often appear relative, variable,
and questionable; whereas in the nineteenth century, gender
roles usually were assumed to be fixed, moral, and supported
by the highest religious, political, and social authorities. Encounters with other cultures, through travel or the reading of
history, offered the possibility of recognizing the relativity of
cultural values, including those involving gender and sexuality;
but such encounters also often served to confirm previously held
beliefs and attitudes. Part of the appeal of travel writing for
Mark Twain, as it had been for Cooper, Hawthorne, Irving, and
others before him, was the opportunity it offered for defining
American customs and values through judgments about foreign practices and beliefs, just as the same form allowed Alexis
de Tocqueville (in *Democracy in America*) and Frances Trollope
(in *Domestic Manners of the Americans*) to describe America in
ways that clarified European values by implicit or explicit comparisons. Furthermore, historical fiction allowed Mark Twain
great latitude to imagine clashes of value systems and practices,
often with comic as well as moral and political overtones. Thus,
through his actual and imagined travels, Twain became in one
sense truly a world citizen—he traveled and lived abroad as few
of his contemporaries did—and his writing draws on references

to an enormous range of cultures and nations. European culture is prominent in this range not merely for the obvious reason that Samuel Clemens lived in Europe for more than a decade but because for many Americans European culture, by which I mean its traditions of history and class in particular, had (and continues to have) an almost hieratic authority, which Mark Twain both challenged and exploited.[2]

The Duke and the Dauphin, like other more or less fake European aristocrats in Twain's works, illustrate in powerful ways both the artificiality and the force of social roles and cultural conventions. Clemens was always keenly conscious of the paradox that our social identities are invented, improvised, and staged—but also forceful, effective, and defining. Gender, culture at large, and character form a complex mixture of contradictory and variable patterns in Twain's fiction and thought. European history provided him with a wealth of illustrative material from which he fashioned fables of slavery and exploitation, character versus training, superstition in conflict with enlightenment and progress, and other favorite themes. Some of the most striking if schematic of his images of gender and power are persistently drawn from this realm: the Machiavellian queen, for example, and the saintly woman martyr immolated. Clemens's concept of culture was strongly influenced by nineteenth-century faith in progress and technology and the widespread belief in the "savagery" of "primitive" peoples (see Johnson and Cummings). At the same time, he was caught in a conflict between chivalric, romantic notions of manhood and a more complicated, hardheaded realistic quest for self-knowledge, a conflict mirrored in shifting ways in his European fictions. My purpose in this book is to trace some of these patterns.

When I write of American conceptions of gender and European cultural practices in this book, I recognize of course that gender is a large subheading of culture. European and American cultural practices in the realm of gender, though they displayed noteworthy differences, also shared much in common during Clemens's lifetime, as they still do today. "Culture" is a term with many definitions, of which some are mutually irreconcilable and many divergent. I employ "culture" in this book in two major ways: first in the sense of a broad historical tradition of beliefs, values, customs, and practices, with a touch of the German sense of *Kultur*—civilization, high culture—but also a bit of the anthropological sense of the folkways and mores that give a succession of generations a sense of continuity and identity. The second major sense in which I employ the term is in relation to America: American culture, as described in this book, is of necessity a somewhat different thing, though in many ways it derives from European culture. By American culture I mean something more self-consciously national. American culture in this sense is also mass culture, at least incipiently, and Mark Twain's contribution to the shaping of mass culture in America is an implicit part of the background to my study. The fact that Clemens turned to early mass-market techniques, specifically to subscription-sales publishing, to sell his books and that he aimed at a broad popular audience is a significant part of what has made American culture distinctive (see Budd, *Our Mark Twain*).

The functions of history, class, and religious ideology in European culture (as defined above) were supplanted in nineteenth-century American culture by literature, wealth, and a gender ideology of separate spheres which ensured male privilege, dominance, and political power. In particular, I focus on the ways in which Mark Twain took elements of European culture (or what he represented as European culture) and redefined them into terms that served to constitute and reinforce nineteenth-century American culture. In acts of historical interpretation that were highly selective (largely ignoring the existence of Native American cultures, for example, except to associate them with what he regarded as the worst extremes of European culture, as in "The French and the Comanches,"

Letters from the Earth), he employed decontextualized images of European culture to replace the centrality of old narratives of class and national conflict with the new narratives of gender and wealth. The irony of this conceptual translation is that democracy offered a clearer potential basis for a gender-egalitarian society than did Old World aristocratic and religious ideologies. It is this very potential that lies unacknowledged and threatening beneath the surface of many of Twain's fictions and autobiographical narratives interpreting Europe.

How Mark Twain as an American regarded Europe is in some respects analogous to how Sam Clemens as a man regarded women. For example, Europe is personified in *The Innocents Abroad* as seductive temptress, in a letter to the *Alta California* as a witch (Hag Europe, foreshadowing Ezra Pound's characterization of European civilization, in "Hugh Selwyn Mauberly," as "an old bitch gone in the teeth"), and in later sketches as symbolic mother. There are obvious limitations to the range and kind of his perceptions in both cross-cultural understanding and gender as revealed in Twain's representations of masculinity and femininity through encounters with European society. His inability to appreciate the writings of Jane Austen, George Eliot, and Oliver Goldsmith, for example, was not only due to his strong biases concerning style but existed in part because, as Brander Matthews put it, Samuel Clemens disliked writers' such as Austen's "placid and complacent acceptance of a semi-feudal social organization, stratified like a chocolate layer-cake, with petty human fossils in its lower formations" (265). His extreme intolerance of these writers testifies to his lack of sympathy for societies in which the social unit, especially when it is well established, is in some ways more important than the individual. Yet what is perhaps more significant than Clemens's inability or unwillingness to understand certain features of other cultures is the nature, shape, and evolution of his gendering cross-cultural perceptions. Clemens's self-definition as an American author drew significantly on his use of cultural and sexual Otherness as he wrote about the Old World throughout his career, envisioning an American viewpoint by translating Europe into American literature. These translations are reflections of and responses to larger American cultural currents, and the expressions of a powerfully imaginative individual, who works as a cultural interpreter in ways that still influence our understanding of ourselves.

Just as Mark Twain did not have a fully developed conscious philosophy of language but did explore issues having to do with the philosophy of language, as David Sewell has persuasively argued, so he did not have a conscious philosophy of gender, but his fiction and other writings are suffused with perceptions about gender identity and conflict (1–3). As Susan Gillman has recently shown in *Dark Twins,* gender, racial, and other social boundaries are crossed, challenged, and sometimes confirmed in Twain's obsessive stories of cross-dressing, female impersonators, and secret same-sex marriages. The appeal of fluid gender and racial barriers to Twain's imagination is made plain in Gillman's analyses of his accounts of indigenous dress and demeanor in Ceylon in *Following the Equator.* But the dissolutions or variabilities of gender and cultural boundaries were also threatening to Clemens and to his culture, and the imaginative, sometimes dreamlike play with such possibilities in his imagination was often a form of nightmare or exorcism.

Autobiography and fiction are in some respects extraordinarily intertwined in Mark Twain's writing. However, in order fully to understand the extent to which this is true, we must recognize how much his life itself was his writing for Clemens and his writing was and is his life for his readers. In particular, we need to see how involved we as readers, scholars, and critics are in the continued writing of his life. The lines between biography, literary criticism, psychological speculation, cultural history, fiction, and interpretation blur even as we attempt to clarify them.[3] Recognizing our own subjectivity as readers and scholars need not mean abandoning the goal of seeing Samuel Clemens as clearly as possible in the context of his times. It does mean, however, acknowledging the subjectivity and relativity of our—in this case *my*—interpretation of Clemens's life, thought, character, and art.

Twain's interpretations of gender through the grid of European culture were always full of contradictions. In chapter 1 I explore his often paradoxical search for cultural authority. For example, in *The Innocents Abroad* he lambasted European filiopietism, such as Portuguese reverence for customs inherited from their fathers on the Azores, but he revealed his own profound need for legitimation through the search for symbolic and authoritative yet sympathetic fathers in *The Prince and the Pauper,* a psychologically potent historical myth of identity exchange, loss, and reinstatement. He portrayed powerful women, such as Morgan le Fay in *A Connecticut Yankee in King Arthur's Court,* as violent, cold-blooded, and manipulative, yet he could not entirely disguise the great similarities between his hero Hank Morgan and the cruel queen. The Yankee Morgan expresses bemused and bewildered contempt for his aristocratic British companion Sandy's "womanly" conversation, yet he marries her and she becomes his idealized mate and the symbol of all he desires. Mark Twain's attacks on "backward," superstitious, feudal European customs and values in his historical fiction expose some of the ideological inconsistencies of gender roles in industrial, democratic, individualistic America. In the writings of his last two decades, cultural differences between Europe and America receded as Twain explored the arbitrary nature of gender divisions, the power struggles between men and women, and the complexities of sexual attraction in new ways. Acquainted though Clemens was, through his wife and her family, with some of the most prominent suffragists and women's rights activists of his time, his public statements and private attitudes toward gender issues were largely conventional for his time. Yet his fiction and travel writing reveal sometimes surprising uncertainties, anxieties, and yearnings to reconcile gender divisions that were articles of faith in the Victorian era. Though to his daughters he was an intimidating, often overbearing and overprotective father, in his late fiction he filtered questions of authority, sexuality, and gender through the screens of European settings, magical duplications of identity, and exploratory fantasies that cast doubt on patriarchal rule and on strict divisions between the sexes.[4]

One of the commonplaces of Twain criticism is that Clemens used European material to define an American stance of independence towards Old World culture. The underlying metaphor in this discourse frequently is one of adolescent rebellion: the young author established his identity as an American and helped set the tone of a vigorous, bold, independent new American literature, partly through his innovative and unapologetic use of a fresh American vernacular, partly through an irreverent humorous stance in the face of the shrines of Culture on the European continent. Like many powerful figures, this metaphor contains some elements of truth, but it is also misleading and overly simple. It is analogous to and has connections with the fallacy propounded by Van Wyck Brooks that Mark Twain's artistic vigor was subjugated by a circle of genteel women and with the more plausible but still insidious and narrowly exclusionary theory of Leslie Fiedler and other critics that Mark Twain's writing exemplifies and stands at the origin of the quintessentially American tradition of literature the central theme of which is the male's flight from the taming and entrapping company of females, who represent marriage, society, and self-suppression (see *Love and Death in the American Novel*). However, careful investigation shows that Twain incorporated and appropriated European symbols and values as well as feminine gentility and innocence in his imaginative explorations of the frontier, of the South of his childhood, of Europe both real and imagined, and of many nations and regions. In this study I explore some of these manifold appropriations, which he conducted in many different forms of writing. My primary focus is on how the European material illuminates Twain's concepts of gender.

In *The Innocents Abroad* Mark Twain largely excluded the women who actually traveled to Europe on the *Quaker City* and who played a significant role in his social life on the trip. Having eliminated them from his cast of characters, he claimed for himself an almost virginal innocence that allowed grown men to be "boys" and himself to be the prime Innocent adventuring amidst the ruins and wonders of a mature, often (in his eyes) corrupt Europe. Thus he claimed for himself the equivalent of a "feminine" sexual and social innocence valued by his culture, an appropriation which allowed him to invent and stage scenarios or anecdotes of virginal masculine American innocence as it encounters entrapping or demanding female European experience. In these little American dramas about an unsuspecting boyish American tourist confronting wily, assertive, or knowing Old World women, sexual tension, curiosity, or byplay is often an important if half-disguised theme. Also in these miniature dramas, the American male has the financial power, but the European woman has the sexual and social power, as in other fictional American representations, such as Henry James's *The Ambassadors* and *The American*.[5] The conflict between the two clearly was both titillating and disturbing to Twain. He derived humor from it, sometimes at his own expense, but it also drove him toward a moral condemnation of what he regarded as licentiousness clearly motivated by fear of losing control. Sexuality for Samuel Clemens was almost always associated with guilt and anxiety, freedom from sexuality (real or imagined) with innocence and bliss. This is one reason why so many of his heroes are boys or childlike men and why his female cast of characters is underpopulated with married or positively portrayed sexual women (see Diel and Jones).

When the European cultural myths were at odds with his preconceptions, he rewrote them, as in the case of the story of

"Torn Away by the Officers," from *The Prince and the Pauper*.
Illustration by Frank T. Merrill and John J. Harley.

Abelard and Heloise, where to acknowledge the implications of
the story as it stood would have meant ascribing to an innocent, "good" woman sexual desires, even sexual initiative, an
acknowledgment that would have threatened his own image
of innocence. He wrote in defense of "Mr. Laura" (Laura's
husband) and against the "one-sided sentimentality that celebrates Petrarch's love for Laura" (183–84), aligning himself
with an innocent, victimized male hidden behind the female
name. When, by contrast, European women were powerful and
clearly not sexually or politically innocent, he facetiously cele-
brated their power: "We saw also an autograph letter of Lucrezia
Borgia, a lady for whom I have always entertained the highest respect, on account of her rare histrionic capabilities, her
opulence in solid gold goblets made of gilded wood, her high
distinction as an operatic screamer, and the facility with which
she could order a sextuple funeral and get the corpses ready for
it" (185). On the other hand, the lack of soap in Italian hotels
(itself emblematic to the "clean" young American) further encouraged him comically to claim for himself the female role.
To the woman who tried to enter the bathroom in Italy when
he was in the bath, he said, "Beware, woman! Go away from
here—go away now, or it will be the worse for you. I am an
unprotected male, but I will preserve my honor at the peril of
my life!" (188). But between these comic extremes of European
female aggression and American male defenselessness, he found
subtler areas of contradiction, where he was able to play off
American gender roles and expectations against European cultural values and practices and the veneration in which Europe
was generally held by Americans, as I explore in chapter 1. *The
Innocents Abroad* at its best illuminates American values through
complex implied comparisons of cultures.

In chapter 2 I address the distance between the dominant
public veneration for European cultural artifacts and a submerged private fascination with "corrupt" European morals,
which is nowhere clearer than in the contrast between "A

Memorable Midnight Experience" (collected in *Mark Twain's Sketches, Number One*, 1874), his polished, reverential account of a visit to Westminster Abbey, and *1601: Conversation As It was by the Social Fireside in the Time of the Tudors* (1876), his bawdy and scatological reenactment of conversation among Queen Elizabeth's private circle. The queen is the subject of both sketches, although one concerns the grandeur and romance but also the evanescence and deceptiveness of her female power, while the other ambivalently jests about a woman's sexual and political power. The European queen served the American male writer as a potent cultural symbol of his own culture's anxieties about gender, symbolizing sexual and social freedom and power that he both desired and feared, just as later on Mary Baker Eddy became a symbol of fascination, loathing, and dread yet also curious attraction for Mark Twain, who fictionally transformed her, in "The Secret History of Eddypus, the World-Empire," into a pope and ultimately into himself, through a process of projection and transference (*Mark Twain's Fables of Man* 318–85). *1601* amused Clemens immensely, though he also took pains to keep it private. It belonged to that category of literature and art that had to be kept sub rosa in sexually repressive Victorian society. The repression and the hiddenness of the transgression intensified the hilarity of the subject. Flatulence and copulation, bodily functions, provided a satiric, lubricious, and salutary reminder of the force and elementary truths of physicality but also contained hints of mortality, limitation, and fear. These hints and fears were given shape in Twain's narrative of Westminster Abbey as well, but in a very different form, through contrasts between the monumentality of the edifice and the living presence of a small female cat, and between the reach and reputation of Queen Elizabeth's power and her death, hinting at the ruling Queen Victoria's mortality and at the mortality of all powerful women. Twain's *1601* celebrates female sexual appetite but also reveals a covert anxiety that that appetite is linked to female dominance and the threat of death, as in the myth of Adam and Eve. Speech, rhetoric, and even literary art are implicitly linked to flatulence, while the social proprieties are mocked. Death, sex, and all the elementary realities of the body are democratic, Twain appears to assert, but if that is so, there is a tenuous and uncertain connection between these truths and the artificialities of society.

Monarchy and aristocracy contained for Mark Twain, as no other social reality did, the paradox of social prestige and power joined to the cruelty, corruption, flimsiness, and falsity of human character. Gender complicated and intensified the paradox. To put it most simply and crudely: sometimes kings were weak and queens were brutal. How could this be, when men were supposed to be strong, women were supposed to be kind and virtuous, and kings and queens occupied the pinnacle of society?

On a psychological level, Twain perceived the masculine side of this troubling paradox as rooted in anxieties about paternity. In his writing, men need fathers (or father figures) to give them a sense of identity, to become men. On the feminine side, girls need children to become women; motherhood is essential to womanhood, in Mark Twain's representation. Therefore, Twain's anxieties about mature manhood and womanhood concern, interestingly enough, failures of cross-generational linkage, of inheritance and nurture, failures at social connection and transmission. Twain's boys yearn for a sense of identity conferred by real or surrogate fathers; his women are defined by the identities they nurture in their children (the clearest example of Twain's fascination with this theme is, of course, *Pudd'nhead Wilson and Those Extraordinary Twins*). My analysis in chapter 3 shows that the cross-cultural dimension of this paradox leads in several directions: Twain has no more powerful symbols of fatherhood than kingship and aristocratic nobility, for they imply the transmission of authority, identity, property, and prestige from father to son, a theme almost obsessively explored in *The Prince and the Pauper*.

Yet that idea is fundamentally undemocratic and antiegalitarian. As a result, as an American, Twain seeks to envision male heroes who engender their own authority, identity, property, and prestige, the type of hero perhaps best represented by Hank Morgan, "self-made man." This perception of the vast (and to Clemens often outrageous) distance between "manhood" and kingship lies behind his decades-long vituperative attacks on European monarchy for its brutality, hypocrisy, and "sham," though this perception also helps explain why Clemens could be on friendly terms with individual kings without a sense of contradiction. This view also lies behind Twain's ambivalent fictional portraits of kings, however: Henry VIII as tyrannical ruler but benevolent father, for instance, or King Arthur as a lovable, ineffectual, but compassionate bumbler in *A Connecticut Yankee*. In the novels of Mark Twain's middle years, some forms of kingship and aristocracy remain attractive images, combining as they do masculine authority and social adulation. The pauper desires to become a prince, Hank Morgan becomes something very like a king when he becomes "the Boss," and Samuel Clemens in his white suit fancied himself as a kind of aristocrat of talent. There are times in his fiction when these paradoxes come close to appearing as conscious acknowledgments of contradiction. Fiction, for Clemens, was a kind of exploratory imaginative autobiography, which may be one reason why he had difficulty in seeing value in fiction which did not provide him a figure with whom to identify.[6]

The element of sexuality provides the most explosive ingredient in Mark Twain's representation of the female side of the complex cultural paradox outlined above. In chapter 4 I investigate the psychological ramifications of this theme in *A Connecticut Yankee*. A cruel queen such as Morgan le Fay could retain her sexual attractiveness, and Elizabeth in *1601* could celebrate female sexual prowess. But both women are also portrayed as cold-blooded murderers. Their sexual identity, as Twain represents it, consists of self-gratification, which makes them ruthless, immoral. They are emphatically *not* mothers, not martyrs, not saints. Morgan le Fay calmly slips her phallic dirk into her page, in contrast to Hank, who cultivates a stable of pages as if they were surrogate sons. Elizabeth threatens her ex-lover, Sir Walter, and the possibility of execution chastens and silences her subjects. Yet in their very "masculinization," these female figures point toward a critique of male values. Hank Morgan at certain moments uncannily resembles Morgan le Fay in cruelty, ambition, and ruthless desire for domination. In *1601* Samuel Clemens possesses a rhetorical control that more closely resembles that of Queen Elizabeth within the sketch than that of the male narrator, the cupbearer to the queen. These similarities between male and female characters and between male author and female character suggest at least a subliminal awareness of cross-cultural and cross-gendered traits, traits that appear to vitiate rather than confirm the gendered side of the paradox.

But the presence of shared negative traits in both sexes is more than counterbalanced by the overpowering emphasis Mark Twain places on the association between motherhood and martyrdom, womanliness and self-sacrifice. Womanhood, nurture, motherly love, and virtue are equated with victimization. Spiritual strength leads to physical immolation, never more clearly than in *Joan of Arc*. Twain's ideal of womanhood is the woman who sacrifices herself—for her virtue; for her beliefs; for her children, her husband, or her nation. A queen could be virtuous if she sacrificed for her people. But if, on the other hand, she became queen through personal ambition and sexual intrigue, as various mistresses of French kings did, nothing could demonstrate more forcefully for Twain how viciously evil monarchy could be and how terribly womanhood could be debased. This combination of the artificiality of the institution of royalty and what he regarded as the perversion of female character explains the white-hot fury of Twain's attacks on the French, an animosity which he sustained for decades (Baetzhold 38–39, 42–45). The notion of a woman coming to power through sex was frightening and hateful to him: an aberration of culture and gender—and the French had done it. Twain commented on Andrew D. White's *Warfare of Science with Theology,* in which Saint-Simon claimed that the king's mistress, Madame de Montespan, was very religious, "From the year AD300 to the year 1800 may be described as the age of pious w----s."[7] Such vituperative exaggeration and distortion of history recurs throughout Twain's historical fiction and is an indication of feelings strong enough to overrule his otherwise powerful desire for historical accuracy, demonstrated in his extensive research. Such a strong emotional investment helps to explain glaring historical falsifications such as his projection of an age of chivalry into sixth-century Britain in *A Connecticut Yankee* or his invention of identical boys who accidentally change places in *The Prince and the Pauper.* His expression of deeply felt American beliefs about gender also helps to explain his habitual and, to later generations of critics, notorious overvaluation of his most conventional and flat-footed works.

Reaching back into a freely fictionalized world of European history enabled Mark Twain to give shape to some of his most deeply rooted psychological concerns and to give them cultural potency. Thus *The Prince and the Pauper,* with its Renaissance British trappings, allowed him to explore his very American preoccupation with fathers and sons, particularly sons in search of fathers. This preoccupation is American in its effort to give expression to the New World discontinuity between generations and the concomitant desire for self-creation.

As I explore in chapter 3, Twain's three symbolic sons, Edward, Tom, and Miles Hendon, engage in parallel quests for real or surrogate fathers who will confer upon them legitimacy, identity, and an empowering social place. Ironically, and in profoundly American fashion, these sons also in some sense choose and even create their own fathers. The psychological drama of this folktale-like myth of sons searching for lost fathers is located almost exclusively on the male side. The simplistically conceived women in *The Prince and the Pauper* mirror the Manichaean dichotomy displayed in the father figures, with the difference that benevolent women are almost all victims; malevolent women are the only powerful kind. The male characters sometimes display admixtures of good and bad qualities, and even what one might call androgynous qualities, such as combinations of compassion, gentleness, courage, and forcefulness. These combinations demonstrate, at different extremes, the most terrifying as well as the most attractive and idealized images of fatherhood in the mad hermit and Miles Hendon. The fanatical, deranged hermit shows us Twain's fascination with a chillingly paradoxical alliance of tenderness and bloodthirstiness. Gentle and solicitous as a kind mother at one moment, the hermit, who aspires to be pope, is sadistically vengeful and murderous the next. If the hermit, like pap Finn, is Clemens's worst nightmare of a father, with a satiric thrust at the patriarchal claims of the papacy, the brave and kind Miles Hendon is his most desired fantasy of a good father, with the patina of aristocracy but an innate nobility meant to outshine the social distinction of his rank. Miles moves through a plot designed to prove his superiority of character and, in a sense, legitimate the accident of honorable birth. Miles Hendon is to Edward what Jim might have been to Huck if race were no barrier. The psychological theme of yearning for a father is tied in *The Prince and the Pauper* to the desire for an inheritance, which is interpreted in Twain's fiction dually as a sense of legitimacy through parentage and as social position. The aspect of social position is treated in a very American way: Tom earns his position as King's Ward and chief governor of Christ's Hospital through his gentle and just rule as king and through his honesty in restoring Edward. Edward in a sense earns his right to rule through his education by hard knocks among the lower classes. But Clemens is not merely enthralled (as he obviously is) with the trappings, the "gaudiness," of royal pomp and ritual; he employs the historical European setting and characters to express his complex explorations of fathering, masculine identity, and the paradoxes of social existence.

Those paradoxes are also the subject of *A Connecticut Yankee in King Arthur's Court* (1889), which is far more than a political allegory, as I show in chapter 4. The premise here is significantly similar to that of *The Prince and the Pauper:* a commoner assumes the throne and transforms the nature of rule in a backward monarchy. The potentially corrupting influence of power is a central theme of both works, and both employ European culture as a complicated metaphorical staging ground for a range of gender issues. In *A Connecticut Yankee* Twain largely leaves behind the search for surrogate fathers, so central to the earlier novel, and concentrates instead on rival forms of masculinity and on the threat of different forms of female force and expression. Hank Morgan, as a self-made American philistine, serves as one of the richest and most revealing characters through which Mark Twain illuminates the drives, contradictions, and uncertainties of the Victorian American male. For all his individualism and self-reliance, Hank also displays a profound if poignantly futile yearning for social permanence, the establishment of a cultural legacy, and the cross-generational interconnection so many of Twain's characters seek in the European setting. King Arthur is a kind of father figure to Hank, and at his best Arthur exhibits the same fusion of compassion and courage already seen in Miles Hendon: an "internal" nobility that justifies and even puts to shame the "external" nobility of rank. But Arthur is weak, naive, and ridiculously childlike, a "father" who must continually be protected from his own mistakes. By contrast, Hank's surrogate son, Clarence, is wily and cynical, an effective actor in the world of power struggles. But there is something uncanny and unnatural about Clarence, reflected, among other ways, in the fact that the boys he trains under Hank's supervision are all alike. Clarence lacks precisely that individuality, not merely of characterization but of conceptualization, that comes from a fully realized sense of social context and interrelatedness within a diverse group, the kind of differentiation some of Twain's Mississippi characters have because they are rooted in social reality. Hank, Clarence, and in fact most of the characters in *A Connecticut Yankee* are more rooted in psychological than in social or historical reality. The irony is that Hank's associates, supposedly representative of American frontier individualism, conform to an only partly articulated agenda of masculine fantasy and become disturbingly conformist. The products of Hank's "man factory" resemble the subjects of a tyrannical regime more than self-actualizing democratic citizens.

In Twain's psychological paradox of the incongruity of power and social position, character and place, the female side is more fully developed if in some ways no less schematic in *A Connecticut Yankee* than in *The Prince and the Pauper*. The failure of Hank's political reforms is linked to—if not indeed caused by—the failure to reconcile the feminine with the masculine modes represented in the novel. The cultural critique Twain mounts against European customs and values, especially related to gender, becomes the source for my countercritique of his typically late-nineteenth-century American gender role conceptions as I examine the internal tensions and contradictions of values embodied in the book. The intertextual values upheld and clearly implied through satiric episodes include the separation of public and private realms through the valorization of male public innocence, represented as playful, and the condemnation of female innocence in the public realm as a lack of shame: a shameful shamelessness. Pride is presented as an essential ingredient of manhood, embodied to the point of excess in Hank's arrogance and self-confidence, qualities springing from his (and Clemens's) firm belief in the superiority of democracy, technology, rationality, and progress over ignorance, superstition, and traditionalism. Shame, on the other hand, or a proper measure of shame, is presented as an indispensable test of womanliness, linked to a prurient male possessiveness about the female body, and tied to powerful fears of savagery, primitive sexuality, and male violence.[8] Hank Morgan is trapped between his own primitive drive for power and dominance and the violence that that drive engenders.

Hank's internal struggles with fears of sexuality and violence are given external form through his symbolic relationships with highly symbolic women. These relationships both cast light on some of the psychological dilemmas of male dominance within the context of democratic ideology and provide a revealing palimpsest of Victorian American men's fears and aspirations. In psychological terms, Hank's internal conflict between compassion and contempt for the ordinary victimized human creature is projected onto several symbolic female figures: the martyred mother, on the one hand, who recurs with insistent frequency, as if to underscore her importance to Twain; and on the other hand the overpowering, emasculating female figure of the Church and her human counterpart, Morgan le Fay. Women in *A Connecticut Yankee* represent both the embodiment of virtue—a saintly self-sacrifice—and the essence of vice— sexual potency, ruthless ambition, and political power. Men most closely approach sainthood when they approximate the self-sacrifice modeled by the many angelic, saintly women who die at the stake or through some other form of feudal torture and execution. Women most closely approach demonic evil, on the other hand, when they approximate the self-serving, self-aggrandizing ambition of proud, manly men, embodied foremost, of course, in Hank.

Thus the gendered, self-contradictory nature of Twain's conception of democracy is most clearly exposed in his passionate fictional attack on monarchy, aristocracy, and the Established Church. *A Connecticut Yankee* implies that late nineteenth-century industrial American democracy depended upon female submission just as much as feudal plutocracy, in Twain's representation of it, depended upon the submissiveness of the peasant class. The moral terms with which Hank condemns the feudal ideology of humility and submission are uncannily similar to the moral terms which Hank employs to condemn the *lack* of humility and submission among Arthurian women, who by their "lack" become subject to the accusation of being primitive, savage, even bestial. Morgan le Fay, for all her resemblance to Hank Morgan, becomes, as a "masculine" woman, the object of his projected hatred for all the qualities within himself that cannot be reconciled with the ideals of rationality, tolerance, and equality he claims to represent. Twain's critique of European culture exposes, with great clarity, the inconsistencies and flaws of his own American cultural constructs in the realm of gender, sexuality, and power.

Yet, as if aware of these inconsistencies and flaws, Twain created characters and scenes that suggest an effort to reconcile some of the false and destructive extremes created by idealizing virtue as female martyrdom and representing male self-actualization as alienated domination and cruelty. Deference to genteel feeling about Arthurian legend feeds into the portrayal of Arthur as a self-sacrificing hero when he nurses a child in the smallpox hut. An exceptional priest, in an extended martyrdom scene, is made to articulate a fusion of compassion and legalism—a very rare and noteworthy thing in Twain's fiction. But perhaps most significantly of all, the fate of Hank Morgan, suspended between two cultures and times, yearning for wholeness, companionship, and his child, is to become like a martyred mother, dying for a virtuous cause. Significantly, in his final delirium Hank mistakes Mark Twain, the narrator of the second and concluding postscript, for Sandy, suggesting that Hank Morgan, the creation of Twain's imagination, seeks a reconciliation of his tortured delusions in Twain himself through the vanishing veil of a character who was once Alisande la Carteloise, British lady, metamorphosed into Sandy the ideal Victorian American wife and finally transformed into a symbol of release from the anguish, delusion, and alienation of unbounded male ambition.

The conclusion of *A Connecticut Yankee,* in its psychological turning inward, signals a movement away from the grandiose dreams of conquest, reform, and progress toward the interior world of self-scrutiny, fantasy, and desire for release from the constraints of society; and it foreshadows the late writings with their psychological speculations. The male dream of kingship proved itself bankrupt and self-alienating in *A Connecticut Yankee,* and this development leads to the search for a new relationship between virtue and power, feminine innocence and masculine action in *Personal Recollections of Joan of Arc* (1896).

Joan has been of particular interest to feminist critics, who have seen in Twain's efforts to envision a superhuman heroine everything from protofeminism to a major failure of the masculine imagination to comprehend a female character.[9] In chapter 5 I analyze the complex narrative psychology of Clemens's fictionalizing biography. Twain's Joan is his attempt to create a perfect human being: a saintly innocent who yet has power in the world of male ambition, conflict, rhetoric, and war. His failure to grant Joan any sexuality (sexual traits being flaws in his mind) is connected with the transfer of erotic passion into rhetorical passion (see Jones). Storytelling, oratory, song, and poetry become the means through which erotic energies are expressed. The narrator, Sieur Louis de Conte, whose name is itself telling, is a man caught between the brutality of martial masculinity and the passive saintliness of femininity embodied in Joan. Joan is the quintessential woman who inspires men to be men, in Twain's eyes. Yet her power is represented as exclusively moral and spiritual, not sexual or rhetorical. It is left to de Conte to seek to mediate between brutes such as the warrior affectionately nicknamed Satan and the bloodless "little woman" who inspires such idolatry and patriotic passion. The means of that mediation is de Conte's storytelling, by which he seeks to comprehend and memorialize Joan. For de Conte, storytelling takes the place of sexuality: storytelling is his form of romance, self-engendering, and parenting. De Conte is implicitly in competition with males who achieve popularity and power through storytelling prowess or martial feats. But, as Twain's *Joan of Arc* shows, though the rhetoric of poetry (sung by male singers) can inflame patriotic passion, it also risks being transparent and ridiculous, and it is associated with anxiety about ancestry, legitimacy, and identity. On the other hand, without the redeeming innocence of an angelic child, the realities of war and vengeance mean that martial power culminates in horrors of cruelty and killing, infused with arrogance and brutality that are the moral equivalent of rape. Capable neither of the saintly compassion and invincible courage he sees in Joan nor of the masculine ruthlessness and thoughtless boldness he sees in Satan (mirrored in the evil Cauchon), de Conte tries to negotiate a masculinity that admires both yet is oddly detached from both as well. Paradoxically, Twain's Joan serves an unconvincing and unattractive king who is the utterly unsatisfactory focus of French patriotism. Twain did not have the boldness or the vision to make *Joan* a convincing critique of patriarchal law and rule as, for example, Bernard Shaw did in his version of the story of Joan (Searle 121–27). But Twain does show the dilemmas of a male narrator who is not at ease with the alternatives a gendered society and imagination present him with and who seeks in literary art solutions to his dilemmas. Interestingly, de Conte, like Miles Hendon, belongs to the middle ranks of aristocracy and, as Susan K. Harris has pointed out, is deeply attached to but not a part of the village society he writes about.[10] Social rank is an important feature of symbolic autobiography for Twain as an American writer, but some form of disinheritance is also. The quest for an identity that will answer the male anxieties about lineage, inheritance, and place in history undergoes a significant shift from *The Prince and the Pauper* to *Joan of Arc*, from the exteriority of bravery in the face of social and physical danger to the interiority of battle with fears about literary art, emotional dangers, and private sense of self. This shift is further reflected in Twain's late fantasies about mysterious strangers.

In chapter 6 I unpack some of the complex layerings of gender socialization in the multiple versions of the "Mysterious Stranger" manuscripts. The preoccupation with Satan in various disguises signals a continued concern with masculine identity already revealed in the callous cruelty of the supposedly heroic Satan in *Joan of Arc* who is there represented as Joan's perfect masculine opposite and companion. In "The Chronicle of Young Satan," adolescent male American fantasies about kingship are displaced by a different kind of speculative male fantasy: an ambivalent embrace of amorality and evil in the form of Satan. Satan is now the aristocrat—a prince—but in the various manuscript versions he is also a boy or a young man, and larger social structures mostly fade away to give prominence instead to a sort of feudal village and, more significantly, to psychological exploration through doublings and experiments with identity, perspective, and role-shifting. Satan transcends his sex but not sexuality. He has a spiritual force with an erotic spark; he induces ecstasy in other beings. In "The Chronicle of Young Satan" we find attractive strong women and women allied with or representative of progress, while good men are weak, and rapacious men are the primary villains. Perhaps even more significantly, women are seen as representative of humanity in its flaws and its virtues, a movement that indicates the mature Twain's increased willingness to represent sexuality and gender difference positively.

In all three versions of his "Mysterious Stranger" manuscripts Twain presents a mixture of his familiar gender stereotypes and some more complex and interesting departures. The doubling of male and female characters in "No. 44, The Mysterious Stranger" allows him to explore the conflicts between physicality, spirituality, and social controls within sexuality. In "No. 44" we have varieties of the male self that are extremely revealing about the attitudes of his time and culture. Of particular interest are the male patriarch's partial retreat from authority, as if he recognized its limitations, and the young male lover's blindness about his self-centeredness in courtship, leading him to "worship" the young woman he thinks he loves but to accept her silencing without question as soon as a social crisis emerges. While Twain creates several versions of the strong, shrewd, forceful servant woman, she is made to humiliate herself at the feet of her adopted son; and though the multiple perspectives of doubling permit Martin and the reader to see clearly that the young woman he desires also has strong reciprocal sexual urges, that recognition is quickly overshadowed by the male social control exerted over female sexuality. Finally, one of the most attractive and vital female characters, an independent, vocal, rebellious young servant woman, is treated with a mixture of affection and contempt, and eventually is turned into a cat. In all of these ambivalent explorations Twain reveals a new willingness to reach through what he perceived as the limits imposed by sex, a speculative awareness of some of the ambiguities of gender, but also a sense of the force of social conventions and a profound ambivalence about humanity itself. In the widening of perspective of his later years, Twain was able to acknowledge to a greater degree some of the cultural relativities and complexities of gender and identity; but in striving to transcend time and place, physicality, culture, and social constraints, he was increasingly seeking to transcend being human.

The fact that, throughout his writing career, Mark Twain appropriated images and themes from European history and culture primarily to express his own American cultural and psychological themes does not diminish their authenticity and significance. On the contrary, his shaping of material frequently taken out of its original context, distorted, transformed, parodied, simplified, or elaborated represents an extended process of interpretation in which Samuel Clemens the private individual and Mark Twain the public author and personality took a major part in the definition of their own culture—not only the emergent nation of Americans whom Twain came to represent to many but also, through a worldwide readership, something of the perhaps more tentatively emergent world culture of which he is still—and will long continue to be—a not insignificant part. In light of this process and its influence, the merging of his images of European culture seen from an American perspective and of his representations of gender deserves our close and continuing scrutiny.

Chapter One
~❧~

THE INNOCENTS ABROAD:
PRIVILEGE, GENDER, AND
SELF-DEFINITION

The importance of *The Innocents Abroad* (1869), Mark Twain's first full-length, coherent book, which Robert Regan calls "the first great monument of American prose" (*American By-paths* 187), lies largely in its creation of a powerful, distinctively American way of confronting Europe, embodied in what James M. Cox has called "the character, the personality, the *humor* of Mark Twain" (38), a form of humor combining within itself many frequently contradictory attitudes ranging from burlesque mockery to reverence to realistic reporting.[1] If one focuses on the contradictory attitudes themselves, the book falls apart. Twain can be seen as an irreverent American, an advocate of gentility, a fierce critic of the social order of the Old World, or a worshipper at its shrines. All these are poses that make up the larger pose. The unity of the book finally seems to reside in the narrator's ability to convince the reader that he is writing honestly and authentically. The claim to that effect is contained within the preface:

> THIS book is a record of a pleasure-trip. If it were a record of a solemn scientific expedition, it would have about it that gravity, that profundity, and that impressive incomprehensibility which are so proper to works of that kind, and withal so attractive. Yet notwithstanding it is

only a record of a pic-nic, it has a purpose, which is, to suggest to the reader how *he* would be likely to see Europe and the East if he looked at them with his own eyes instead of the eyes of those who travelled in those countries before him. I make small pretence of showing any one how he *ought* to look at objects of interest beyond the sea—other books do that, and therefore, even if I were competent to do it, there is no need.

I offer no apologies for any departures from the usual style of travel-writing that may be charged against me— for I think I have seen with impartial eyes, and I am sure I have written at least honestly, whether wisely or not. (v)

Upon closer examination, several contradictions emerge from this seemingly straightforward program as it applies to the text that follows. As Twain impersonates "the most genteel travel rhetoric" (Cox 58), he causes us to doubt the truth of even the most eloquent and apparently serious presentation of his emotions, such as his apostrophe to a tear-jug or his description of the Sphinx. The stance of humor which opposes the known to the unknown, flights of fancy to shattering disillusionments, and the rhetoric of elevation to the comically puncturing hardness of the vernacular depends upon our seeing Europe *not* through our own eyes but through the eyes of more conventional travel writers, whom the writer frequently quotes, imitates, or parodies, *and* the eyes of Mark Twain. Thus there is complication and difficulty in the seemingly transparent assumption, as stated by Cox, "that as long as the narrator is honest, there is no real distinction between narrator and reader" (41). In this assumption, and in its implicit claim to representativeness, in its staking out of Americanness as the region of honesty where narrator and reader share an identity in the confrontation with the Old World, lies the innovative, audacious, and successful yet complicated and troublesome character of Mark Twain's stance. Epistemologically, the paradox of his stance lies in his claim to be able to see as his readers would see, because he sees honestly, while the honesty of his vision depends upon his seeing from the particularity of his own perspective, not from the generality of his predecessors. This paradox requires the enactment of a continual series of tensions between convention and originality; tradition and attacks on tradition; rhetoric and plain, "honest" language; illusion and innocence. These tensions are the source of humor and entertainment; they give the book its vitality, freshness, and air of originality.

Underlying that air of originality is the book's fusion of cultural and sexual themes. To understand the particularity of Mark Twain's vision, we need to disentangle some of the complicated strands of opposition that are woven into the text of *The Innocents Abroad*. Two pairs of opposites that are intricately interrelated and that foreshadow lifelong themes of his imagination are male-female relations and comparisons between America and Europe. Twain's use of dramas of gender to illuminate conflicts of cultures and vice versa is important for understanding both the central position he has occupied in American culture and the limitations of his—or any American writer's—representativeness. Not surprisingly, his perspective is masculine—but what does that mean? Similarly, he unquestionably writes as an American, but again, how, besides in the most obvious forms of self-identification, does his American perspective reveal itself? And how do his youthful 1860s American qualities merge with his own and his society's representations of maleness? As I will show, these questions are all related.

The perspective of *The Innocents Abroad* is predominantly masculine. The tone, interests, humor, and style of the narrator are both obviously and subtly male. This perception is reinforced by the fact that Mark Twain surrounds himself with a group of "boys" whose escapades and mutual tauntings frequently form the subject of his narrative. In a way that is not true to his private experience of the trip, Twain omits the part women played in his actual travels: his friendships and association with Emeline Beach, Emily Severance, and Mary Mason Fairbanks, in particular. Yet women are not entirely excluded from *The Innocents Abroad*. The text dramatizes an uneasy, frequently ritualized relationship to the European and female Other. Underneath the bold posture of confidence and the pervasive claim to honesty, the comic travel narrative reveals uncertainties about male power and privilege, linked to national identity. The confidence of the narrator's often contradictory poses seems to offer freedom, comprehension, and control in his encounters with strangeness and cultural difference. But the intrusion of the feminine, which at first seems marginal, suggests otherwise. For the encounters with female figures in *The Innocents Abroad* reveal a fear of involvement and of entrapment. In the face of the Otherness of European culture and of woman, the strategy of humor displays a beleaguered self: a boy-man, an innocent who ambivalently seeks to lose and to preserve his innocence.

Part of the confidence that distinguishes Mark Twain's voice as a new American voice in the history of American letters stems from the newfound economic and cultural self-confidence of post-Civil War America. That confidence is linked to a sense of male privilege and power in Twain's imagination. The narrator of *The Innocents Abroad* dramatizes the connections between national identity and masculine prerogatives, showing us both their attraction and an uneasy awareness of their limitations.

The confident, representative American narrator is ironically enough portrayed in a series of stylized comic encounters of the American young man with a European woman in scenes which display the young man's innocence, inexperience, and insecurity. These episodes include his first encounter with a French waitress, an anecdote about buying gloves from a clerk in Gibraltar, and a burlesque story, omitted in revision, of fending off the advances of a Portuguese woman in the Azores. These dramatic encounters follow the pattern of

Mark Twain's general comedic strategy of building up excessive or misguided expectations which are then undermined or destroyed by harsh "reality." These theatrical episodes present us with two ways of knowing: the one romantic, extravagant, embellishing; the other disillusioned, reductive, and self-protective. Both ways, it is important to note, are imaginative interpretations of events. The disillusioned, "realistic" conclusion the narrator arrives at is no more objective and truthful than the self-consciously false view the storyteller sets up for deflation at the beginning. The process itself, the movement from grand expectation to sober, hard-won experience, is an American cultural paradigm, American in its ambivalent celebration of naïveté, in its seeming faith in eventual enlightenment, and in its innate disposition to discredit tradition, authority, and inherited knowledge in favor of individual experience, novelty, and immediacy.

The miniature drama of the innocent American male confronting the experienced European female, as Mark Twain stages it, is enhanced and emphasized by the presence of a group of observers and commentators. The surrounding male chorus has an important function in this cultural drama. It criticizes, mocks, applauds, and in other ways participates in the action. It often serves to represent or express values that have a bearing on the cultural and sexual themes of the comedy. The group is frequently not individualized but rather represents collective values and attitudes. It thus represents the narrator's awareness that his experiences and attitudes do not exist in isolation: they are being perceived and judged by others. The group dramatizes the often unacknowledged pressures toward conformity in American society, a reality that runs counter to the individualism Twain asserts and assumes.

In his letters to the *Alta California,* Twain had included a revealing prototypical anecdote telling of his encounter as an American male with a European woman, which he discreetly omitted from the travel book. In the early episode, a woman approaches him on Fayal in the Azores. The "bent, wrinkled, and unspeakably homely old hag, with her capote [a Portuguese cap] standing high aloft" (*Traveling with the Innocents Abroad* 14), holds out her hand to him. Twain pretends not to have understood that she was begging and makes of their interaction a burlesque of courtship, with himself as the embarrassed suitor:

> "Away, woman—tempt me not! Your seductive blandishments are wasted upon one whose heart is far hence in the bright land of America. The jewel is gone—you behold here naught save the empty casket—and empty it shall remain till grim necessity drives me to fill the aching void with vile flesh, and drink, and cabbage. Avaunt, temptress!" But she would not avaunt. She kissed her hand repeatedly and curtsied over and over again. I reasoned within myself, This unhappy woman loves me: I cannot reciprocate; I cannot love a foreigner; I cannot love a foreigner as homely as she is—if I could, I would dig her out of that capote and take her to my sheltering arms. I cannot love her, but this wildly beautiful affection she has conceived for me must not go unrewarded. (15)

He decides to recite his "poetic paraphrase of the Declaration of Independence" to her as her "reward." Here Twain presents a burlesque allegory of the relationship between Europe and America in comically sexual and mercenary terms. Europe is represented by the "old hag" who is by implication witchlike ("Avaunt" confirms her identity), while Twain humorously identifies himself with patriotic emblems and claims a physical need that supplants the romantic desires of the heart with lust for meat, drink, and cabbage. Ironically, the woman is driven by genuine material need, which, in his parody of romantic fiction, Twain distorts for the purposes of comedy. He is the virgin; she is the whore. As in his comic sketches of battles with guides, the subject is the American male's economic power, here translated into sexual terms as the power of evasion through rhetoric. He displays through comedy his discomfort at dealing with a seductive but threatening Hag Europe. As his later writing will show, he found it easier to allegorize Europe as American Fatherland (particularly in *The Prince and the Pauper*) than to acknowledge the seductive force of Europe as a dangerous Motherland (the subject of *A Connecticut Yankee in King Arthur's Court*).

At the beginning of *The Innocents Abroad*, Mark Twain defined the nature of the *Quaker City* excursion by contrasting it with two forms of travel as social experience: the one by implication masculine, the other implicitly feminine. Establishing the character of his "record of a pleasure trip," he contrasts it first with "a record of a solemn scientific expedition," a venture to which he attributes "gravity," "profundity," and "impressive incomprehensibility," terms that are gender-marked as masculine. The vision of such an implicitly masculine voyage is supplanted by that of a "pic-nic," a term that has connotations associated with the world of feminine leisure. However, he redefines this leisureliness in masculine fashion by claiming that it is a picnic that "has a purpose," "to suggest to the reader how *he* would be likely to see Europe and the East if he looked at them with his own eyes instead of the eyes of those who traveled in those countries before him" (Preface v). This potentially domestic, feminine "pic-nic," furthermore, is made exotic in Twain's ironically grandiose description of it. He purposely distinguishes the "great pleasure excursion" he is about to narrate from the supposedly more ordinary picnics that implicitly resemble the one conducted by the Sunday School teacher in *Adventures of Huckleberry Finn* or the matriarchal pleasure party in Louisa May Alcott's *Little Women:* [2]

> Instead of freighting an ungainly steam ferry-boat with youth and beauty and pies and doughnuts, and paddling up some obscure creek to disembark upon a grassy lawn and wear themselves out with a long summer day's labori-

Entertaining an Angel, from *The Innocents Abroad*.
Illustration by True Williams and Roswell Morse Shurtleff.

ous frolicking under the impression that it was fun, [the participants] were to sail away in a great steamship with flags flying and cannon pealing, and take a royal holiday beyond the broad ocean in many a strange clime and in many a land renowned in history! (19)

The trip, as Mark Twain presented it, called forth in the imagination of the youthful male author a tension of desire, embodied in the "seductive nature" of the "enterprise" of the excursion: a clue to the sexual features, only glanced at by previous critics, of Twain's self-discovery through the journey.[3] Travel writing, as Mark Twain represented it here, was a masculine mode of writing. Furthermore, he dramatized his encounters with European women in terms that emphasized the privileged status of a paradoxically innocent American male in contrast with experienced, sometimes attractive, sometimes repellent European femininity. The encounter of New World explorer with Old World culture, which had often been an experience of education into the cultivation of the upper class in previous American writers' representations, became a drama of gender confrontation, a comic conflict of assumed innocence with projected female seducers.

The degree to which Twain assigned the role of destroyer of male illusions to the female is indicated by the anticlimax of his story of "the boys'" attempting to impress each other with their knowledge of French in Marseilles. Their hapless imitations of the language as they try to order wine and food at a café culminate in the waitress's exclamation: "Bless you, why didn't you speak English before?—I don't know anything about your plagued French!" (94). Twain interprets the experience as follows:

> The humiliating taunts of the disaffected member spoiled the supper, and we dispatched it in angry silence and got away as soon as we could. Here we were in beautiful France—in a vast stone house of quaint architecture, sur-

rounded by all manner of curiously worded French signs—
stared at by strangely-habited, bearded French people—
every thing gradually and surely forcing upon us the
coveted consciousness that at last, and beyond all question
we *were* in beautiful France and absorbing its nature to the
forgetfulness of every thing else, and coming to feel the
happy romance of the thing in all its enchanting delight-
fulness—and to think of this skinny veteran intruding
with her vile English, at such a moment, to blow the fair
vision to the winds! It was exasperating. (94–95)

While the anecdote follows his typical sequence of raising expectations which are then comically shattered, the culprit is
a woman who is significantly characterized as a "veteran" and
whose sexually unattractive appearance is part of her offen-
siveness.

The sexual undertones of Twain's anecdotes are never clearer
or more revealing than in his account of his encounter with
an attractive young woman clerk in a shop at Gibraltar.[4] It is
a comedy in which the sexual symbolism is too obvious to be
ignored.

> A very handsome young lady in the store offered me a
> pair of blue gloves. I did not want blue, but she said they
> would look very pretty on a hand like mine. The remark
> touched me tenderly. I glanced furtively at my hand, and
> somehow it did seem rather a comely member. I tried a
> glove on my left, and blushed a little. Manifestly the size
> was too small for me. (73)

She teases him with the pretense that the glove fits him precisely, that he is "accustomed to wearing kid gloves," and that
he has not ruined the glove that was too small for him. His
friends, "the boys," continue to tease him, after they leave the
shop, by repeating the woman's ironic statements in praise of
his skill at putting on gloves. The point of the jokes is pre-

cisely Mark Twain's lack of experience—his awkwardness and embarrassment in a situation of sexual innuendo. However, the circumstances are clearly titillating and enjoyable also: "I was too much flattered to make an exposure and throw the merchandise on the angel's hands. I was hot, vexed, confused, but still happy" (74). He persists in calling the young woman an angel, though the term begins to take on an ironic edge: "We had entertained an angel unawares, but we did not take her in. She did that for us" (75).

If we read *The Innocents Abroad* as an American comedy of manners, one of its themes emerges in sharper outline: the contrast between clear American ideas of masculinity and femininity and European subtleties about gender, a theme that reaches back to Royall Tyler's *The Contrast* (1787). Twain initially admired the orderliness and punctuality of trains in France and Italy. The "masculine" rationality of these systems of transportation furnished a counterweight to his condemnation of the effeminate luxury of priesthood, a luxury he was later, in *A Connecticut Yankee,* to associate repeatedly with secret concupiscence (as in his jokes about foundling asylums located between monastery and nunnery). Nonetheless, a certain ease and domestication attracted Twain in Europe. One of his accolades of European culture concerns a public form of family life: "I do envy these Europeans the comfort they take. When the work of the day is done, they forget it. Some of them go, with wife and children, to a beer hall, and sit quietly and genteelly drinking a mug or two of ale and listening to music. . . . They are always quiet, always orderly, always cheerful, comfortable, and appreciative of life and its manifold blessings. . . . We grow wise apace" (187). Yet in this apparently straightforward tribute, Twain was mischievously contrasting value systems: the teetotalism of his youth is subverted by his calm, ironic assertion of the respectability of European women's use of alcohol, the public consumption of alcohol being in America largely a male prerogative.[5] Thus Mark Twain was subtly subverting the

cultural authority of Europe and at the same time criticizing
American rigidity.

It is not surprising to find that his anecdotes reveal a subtext
of sexual curiosity and anxiety on the voyage on which Clemens
claimed to have first seen the portrait of his future wife and to
have fallen in love at first sight. Sexual conduct on the European
scene provided material for Mark Twain's comedy and for his
moralizing in ways that are not as straightforward as they might
at first appear. Although in public he predominantly affirmed
the ruling morality of Victorian America, the implications of
his anecdotes and observations about sexual matters frequently
reveal a more troubled, conflictive awareness than his manner
and tone admit. The most self-evident example of this awareness in *The Innocents Abroad* is furnished by his description of
the cancan at the Jardin Mabille in the Paris suburb of Asniéres.
The description reveals a powerful sexual curiosity evident also
in other episodes in the book. Yet an equally strong element is
the negative one of feigned or real restraint, embarrassment,
even guilt: "Twenty sets formed, the music struck up, and
then—I placed my hands before my face for very shame. But
I looked through my fingers. They were dancing the renowned
'Cancan'" (136). Leslie Fiedler states that Twain shared with
his generation a "sentimental-hypocritical . . . morality . . .
complementing a theoretical abhorrence for European frankness about sex with an actual eagerness for seeking out occasions
to put that abhorrence to work" ("An American Abroad" 82).
Here Twain indulges in satire both of himself and of his culture.
Sexually bold women become the focus of a curiosity that he
uses to tease his readers with by displaying it while pretending
to be ashamed. He has found a way to tease his audience and
perhaps also the censorious mother figure, of the kind that he
made "Mother" Fairbanks out to be, by both enacting propriety
and mocking it at the same time.

Mark Twain finds opportunities to express his sexual curiosity in allusive terms that betray the polarization of his image

of women and of erotic experience through religious metaphors: women in *The Innocents Abroad* are represented as angels or demons. Yet while he uses these polarized images, he clearly knows they are distortions and plays with them. One pole of this dual vision, the one which Twain affected to favor at this stage of his life, is that of heavenly purity. His rapturous tribute to the women of Genoa exemplifies this view of erotic attractiveness: "At least two thirds of the women are beautiful. They are as dressy and as tasteful and as graceful as they could possibly be without being angels. However, angels are not very dressy, I believe. At least the angels in pictures are not—they wear nothing but wings" (160). In this manner subversively linking his erotic associations to European art, where nudity was acceptable, he could question American prudery by means of the conventional prestige of art, but he could also appear to dignify his erotic attraction.[6] Though he similarly appealed ironically to the authority of the "staid, respectable, aged people" (136) who witnessed the cancan with him, he also had visions of another kind of spectatorship as he watched the furious finale of the dance: "Nothing like it has been seen on earth since trembling Tam O'Shanter saw the devil and the witches at their orgies that stormy night in 'Alloway's auld haunted kirk'" (137).[7] If Mark Twain could sublimate female sexuality through angelic associations, he also clearly could evoke diabolic images that suggest its threatening aspect for him.

Submerged in Twain's oblique references to sexuality is not merely the fear of being "taken in" but the association of sex with the bane of nineteenth-century morality: idleness. Aziz, the Turkish Sultan whom Twain portrays as the opposite of the progressive, and hence practically American, Napoleon, is represented as weak, childlike, dominated by his mother, and fatally sensual: he "sleeps, sleeps, eats, eats, idles with his eight hundred concubines . . . is surfeited with eating and sleeping and idling"—a description in which idling becomes virtually synonymous with an activity Sam Clemens could not name here, or, at any rate, with the exhaustion that follows that unnamed activity.

The fear of dissipation could be overruled by its attraction, particularly in circumstances in which the romantic appeal of illicit activity could be exposed as meretricious. So, for example, he was disappointed to find that the famed Grisettes (according to Twain, the guidebooks described them as "oh, so charmingly, so delightfully immoral," 150) "actually had large hands, large feet, large mouths . . . pug noses as a general thing, and moustaches that not even good breeding could overlook." The masculinization of such figures permitted Twain to conclude that "it would be base flattery to call them immoral" (151). Again and again he sought out and exploited the comic potential in incidents or observations that illustrated the conflict between romantic and realistic views of relations between the sexes. One particularly significant example of the comic juxtaposition of values is to be found in the story of the doctor's offer, "in jest," to kiss the "good-looking" young girl who was their guide at the Palazzo Simonetti, a building that featured an echoing courtyard. Though the doctor was "a little taken aback" when she gave him permission to kiss her for a franc,

> the commonest gallantry compelled him to stand by his offer, and so he paid the franc and took the kiss. She was a philosopher. She said a franc was a good thing to have, and she did not care any thing for one paltry kiss, because she had a million left. Then our comrade, always a shrewd businessman, offered to take the whole cargo at thirty days, but that little financial scheme was a failure. (198)

The commercial relationship of employer (tourist) and employee (guide) had been turned into something a bit more than mere parody by the young woman's frank acknowledgment of the nature of the relationship. Twain acutely revealed the convergence of chivalry, masculine privilege, and the cash nexus, reinforcing his vaguely uneasy approval of male power with irony.[8] The cultural confidence Cox names as one of the distinguishing marks of Twain's stance as an American clearly was reinforced by economic power but threatened by sexual privilege (40–44, 69).

American concepts of courtship versus European degeneracy and the nature of manhood are also the unacknowledged subjects of Mark Twain's well-known parodistic rendering of the story of Heloise and Abelard. Ostensibly the "history" presented "for the honest information of the public" to discredit a false sentimentality about Abelard, Twain's version of the story has as its subject the despicable behavior of a "cold-hearted villain," the "dastardly seducer," the "unmanly" Abelard against a "confiding, innocent girl," the "pure-souled" Heloise. The story expresses Victorian ideas of male seduction and female victimization. Part of the implied message of the story is Twain's very American refusal to acknowledge that a "good woman" could have unsanctioned sexual desires. However, the half-humorous, half-enraged Twainian story also betrays a mixture of anxiety about the function of a father-in-law and the failings of a son-in-law. Though he professes sympathy for the naively wronged Fulbert, Heloise's uncle and guardian, Twain's extended joking about him is a form of verbal aggression against the authority he represents. He describes the (comically phallic) canon as "a sort of mountain howitzer," "the good old swivel," "the old gun, or son of a gun," and "the old smooth bore." Similarly, the violence of his railing against Abelard testifies to a desire to place as much distance as possible between himself and the role model his medieval counterpart represented: according to Twain, Abelard deliberately intended to seduce and deceive, employing "the chilly phraseology of the polished rhetorician" to address Heloise "from the North Pole of his frozen heart" (145) in a religious innocence that was not genuine.

Authenticity of feeling and sincerity were standards by which many Americans measured probity of character, standards which Mark Twain's pose of honesty and sincerity reinforced.

Calculation and coldheartedness so aroused Twain's ire that he vigorously applauded Abelard's castration. The judgmental tone of his revisionist account may have had its roots in fears about his own conduct in courtship. For during the later stages of his revision of the *Alta* letters, Samuel Clemens engaged in a campaign of representing himself as more innocent and more religious than in fact he was in his determined courtship of Olivia Langdon, one expression of his bid for membership in the moneyed class.[9] His relations with Jervis Langdon, his prospective and later actual father-in-law, were in fact generally cordial and satisfactory. Twain exorcised in advance, through comedy, the unacceptable ways for a future son-in-law to behave, unworthy as he clearly felt himself to be. If Abelard's "seduction" of Heloise was "unmanly," Sam Clemens was himself in danger of an "unmanliness" that lay within the rhetorical strategy of his sexual self-definition and self-revelation. Clearly, "manliness" had to do not only with intentions but also with the acknowledgment of patriarchal authority: the "honest" declaration, the transfer of authority, the gaining of the bride's father's permission to consummate courtship.

Mark Twain's effort to distance himself, as an American man, from the threatening, "unmanly" European male's seduction of an "innocent" woman in his version of the story of Heloise and Abelard suggests a larger cultural dimension of Twain's definition of masculinity. Honest manliness is identified with the clarity of Victorian American gender roles and rituals, while sophistry, clerical hypocrisy, and sexual licentiousness are identified as European. Indeed, there is more evidence to indicate that, for Twain, American identity was in some ways inherently gender-related. The kind of American who pretended to be a Frenchman aroused a vituperative ire in Twain: a "poor hermaphrodite, neither fish nor fowl," he called him. Suggestively, the implication here is that a true Frenchman may be one sort of thing while a true American is another (both without provoking contempt), but the *pretense* of being European makes of an American a sexual oddity, a confusion of genders. Significantly, then, Twain's aim on his "pleasure trip" was not by any means to become European, as the hostile portrayals of Abelard and of M'sieu Gor-r-*dong,* the Frenchified American, show.[10] Nor, it is important to see, was his aim a kind of sexual conquest, as his embarrassment and irony regarding the commercial overtones of "being taken in" in Europe reveal. Instead, Twain was aiming for a kind of cultural authority that combined masculine privilege and feminine innocence. He was engendering himself androgynously. In fact, some of the most telling metaphors Twain uses to display his relation to the excursion reveal an image of both masculine and feminine parental functions: "a brave conception," he calls the tour, and "the offspring of a most ingenious brain," an image extended in a most revealing way in his famous comment to William Dean Howells concerning Howells's review of *The Innocents Abroad:* "I felt like the woman who was so glad that her baby had come white." [11] Sexual purity and respectability had been potentially compromised, in Twain's mind, by his intercourse with a crude, Western approach to Europe, the embodiment of civilization. But ironically he saw *himself* as the woman who had known more than one kind of man. In venting his relief that his literary "conception" had met with the approval of the Eastern establishment, he availed himself of the worst fear of his society of origin, the South: miscegenation, the violation of sexual and racial (thus cultural) boundaries. The image of maintaining a fictitious purity—of race and of sex—should not obscure the fact that Twain had, in a fundamental way, claimed for himself a condition of innocence that could be only an *appearance,* the same claim he implicitly made for himself as narrator in *The Innocents Abroad.*

A comparison of the significance of Europe in Louisa May Alcott's *Little Women* (1868) with Twain's relation to Europe in *The Innocents Abroad* helps to set the issue into context. Though in many ways Europe in Alcott's contemporaneous novel is continuous with America, Europe also acts as a seat of art and polite society. Italy is the place where Amy March learns the limitations of her artistic inclinations; thus her education by Europe is consistent with the education of her sisters, who must all learn to accept and come to terms with limitations, personal and social. Europe for Alcott is a charming vista but not one that essentially enlarges the awareness of restriction that surrounds her heroines: they must all internalize constraint. By contrast, Mark Twain sets out with visions of the "bold originality," "the extraordinary character," and "the vastness of the enterprise" he embarks upon. When he encounters limits, as often happens, he rails against them. The encounter with Europe becomes the occasion for vilification of his own illusions and of the deplorable conditions on the Continent as often as for rapturous (if often ironic) glorification. In other words, at this phase of his career, Twain can hardly be said to internalize the restrictions presented to him by Europe but rather regards them as alien and extraneous to the self. Unlike Alcott, Henry James, or William Dean Howells, he rejects limitations. As Cox has argued, Twain impersonates disillusionment but ironically retains his innocence. This contradictory and ambivalent endeavor is the result of a gendered series of acts of cultural self-creation.

Significant to the gender images in *The Innocents Abroad* is the peculiar, noteworthy absence of the woman who played such an important role in Mark Twain's shaping of his narrative: the absence of "Mother" Mary Fairbanks.[12] She who was among the passengers on the *Quaker City*, who read his dispatches, who offered suggestions that were often welcomed and incorporated, to whom Twain turned with enthusiasm to report about the progress of his writing—she is missing in the book, just as the image of the powerful, witty, urbane mother (Sam Clemens's own) is largely absent in his fiction generally. In the fiction this absence can perhaps be explained by the predominance of, even obsession with, fathers that is characteristic of Twain's imagination. In *The Innocents Abroad,* too, it seems tempting to see the "pilgrims" as father figures, a notion supported by the nature of the potentially antipatriarchal juvenile society (almost a "gang") formed by Twain and "the boys." But the exclusion of "Mother" Fairbanks can also be partly understood by recognizing the cultural imperative of conventional gender definition that required the son to reject or disentangle himself from the mother figure in order to achieve adult identity.[13] However, the reality is even more complex, since, in many respects, Twain incorporated the genteel values of Mary Mason Fairbanks into his narrative. In excluding the female from his narrative, he claimed for himself an innocence he might otherwise have had to share with her. Instead, Twain *himself* posed as that female pilgrim. To have Mary Fairbanks aboard, to recreate *her* experiences, would have been to diminish his own role as the quintessential American Innocent. He claimed the equivalent of female innocence for his own purposes.

Yet he was male, and this paradox led him to project onto women a degree of experience that implicitly became a threat to him, the putatively virginal male. Thus he invented, staged, and elaborated cultural dramas in *The Innocents Abroad* in which he confronted European females whose supposed experience and sophistication confirmed his innocence. These dramas reveal the merging of sexual anxiety and cultural anxiety. Economic power was a less equivocal symbol of American confidence than sexual maturity, yet both the confidence of American purchasing power and his fears about courtship provided the young American male author with material to dramatize what it meant for him to confront, challenge, and incorporate European culture in an extended act of declaration of American identity.

Chapter Two

MARK TWAIN
AND FEMALE POWER:
PUBLIC AND PRIVATE

In the 1870s Mark Twain wrote several sketches that show him confronting female privilege, sexuality, and power. Significantly, the exploration of these themes derives from his attention to British royalty and class structure. As Twain turned from the travel narrative of *The Innocents Abroad* (1869) to fiction, he was simultaneously delving into the European and the American past: the period of the Renaissance in England and the period of his childhood in the Mississippi valley of the 1830s and 1840s. It is no accident that the shift in tone and substance referred to here was happening during the years after he was first married, which were also years of prosperity and the expansion of his reputation. The experience of living intimately with a woman in marriage almost certainly exerted a subtle pressure on his perspective, though he often tried, perhaps to the detriment of his art, to maintain the tone and persona he had established in his bachelor days.[1] Nonetheless, marital and professional fulfillment seems to have temporarily muted Twain's tone and diminished the range of his poses. This is partially substantiated by his not having found sufficient material in England to satirize; he gave up the attempt to write another book like *The Innocents Abroad* but exclusively about England. At the same time, he was gaining greater mastery in the use of limited perspective. The sketches he wrote in an attempt to repeat the approach of *The Innocents Abroad* form his unpublished English Notes. In the best of these sketches, "A Memorable Midnight Experience" (published in *Mark Twain's Sketches, Number One*), and in the scatological, bawdy *1601*, which Clemens composed for his own amusement and that of a few male friends, we can see the increasing tension between public and private utterance that became a key to Clemens's attitudes toward gender at this period. The relationship between the restrained sketch written for general publication and the bawdy, body-function-oriented one written for private entertainment is the same as that between a book such as *The Adventures of Tom Sawyer* and the notes "Villagers of 1840–3" (published in *Huck Finn and Tom Sawyer Among the Indians*) that Twain never intended to publish, in which he recalled some of the physical and moral realities of life in Hannibal that he considered improper for publication.

The fact that "A Memorable Midnight Experience" was written for publication and *1601* was not is itself part of the dichotomy in Twain's consciousness, as well as in the consciousness of his contemporaries, about what was considered appropriate for public acknowledgement and discussion and what was not. While Twain was indubitably keenly attuned to the limits and taboos concerning the border between public and private in the consensus of his time, his writing also reveals the fact that for him, the duality was fraught with paradoxes—that it did indeed present tensions and at times the temptation to overstep the bounds, playfully or seriously. In "A Memorable Midnight Experience" Twain visits a public monument in London—but at night, in the company only of a friend, a guide, and a cat. He protects the privacy of his friend, Charles Kingsley, by never naming him and preserves his own through a certain self-effacement in tone and theme. Conversely, though the subject matter of *1601*, flatulence and copulation, is private, the arena in which it is discussed within the framework of the sketch is at least semipublic—the "Social Fireside" of Queen Elizabeth, including in its circle some of the most prominent Tudors: Shakespeare, Sir Walter Raleigh, Ben Jonson, and Lord Bacon. Furthermore, these Tudors refer to Continental figures such as Montaigne, Rabelais, Cervantes, Rubens, and Margaret of Navarre as they "talk about ye manners and customs of many peoples"; they are hence far less provincial, more cosmopolitan, than the narrator, who seems still to cling to Lyly's false euphuism as emblematic of queenly "grace" and the true English style. This ironic use of the freedom of conversation of famous historical figures in an earlier, much revered era is part of its fascination for Mark Twain and a prime reason for his creation of the sketch as an outgrowth of his historical research in preparation for writing *The Prince and the Pauper*. [2]

Roger Salomon has pointed out that, in Twain's work, "the aesthetic moment is one of escape from time and reality" and that the "best example of this quality of temporal suspension is found in Twain's sketch 'A Memorable Midnight Experience'" (64).[3] The aesthetic experience of history for Mark Twain, then, is itself often, paradoxically, a moment of stasis, outside or beyond history. It is a moment accompanied by the frisson of contact with the totally Other, a brush with death and transcendence, and, as Salomon and other critics have shown, frequently expressed in the imagery of sleep and dream. However, for Twain, the confrontation with history as an aesthetic experience removed from the flux of time always depends upon a contrast with the living present. As in *The Innocents Abroad*, where the awesomeness of antiquity is sometimes affirmed but at other times undercut by the "bustling" nineteenth-century present, so in Twain's sketch of the London memorial the effects of historical experience are mediated by a contrasting awareness of present-day life.[4]

"A Memorable Midnight Experience" presents a dialectic between past and present; familiar and unfamiliar; living and dead; and, most subtly, between male and female modalities.

Female beings in the male narrator's consciousness are represented primarily through three widely different presences: a "little half-grown black and white cat," the statue and the historical memory of Queen Elizabeth, and the great Abbey of Westminster itself. Each being—the independent little cat, the powerful queen, and the didactic yet womblike cathedral, anthropomorphized—functions to extend and complement the masculine experience of entrance into the vast, dusky unknown of time and space represented by the excursion of the title.

In the opening paragraphs, the narrator stresses the originality and urgency of this nocturnal male "Expedition" (just as the narrator of *The Innocents Abroad* had done in that book's opening). While the writer's curiosity grows "with the minutes," he keeps it "manfully under the surface" as he and his companion approach their destination. The carriage passes through the London streets where the author feels lost, the crowds grow thinner, and the wintry cold seems to increase. In silence the two companions pass through a dark tunnel into their destination, led by a "conductor." The moment of arrival and recognition is also one of awe—all three men remove their hats in the spacious silence and the presence of the dead. Twain evokes some of the nocturnal melancholia Huck Finn experiences; here, too, the narrator becomes receptive to the eerie sounds and silences of the night. He finds himself among statues which almost seem alive in the gloom. Yet the immobility and irrevocably *dead* quality of the "effigies" are emphasized by the presence of the undaunted cat:

> Now a little half-grown black and white cat squeezed herself through the bars of the iron gate and came purring lovingly about us, unawed by the time or the place—unimpressed by the marble pomp that sepulchres a line of mighty dead that ends with a great author of yesterday and began with a sceptred monarch away back in the dawn of history more than twelve hundred years ago. (4)

This independent, affectionate feline is not subject to the dictates of the very Dickensian Mr. W——— , their guide, whom the narrator describes thus: "He is a man in authority, being superintendent of the works, and his daily business keeps him familiar with every nook and cranny of the great pile" (4). The narrator even employs Dickensian vocabulary to describe this "man in authority." Yet the cat defies this seriocomic beadle: though they would have turned her out of the Abbey, "her small body made light of railed gates, and she would have come straight back again" (7). Thus she represents a challenge, if a small one, to the self-legitimizing dignity and authority of the "august relics," the venerable "works" maintained by men such as Mr. W——— .

While the nocturnal explorers encounter the tombs and effigies of many historical figures (in *The Innocents Abroad,* Mark Twain ventured onto the Acropolis at night in an illegal excursion from a quarantined ship), the most prominent and memorable of these is the sculpture of Queen Elizabeth, a figure who exercises quite a different grip on Clemens's imagination in *1601.* The figures of queens appear in a dual incarnation that subtly reveals something about the ambivalence the narrator feels about aristocracy, power, and specifically female power. On the one hand, Twain encounters a queen in the form of delicate, venerable statuary. Significantly, he first discovers this shape of a queen through touch, in the dark, having lost his way in the wake of his companions. "I touched a cold object, and stopped to feel its shape. I made out a thumb, and then delicate fingers. It was the clasped, appealing hands of one of those reposing images—a lady, a queen." Hands seem to function in Twain's imagination as emblems of sexual or quasi-sexual contact that does not satisfy or truly connect. In a related anecdote in *The Innocents Abroad* (discussed in chapter 1), Twain playfully reduced and feminized his hand, which he referred to as a "comely member," in an encounter with an ironic woman clerk at Gibraltar. Both incidents point to the same apprehension. This stone image, female, dead, causes him to feel the cold touch of mortality and its concomitant fear: "I touched the face—by accident, not design—and shuddered inwardly, if not outwardly." But his fear soon increases: "Then something rubbed against my leg, and I shuddered outwardly and inwardly both. It was the cat. The friendly creature meant well, but as the English say, she gave me 'such a turn' " (6–7). Again, as with the "man in authority," Twain self-consciously adopts British idiom. The living animal being reminds him forcibly, through her unexpected appearance, of his own aliveness, of his own being's recoil from death. "I took her in my arms for company and wandered among the grim sleepers till I caught the glimmer of the lantern again, and then put her down." Comforted by her humble, live presence, he is able to return to the realm of the living.

But this is only a prelude to a didactic tableaux: "Behind us was the stately monument of Queen Elizabeth, with her effigy dressed in royal robes, lying as if at rest. When we turned around, the cat, with stupendous simplicity, was coiled up and sound asleep upon the feet of the Great Queen!" Here Twain sets out to teach the reader a lesson in the best genteel tradition, as he was also to do in *The Prince and the Pauper.* The identities of cat and queen become intermingled in a symbiotic union upon which Twain cannot refrain from moralizing. In characteristically Victorian fashion, he concludes, "Truly this was reaching far towards the millenium, when the lion and the lamb shall lie down together. The murderer of Mary and Essex, the conqueror of the Armada, the imperious ruler of a turbulent empire, become a couch, at last, for a tired kitten! It was the most eloquent sermon upon the vanity of human pride and human grandeur that inspired Westminster preached to us that night." Not only has the statue come to represent the historical personage of Queen Elizabeth herself while the cat represents a humble quotidian reality of life in the present, Elizabeth's power is represented as cruel if not immoral will. She is a woman who, by nineteenth-century standards, has acted beyond her sphere. Thus to Twain she is not merely ruler or conqueror but murderer. Mary, Queen of Scots, by contrast, is simply mentioned, in connection with her effigy, to point out how all the portraits are copied from it. Elizabeth the Queen and the kitten, associated and contrasted by their presence together in Westminster Abbey, represent another version of the demon/innocent split of the female Other in Twain's consciousness already seen in *The Innocents Abroad*. To contrast the queen with the kitten is one of the means by which Twain shifts the emphasis of European culture, in his transformation of it, from the realm of politics of state to the realm of gender.

Elizabeth, then, is singled out as representative of that human vanity lamented by Solomon, tinged here with ruthless cruelty. The subtext is not too difficult to decipher: not only is Elizabeth representative of the ironic pride of human grandeur that is belied by death and eternity, she is for Twain a vivid example of the unnatural function of female rule in bringing about death rather than bringing forth life. If, as seems evident, Twain was more interested in exposing the obscenity of power than the obscenity of sex, his vision of monarchy here, mild as it appears, is a symptom of his impulse in that direction. Even the fact that his journey to Westminster has the surreptitious quality of a nocturnal escapade suggests such an interpretation. The metaphysical shudder of being in the presence of corpses at midnight—venerated though they may be—invests his visit to the national shrine with an ironic undercurrent. Antiquity may be a curiosity, as he emphasizes again and again, but the proximity of death is a horrifying reality that puts the lie to the pomp of aristocracy and European cultural prestige. This point is driven home by one anecdote after another: the burlesque story of the confusion over the three skulls of Jonson, the tales of the murder of "Annie, Queen of Richard III and daughter of the kingmaker, the great Earl of Warwick—murdered she was—poisoned by her husband" (6) and of the knight who took sanctuary in the Abbey but was "butchered . . . right before the altar." It is further underlined by the guide's dispassionate statement that a resting place beneath the pavement is a "very comfortable" place, which Twain says "made the cold chills creep up my back" (6).

Queen Elizabeth is, at the very least, an ambivalent model of female power. Yet there is another example of female influence in Mark Twain's imagination here, one which enables him to deflect the sordid conclusions that his concentration on the image of the murderous queen might lead him to: Westminster Abbey. The Abbey itself, apotheosized as a stately being, referred to with the female pronoun, is an alternative model of female nature. "She" is designated as the moral educator of the British nation:

> As we turned toward the door, the moonlight was beaming in at the windows; and it gave to the sacred place such an air of restfulness and peace, that Westminster was no longer a grisly museum of mouldering vanities, but her better and worthier self—the deathless mentor of a great nation, the guide and encourager of right ambitions, the preserver of fame, and the home and refuge for the nation's best and bravest when their work is done. (8)

Twain is here praising *her better and worthier self* (my italics) in terms that correspond to the Victorian conception of the ideal wife and mother: she is the mentor, the guide, the provider of moral support and discernment, the one who "preserves" the memory of valiant deeds, and finally "home and refuge" when that which must be done outside the home is completed. In fact, the Abbey is very like Victoria herself.[5] Westminster Abbey, in Twain's concluding image, is without doubt a woman.

As Susan K. Harris has noted, Twain saw in "home" a " 'type and symbol of heaven' from which he felt he was in exile" (*Mark Twain's Escape from Time* 70). In exile he searched for "that pillow of weariness, that refuge from care, and trouble, and pain . . .

Home." If Westminster Abbey indeed represents a symbolic form of home to Twain, as he claims, it is not difficult to detect that the "refuge from care, and trouble, and pain" also has another name: death. The equation of home with the womb and with the repose of death signals that the Abbey is a womb for the dead. As Twain dramatizes, the dead who reside there have an enduring form of life in the public consciousness, particularly in a national memorial such as Westminster Abbey represents. The Abbey herself is not death, but to be sheltered there, to find sanctuary there, requires a noble life culminating in an honored death. Only the cat, one might say, is human in Westminster Abbey: kings and queens, poets and statesmen, all are caught in the paradox of their fame preserved in history after their deaths, like flies in amber.

The extremes of female power—the queen as murderer, the Abbey as all-embracing moral influence—illustrate Twain's ambivalent desire for transcendence of the self through the female. As he reaches for images of the powerful Other, he is both attracted and repelled. But he cannot stay in either mode for very long: though he can be reverent and moral, or he can be judgmental and sentimental, he will always return to the simple cat with its freedom, ease, and comfort but also its disregard of human self-consciousness, guilt, and history.

Twain's *1601* extends our understanding of his dual response to Queen Elizabeth and to the culture she represented for him. Here the queen is center stage, and the setting is no longer the vastness of Westminster though still the semipublic "closet" of a monarch. The assembled company is balanced between the sexes: five men and five women, not counting the queen herself and her male cupbearer, "the Pepys of that day" (32). Significantly, the men are defined simply by the fame of their achievements. (Francis Beaumonte, the only male whose age is named, is also the only one whose achievement needs to be stated: "being but sixteen, hath yet turned his hand to ye doing of ye Lattin masters into our Englishe tong, with grete discretion and much applaus.") The women, equally significantly, are all defined by the narrator by stating their ages, and since we are told that Lady Alice Dilberry has "turned seventy, she being two yeres ye queenes graces elder," Elizabeth's age is made clear as well. The Duchess of Bilgewater (foreshadowing the character in *Adventures of Huckleberry Finn*) has a name that proclaims her absurdity from the start.

The perspective of the narrator is by no means a simple one. To begin with, he is ostensibly scandalized by the democratic, "righte straunge mixing truly of mighty blode with mean" in this gathering, yet he reports the event in faithful documentary detail. Furthermore, he objects more vehemently to the spectacle of "rank forgot" in which "ye high holde converse wh ye low as uppon equal termes" (33) than to the vulgarity or obscenity of the conversation itself. Clearly, Twain's amusement is aroused as much by the social joke of the aristocratic snob distressed by the mixing of ranks as by the off-color subject matter of the conversation, and particularly by the juxtaposition of the two.[6]

The subject matter of *1601* has caused it to be frequently ignored by critics, except to be surprisingly reviled in extreme terms far into the twentieth century. As Franklin Meine pointed out, Edward Wagenknecht misleadingly called it "the most famous piece of pornography in American literature" (27). Van Wyck Brooks found handy use for it in defending his theory of the waste of Twain's genius:

> Consider the famous book, *1601, that fireside conversation in the time of Queen Elizabeth:* is there any obsolete verbal indecency in the English language that Mark Twain has not painstakingly resurrected and assembled there? He, whose blood was in constant ferment and who could not contain within the narrow bounds that had been set for him the riotous exuberance of his nature, had to have an

escape-valve, and he poured through it a fetid stream of meaningless obscenity—the waste of a priceless psychic material![7]

Maxwell Geismar treats it more sympathetically in recognizing that "this pamphlet, hardly so much pornography as erotica, showed a remarkable virtuosity in Clemens's use of an earlier, franker English language; and, despite a stress on anal-erotic as well as genital humor, it is an entertaining satire" (50). While explicit critical discussion of the physical functions in D. H. Lawrence's or James Joyce's work has become commonplace, the Puritan legacy has clung to much of Twain scholarship in relegating *1601* to the realm of obscenity or, at best, facetiae. Twain's sketch is not meaningless, though it may be obscene.

The issue at stake in *1601,* beneath the "superficies" (to use a Swiftian term) of the scatological and erotic discussion, is power. More specifically, the issue is the power of the physical body in competition with the power of the word, the tongue, the mind. Suffusing the social drama which Twain much later said was the thing that amused him most, "that outraged old cupbearer's comments" on "those people . . . of offensively low birth" who "hadn't a thing to recommend them except their incomparable brains," was the conflict between body and mind, between physicality and spirit (*The Autobiography of Mark Twain* 293). The bowels and the "member" have their power, against which the feeble if embittered remonstrances of the cupbearer can do little. In a backhanded way, Twain pays tribute to the force of social convention, for it is clear that if Elizabeth and her court think nothing of conversing as they do, the cupbearer's opinion is ridiculously irrelevant, "proper" as he may be. The "Pepys of that day" is in a situation remarkably similar to that of the auditor listening to Simon Wheeler's rambling, vulgar tale in "The Notorious Jumping Frog of Calaveras County,"which also features a conflict between words and the capabilities of the body, though cast in the frontier idiom.

As Twain's comment about the "incomparable brains" of
Elizabeth's guests suggests, his sketch pays playful tribute to
the minds—and particularly the verbal skills—of Elizabeth
and her circle. Though he indubitably parodies the Euphuists,
his imitation is skillful enough, especially in the mouths of
Elizabeth, Sir Walter Raleigh, and Master Shaxpur, to represent
a form of tribute to its ingenuity. Furthermore, he gives Elizabeth herself the role of puncturing the pretensions of Euphuism
taken to their extreme. On one level Twain's tale is a contest
of wits in which each participant tries to outshine the other
in eloquence. The hot air of speech is outdone by the performance of passing hot air from the nether mouth when Sir Walter Raleigh farts phenomenally, interrupting the conversation
and causing his "contribution" to become the focus of discussion. With courtly eloquence, the various interlocutors whom
Elizabeth interrogates concerning the source of the fart humbly
disclaim its authorship, calling it in turn "a thundergust," "rich
o'ermastering fog," a "wonder" of "matchless might," a "harri-
cane," "so fell a blast," a "prodigy," and a "miracle." All these
wry tributes to the force of a windy gut are topped by Master
Shaxpur, who soliloquizes,

> Though ye sinless hosts of heaven had foretold ye coming
> of this most desolating breath, proclaiming it a work
> of uninspired man, its quaking thunders, its firmament-
> clogging rottenness his own achievement in due course of
> nature, yet had not I believed it; but had said the pit itself
> hath furnished forth the stink, and heaven's artillery hath
> shook the globe in admiration of it. (35)[8]

As in "The Ode to Stephen Dowling Bots, Dec'd" ("They got
him out and emptied him. Alas! It was too late!") Twain derives comedy from our consciousness of the undignified physical
reality that contradicts the rhetorical grandeur, a reality that
resembles the homely physical simplicity of the cat in Westminster Abbey. With chivalric humility, each courtier denies his

Samuel Clemens with his daughters, Clara and Susy, 1877.
Courtesy, The Mark Twain Project, The Bancroft Library.

or her ability to loose the whirlwind that has awed them all, except for Sir Raleigh, its author, who with scarcely concealed pride denigrates his effort as not worthy of the queen or, he implies, of his own abilities, thus earning the cupbearer's enmity. With Swiftian excremental vision, Twain reveals how courtiers conceal base realities in a cloak of fine words; yet Twain's satiric rapier is directed more against the priggish narrator who fails to see the humor of the occasion than against the imaginative circle of free-spoken Elizabethans. The author, on the contrary, appears to celebrate the rhetorical vigor and ingenuity of Elizabeth's court, amounting as it does to a verbal braggadocio that resembles the swagger and extravagance of such frontier burlesque passages as the raft episode that was omitted from *Huck Finn*.

With organizational neatness, the sketch divides itself into two sections of approximately equal length, the first having to do with the fart and its consequences, the second with sexual prowess. In each section the queen is clearly in control of the conversation, guiding it by reproof and praise. The women prove as eloquent as the men, and though the discussion of sexual powers emphasizes male staying power, as with the ram that "wil tup above a hundred yewes 'twixt sun and sun; and after, if he can have none more to shag, will masturbate until he hath enrich'd whole acres with his seed" (36), female sexual powers are also praised. In fact, each of the anecdotes concerning male members reflects a questionable light upon masculine pride and prowess, beginning with the tale attributed to "Montaine," about the "custom of widows of Perigord to wear uppon ye headdress, in sign of widowhood, a jewel in ye similitude of a man's member wilted and limber," which suggests not only that the women have outlived their husbands but that their sexual desire has excelled that of their men. The queen's joking response, that "widows in England doe wear prickes too, but betwixt the thighs, and not wilted neither, till coition hath done that office for them," suggests that the memory of the husbands who have died is little consolation compared with the live satisfaction of having actual, present lovers. It also suggests a kind of female insatiability hinted at in the cup-bearer's remark about "cunts not loathe to take the stiffness out of them" and in the anecdote of the Duchess of Bilgewater's being "roger'd by four lords before she had a husband" (38). There is an acknowledgment here—and a fear of—the female's greater sexual appetite. The emperor whom Shakespeare mentions, who took ten maidenheads in one night, is surpassed by his empress who "did entertain two and twenty lusty knights between her sheets, yet was not satisfied," to which Countess Granby adds that the already-mentioned ram is "yet the emperor's superior." The story from Boccaccio that Sir Walter relates, about the priest who knelt to offer a prayer of thanks for the maid whom he had "beguiled" into his cell but found that the abbot who spied her through the keyhole already occupied his place when he concluded, also is not designed to flatter male vanity.

With its antiromantic Chaucerian bawdiness, this conversation emphasizes as much the sexual needs and satisfactions of the female as of the male. In response to an argument about the spelling of the word "bollocks," Lady Margery says, "Gentles, what mattereth it how ye shall spell the word? I warrant ye, when ye use your bollocks ye shall not think of it; and my Lady Granby, be ye content; let the spelling be, ye shall enjoy the beating of them on your buttocks just the same, I trow" (37). Lady Margery's comment is one of several reminders that the body has its own reality and its demands which at times supersede those of language. Yet language has its own power which is seen at times as an extension of the body's drives. The two adolescents in the circle, Lady Helen and Francis Beaumonte, prove equally witty in parrying the comments of their elders who seek to expose their inexperience. Lady Helen's response to the queen's question of whether she does not desire to have her virginity protected cleverly refers the issue to the authority and example of her nurse and of the queen: "Mine old nurse hath told me there are more ways of serving God than by locking the thighs together; yet am I willing to serve him yt way too, sith your highnesses grace hath set ye ensample." Beaumonte's reply to the queen's question that seeks to discover his awakening sexuality responds with equal cleverness by deferring graciously to superiority of rank: "Mousing owls and bats of low degree may not aspire to bliss so whelming and ecstatic as is found in ye downy nests of birds of Paradise."

The queen equates Beaumonte's readiness of tongue with sexual prowess: "With such a tongue as thine, lad, thou'lt spread the ivory thighs of many a willing maide in thy good time, an' thy cod-piece be as handy as thy speeche." Yet, as Lady Helen's self-possessed speech indicates, there are women with equal or greater verbal skill and self-determination. The queen herself is in charge in just such a way. When she is displeased at a turn of conversation, a sarcastic comment from her causes the company to fall silent, and a sharp look at Sir Walter causes him to wince. Yet even the cupbearer, who defends Elizabeth against what he perceives as the insulting liberties taken by members of her court, recognizes (and points out) the arbitrariness of her power. He indicates the unfairness of singling out any individual for sexual transgressions. Significantly, the thing that offends her is Sir Throgmorton's failure "to save his doter's maidenhedde sound for her marriage-bed." It would be as much a mistake to see only the patriarchal insistence on virginity as a form of protection of male lineage here as it would be to take the cupbearer's judgments that Lady Alice and Lady Margery were "whores from ye cradle" at face value. The cupbearer also calls the cause of the queen's taking offence "a little harmless debauching" and asks, "Who of this company was sinless?" The point is precisely that Samuel Clemens is not to be easily located in this welter of relative judgments; instead, the version of Queen Elizabeth and her court that he imagines here allows him the freedom to present a circle of equally lusty women and men who are yet all subject to the constraints of power and the body.

These constraints are indicated in the final two anecdotes, which concern two at first seemingly unrelated cases of deflation. Lady Alice's pride in her Euphuistic virtuosity is punctured when the queen punctuates Alice's pretentious speech with a vastly ironic exclamation of "O shit!" Sir Walter's tale, ostensibly from Margaret of Navarre, concerns a maid "being like to suffer rape by an olde archbishoppe, did smartly contrive a device to save her maidenhedde, and said to him, *First, my lord, I prithee, take out thy holy tool and piss before me;* which doing, lo his member felle, and would not rise again" (39). In each case, the physical function—once through its naming, once by naming and action—defeats the desire to dominate and possess, whether through pride or through lust. The word and the flesh vie for domination, and it is by no means clear whether wit or the function of the body is more powerful.

If Westminster Abbey is "the deathless mentor of a great nation," as Twain claims in "A Memorable Midnight Experience," and Queen Elizabeth is the purveyor of "the most eloquent sermon upon the vanity of human pride and human grandeur" that Westminster can preach, the innocent little cat and "pricks" that "were stiff and cunts not loathe to take ye stiffness out of them" are part of the same lesson. The warm animal body, sexual or not, human or not, but breathing in the face of the Great Dark, has its own irreducible meaning, which it was part of Twain's genius to recognize. Far from being meaningless obscenity, *1601* contains its intimations of mortality in the midst of comic celebration of the body, just as "A Memorable Midnight Experience" celebrates mortal, ineffable life in spite of its sentimental moralism about the pervasiveness of death. This grasp of seemingly irreconcilable opposites, like

Huck's "sound heart and deformed conscience," is testimony to the authenticity and importance of Twain's vision, even when the forms he experiments with are inadequate.

Yet there is a shadow side to the celebration of the body that Twain indulges in sub rosa here. In *The Innocents Abroad* Twain had excluded the female among the pilgrims and claimed her innocence as his own, but he also showed his concern with a power he had projected on the females of Europe. In "A Memorable Midnight Experience" we enter the womb of a structure that entombs dead European power. The vision of the kitten versus the power of Elizabeth confronts the nocturnal visitor with conflicting visions of power. He cannot enter and exit as freely as the uninhibited cat; he must thus breathe more easily by escaping the enclosure that can arrest him forever. He must flee its deadening power. In *1601* he confronts that power more directly, and he allows what he has previously avoided: the possibility that the sexual female is more powerful than the male. He introduces another boyish innocent in Beaumonte; at the other end of the scale are the aging queen and the oldest female figure, Alice, "yt foolish old bitch" (who incidentally is exactly the age Elizabeth will be when she dies two years later).

It is interesting to speculate why the twenty-two-year-old Duchess of Bilgewater is given the same name as the most depraved character in *Huck Finn* and why Clemens chose the year 1601 — just two years before Elizabeth's death — to set his story in. Clemens did not, for example, choose a time when she was still the lover of Raleigh, whom she spurned, or of Essex, whom she executed. In other words, he does not renounce his view of her as murderer. As we can see from these examples, the sketch attempts to allay some of the profound anxieties also revealed in "A Memorable Midnight Experience," but it does so more directly and honestly. The misogyny of the cupbearer when he catalogs the instances of female promiscuity is not wholly alien to Sam Clemens, who used European mores to exorcise his American puritanism as well as to work out his own ambivalence toward gender conflict. Clemens's private sketch, like the travelogue account, attempts to come to terms with the perceived cultural paradox of emblematic female power in European history. In the process, the political symbolism of royalty becomes, in Twain's translation, part of the gender symbolism of American culture. The discourse of class structure, aspiration, and conflict is translated by Twain into the language of American gender anxieties, conflicts, and constraints.

Chapter Three

FATHERS AND SONS IN
THE PRINCE AND THE PAUPER

In *The Prince and the Pauper,* the work that Twain was preparing for by researching the language and customs that found their expression in *1601,* there is no figure comparable to Queen Elizabeth. In fact, the queens of Henry VIII do not appear at all. Twain concentrates instead on the relationship between father and son in ways that are intimately rooted in his own childhood. Edward and Tom, the innocents, are not unrelated to the boyish innocent of *The Innocents Abroad* or to the night visitor to Westminster Abbey or to Francis Beaumonte and the other four males who, in *1601,* are at the arbitrary mercy of a queen/parent who can execute them at will—or remove her "mercy" with an "O shit!" *The Prince and the Pauper* continues Mark Twain's evolving appropriation and translation of images and events from European history into the expression of American concerns about gender identity through the language of European social class. The irreducible reality of the body is present here also, though it is less visible in the context of the historical romance. Here the living body is not only that of the child, but, in a fashion reminiscent of the imposing dead weight of the Abbey, the corpse of the father. (The nightmare perpetuated by the death of Edward's father, Henry, is finally dissolved by a kind of public exorcism that takes place in the Abbey itself in the climactic scene in *The Prince and the Pauper.*)

While it may seem at first puzzling that there are so few

female characters in this book that was written to be read first of all to a circle of girls and women, the innocent, partially feminized protagonists and the cruel, judgmental adult male figures are ultimately part of the same dichotomy that we have seen in the early travel book and in the sketches of the 1870s. Whereas *1601* displayed Clemens's uneasiness about the "masculine" qualities of Elizabeth, *The Prince and the Pauper* explores both the terror and the comfort of masculine figures who exhibit qualities his culture frequently considered "feminine": nurture, gentleness, and compassion.

The debate surrounding *The Prince and the Pauper* has tended to equate this work with a genteel tradition whose tone was primarily defined by women and to denigrate the novel as an expression of Twain's literary domestication. Tom H. Towers has argued that *The Prince and the Pauper* is "a major and forthright expression of a cultural and political conservatism which is a minor note in Twain's writing" ("The Prince and the Pauper" 194). Towers interprets this conservatism as the obverse of his "despairing contempt" for human civilization. Kenneth Andrews has similarly stressed the origin of the novel in the genteel values and literary tastes of Nook Farm, the elite Hartford neighborhood where Samuel Clemens made his home in the 1870s and 1880s (190–97). The growing hostility toward England and in particular toward British critics of America that Twain expressed vehemently in the 1880s was still mild and largely unarticulated at the time he wrote *The Prince and the Pauper*. [1] This is not to say, however, that Twain's historical romance was a comfortable concession to the dominant cultural tenor of respectable New England society, as many critics have claimed. [2] Recent critical treatment of the book has frequently tended to be a sophisticated version of Van Wyck Brooks's old thesis: the artist was intimidated into curtailing his criticisms of society or acquiesced in their suppression (106–27). In this view, he sold the honesty of his vision, partially expressed in *Adventures of Huckleberry Finn,* for a mess of pottage.

The dualism of this approach to Twain is exacerbated by a tendency to treat his works of the late 1870s and early 1880s almost as if they had been written by two different authors. The hack writer competes with the literary genius, in this view. In *Huck Finn* the latter won, mostly, this theory holds; in *The Prince and the Pauper* the former has the upper hand. This tendency is further encouraged by the requirement that literary history should focus upon prophetic and ground-breaking works. *The Prince and the Pauper* represents little if any departure from conventional forms and styles, while Hemingway's statement that all modern American literature comes from one book does not sound preposterous anymore. Another dimension of the duality addressed here is that *Huck Finn* records an era of American history, while *The Prince and the Pauper* is set in the distant European past. Furthermore, *The Prince and the Pauper* has frequently been dismissed as a children's book, while critics take satisfaction in suggesting complexities in *Huck Finn* that are beyond the comprehension of children. This ignores, among other things, Twain's subtitle for *The Prince and the Pauper,* which is "A Tale for Young People of All Ages." It is also, presumably, a tale for both sexes. In *The Prince and the Pauper* we can see Twain moving toward an androgynous reconciliation of audiences and of gender traits in his characters.

Mark Twain's own overestimation of the literary value of his Tudor romance appears to have contributed to its denigration by twentieth-century critics. This is due in part to the resounding victory of critics such as H. L. Mencken in the battle of naturalism against gentility and romanticism in American letters. As Arthur L. Vogelback has described, *The Prince and the Pauper* "fitted in perfectly with the tradition of correctness and imitation—with the genteel tradition" and was praised accordingly by contemporary critics, including Clemens's friend William Dean Howells (48–54). The novel's lack of originality and innovation is presumably part of what Leonard Woolf reacted against when he condemned the work as betraying "a commonness and tawdriness, a lack of sensitiveness, which do not matter to the impetuous appetite of youth, but which cannot be ignored by the more discriminating and exacting taste of middle-age" (765). However, the consensus of recent critical assessment has missed a significant dimension of meaning in *The Prince and the Pauper*. This meaning resides in the realm where the themes of Twain's psychological obsessions with gender and his quest for a cultural identity meet.

Despite critics' tendency to dismiss *The Prince and the Pauper,* it deserves serious attention, both as a story that has proven its durability with readers over more than a century and as a significant part of Mark Twain's oeuvre. Though the fact that it is Mark Twain's most carefully plotted novel may not count in its favor artistically by contemporary standards, it is a mistake to discount it entirely in a consideration of Twain's development as an artist.

The European setting that the aspiring young journalist Mark Twain had employed as a comic backdrop for self-dramatization in *Innocents Abroad* served the established, middle-aged father Samuel Clemens as the context for his story of fatherless sons seeking an identity and an inheritance through surrogate fathers. The period between 1877 and 1880 was a time when Twain reached beyond the relatively tame world of the fatherless Tom Sawyer into the imaginative inner life of Huck Finn, who escapes the grasp of his savage, destructive father. *The Prince and the Pauper* abounds with symbolic father-son relationships that are curiously paradoxical in ways that form a significant contrast to *Huck Finn*. Robert Regan and Albert E. Stone, Jr. have commented, in different ways, on the significance of the father-son relationships in the former work.[3] What has not been developed is why and how the European setting freed Twain to write about father-son relationships as a dynamic possibility within a society. Neither *The Adventures of Tom Sawyer* nor *Adventures of Huckleberry Finn* offered this possibility in quite such a form, though Tom Sawyer, Huckleberry

Finn, Tom Canty, and Edward Tudor all have in common that they either are or become orphans in one way or another. Tom Sawyer's father is never mentioned; Huck's father, pap, dies in the middle of *Huck Finn* (though Huck does not find it out until the end); Tom Canty's father runs away at the end of the book and is never heard from again; and the death of Edward's father, Henry VIII, is of course central to the plot. Further, one can argue that Twain turned to the dramatization of father-son relationships because it was easier to manage than that of mother-son. Europe as American Fatherland was something he could control better than the Hag Europe as seductive but dangerous Motherland.

The legacy of beneficent surrogate fathers combined with the strength and efforts of the natural selves of the heroes in *The Prince and the Pauper* creates a better life for the boys and for their society. While for Tom Sawyer and Huck Finn, imaginative expansion and education about social roles through European or pseudo-European models lead ultimately back to where they started from, a relationship to society that has not essentially changed, what Tom Canty and the Prince of Wales learn about social roles in the midst of symbolic European institutions leads to redefined relationships to their society and even to relatively small but nonetheless significant changes in that society itself. "The reign of Edward VI was a singularly merciful one for those harsh times," Twain states in the final paragraph (335). He implies that the improvement of justice under Edward's rule was prophetic of greater progress in that direction made in later centuries, an ameliorative tendency that places his "tale for young people of all ages" squarely in the genteel tradition of literature for youth written by female authors such as his neighbor Harriet Beecher Stowe and Charlotte M. Yonge.[4] That ameliorative tendency was associated with feminization, a domesticating female influence which critics from Brooks to Fiedler have self-righteously deplored. Yet the Twain who is writing about the "softening" of male sadism is returning to one half of the dichotomy he already exhibited in *The Innocents Abroad*.

The conflict between social circumstances and the inner lives and aspirations of his characters is a theme that appears in *Huck Finn* and in *The Prince and the Pauper*. [5] Twain's version of European customs, institutions, and historical events represents a utopian/dystopian world of grand hopes and cruel, amoral realities. The utopian aspect of Twain's Europe is its capacity to represent dream objects of desire. For Tom Canty, the dream object is a life of grandeur, luxury, and comfort as a prince, while Tom Sawyer interestingly enough aspires to a parody of such a life. Twain treats Canty's aspiration seriously, though it has some comic consequences, whereas he treats Tom Sawyer's aspiration comically, though it has some serious consequences (such as the diminution of Jim's dignity and significance). For Edward, Prince of Wales, the dream object is to play without rules or boundaries, social or geographical—a freedom of the sort that Huck Finn attains, but only too briefly. In both cases Twain shows us some of the costs of the desire for freedom. For Miles Hendon, as for Jim in *Adventures of Huckleberry Finn*, the dream object is more poignantly adult: to return home after a long absence, to rejoin the love of his youth, and to gain his share of the inheritance which is rightfully his (in Jim's case, to gain possession of himself—his freedom). Yet during Miles's absence, his brother Hugh has employed his masculine dominance to force Miles's fiancée to marry him instead. Miles, like Jim, is a nurturing male, one who, it could be argued, has already incorporated into himself the positive "feminine" qualities of caring, empathy, and protectiveness, an idea reinforced by scenes such as Miles's wielding needle and thread to repair the pauper-prince's clothes. In his letters, Clemens repeatedly described Mary Mason Fairbanks's "motherly" attentions to him as sewing on his buttons and keeping his clothes in trim, activities he also, more or less humorously, used to define womanhood in his 1868 toast to "Woman." If the boys in both stories yearn for freedom, the most admirable men, Jim and Miles, seek connection. They embody a masculine ideal that appropriates "womanly" qualities, an ideal that is not matched by a female ideal incorporating conventional male strengths. The portrayal of the male heroes seems to imply that the woman is superfluous.

   The Prince and the Pauper clearly contains a strand of mythic story, both in Durkheim's sense of myth as "allegorical introduction, to shape the individual to his group" and in the Jungian interpretation of myth as "group dream, symptomatic of archetypal urges within the depths of the human psyche" (Campbell 382). The cruelty of certain incidents in the story reinforces the mythic quality of parts of the novel, a quality that resembles the folktales in theme and style.[6] For example, there is the hermit's sharpening his knife to butcher the bound boy (an echo of the story of Abraham and Isaac) or the burning of the Baptist women at the stake. The explicit treatment of violence is more consonant with the genteel tradition than we may imagine: Mary Mapes Dodge's maxim that it is important that "harsh, cruel facts" be presented unflinchingly sometimes is pertinent here. According to Dodge, they "must march forward boldly, say what they have to say, and go."[7]

   Twain's orphaned sons seek to accomplish the impossible—to recover their lost fathers—and in the process they invent themselves. *The Prince and the Pauper* reveals the extent to which, even in his minor works, Twain's obsessions coincided with the cultural preoccupations of his countrymen. In *The Prince and the Pauper,* the teleology of the New World individual's psychology and the mythos of American identity merge, given shape yet also disguised by the European setting.

   Europe in *The Prince and the Pauper* is a mythopoetic realm of symbolic social extremes and of fairytale-like father-son relationships. Mark Twain took pains to emphasize the histo-

ricity of his tale, as his facsimile of the birth announcement at
the front of the book suggests. His characters are all supposedly
English, and the action is presented as having taken place in
the real, if fictionalized, past of sixteenth-century England. His
central character is a historical figure: the prince and later boy
king Edward VI. Edward occupies a psychologically and historically significant place in relation to the Elizabeth of Twain's
imagination. He is a boy who will not become a *man* king; and
he reigns, in historical terms, *before* the female monarch who
will treat the boyish Francis Beaumonte as a sex object.

These circumstances point to the fact that, as authentic as
details of the setting and story are, the essential force of the
story is mythic, and the perspective from which the story is told
is distinctly American. Mark Twain's sixteenth-century London is intrinsically a fantasy realm like that of the fairytale, in
which heart's desires are more important than quotidian reality.
Kingship and pauperdom are significant here not primarily as
historical facts but as metaphors for social and personal conditions from which each boy, prince and pauper, imagines escape.
The boys involved are less individuals than types of heroic
innocence. The characters of prince and pauper are stylized
into complementary compatibility, making an exchange of roles
possible. Each boy is inherently noble and imaginative, the
prince of necessity brave and strong enough to meet his mis-
adventures among the rabble, the pauper wise enough to meet
the challenges of life at court.[8] But each boy also requires the
aid of a benevolent father figure.

Mark Twain opposes the boys' natural, authentic characters
to the artificialities and cruelties of a Manichaean Europe. In
the struggle to regain their social identities, each of the three
main characters, Tom Canty, Edward, Prince of Wales, and
Miles Hendon (each of the three in some sense a boy), realizes
his authentic self, which in the end proves to be as important
as the social identity he lost. Though Edward becomes king,
Miles regains his inheritance, and Tom Canty is appointed to

the post of chief governor of Christ's Hospital, these public destinies are not as important as the proving of their authentic private characters that each goes through.

The American nature of Twain's treatment of his special European material becomes clear when one examines his themes closely. The centrality of natural character, particularly in the person of innocent Tom Canty at court but also in the spontaneous responses and positive inner resources of Miles Hendon and Edward, both in manners and in moral questions, suggests the continuity of Europe and America in Mark Twain's imagination at this time. The ultimate aim of each son is to regain his identity, which is initially the identity conferred upon him by being his particular father's son. Though Tom Canty does not desire to claim an identity related to his father's, he does have to renounce an identity based on being the son of a man who is not his father, and he aspires to an identity revealed to him by his surrogate father. Tom Canty represents the outcast seeking to establish a place for himself in a stratified society. The circumstances he is thrown into, which range from extreme poverty and abuse to the pinnacle of wealth and power, present him with tests of character in which he must conduct himself well in order to attain a state in which his inner character is manifested and acknowledged through his social role, a theme consonant with the "rags to riches" genre of American writing.

The symbolic American individual is multiply represented in *The Prince and the Pauper* by the disinherited son, the son who is actually or practically orphaned. The novel reflects a preoccupation with orphanhood that Twain shared with American writers such as Horatio Alger and Frances Hodgson Burnett, a preoccupation that is also central to nineteenth-century American women's writing. Orphanhood, one might argue, is a characteristically American condition; for a nation of immigrants and uprooted persons, losing parents is a common, symbolically potent experience.[9] Oscar Handlin, in *The Uprooted,* has poignantly discussed the loss of parental authority and of continuity between the generations among immigrant families, even when children have not literally become orphans (215–30). The father figures in *Huck Finn* and *Tom Sawyer* are not in a position to bestow a place in society on their sons. Jim, the adult to whom Huck is closest, of course cannot do so because he is a slave. Except for a certain resourcefulness that encompasses trickery and self-serving rationalization, pap has no legacy except cruelty, prejudice, and anarchy to offer his son. (The six thousand dollars Huck comes into possession of at his father's death is money Huck himself found, which his father would have taken away from him if he could have.) Uncle Silas Phelps is too benignly inconsequential to make an impact on either Huck or Tom. The closest any father figure comes to providing a positive legacy is when Judge Thatcher promises at the end of *The Adventures of Tom Sawyer* to see to it that "Tom be admitted to the National military academy and afterwards trained in the best law school in the country, in order that he might be ready for either career or both" (233). The historical romance provided Mark Twain with a context in which he could envision generational succession in positive terms. Whereas in *Huck Finn* his characters develop an authentic self at the cost of social position or a social position at the cost of the authentic self, Tom Canty and Edward are able to achieve both.

While *The Prince and the Pauper* is also circular in the sense that Edward and Miles return to their original social positions (while Tom moves from pauperdom to a comfortable sinecure), in the book with the European setting Twain imagined multiple father-son relationships that issue in a form of generational succession. The paradox is that in this American form of inheritance the son has to win the right to inherit his father's legacy and even, in one case, becomes his father's symbolic father. Twain implies that the aid a father can give is only equal to or less than the inner resources a son must have to achieve his goals.

It is true only on the literal level, as Stone claims, that Mark Twain's historical romance is "not in the least autobiographical in origin" (92). Even on the literal level, coincidences between this story which Twain took such satisfaction in writing and his own life point to psychological, symbolic autobiography. Clemens was eleven years and several months old when his father, John Clemens, died. Though the historical Edward was nine years old when Henry VIII died, Clemens asked that "the artist always picture the Prince & Tom Canty as lads of 13 or 14 years old"—in other words, just at the threshhold of puberty.[10] Thus the ages of the historical Edward and the fictional Edward bracket Sam Clemens's age at the time of his father's death, indicating a probable correspondence between the position of the semifictional boy at his father's death and Clemens's own experience. Furthermore, John Clemens was a judge; judges figure prominently in *The Prince and the Pauper*. Henry VIII, like many fathers who appear in judgmental roles in Twain's fiction, appears in the role of judge when he condemns the Duke of Norfolk to execution, and other characters act as judges in the story as well: Tom Canty in the role of the prince hears and decides the cases of several of his subjects, and a justice of the peace presides as judge in the case against Edward when he is accused of stealing a dressed pig. Sam Clemens, at his father's death, was left in the charge of a mother who would assume a paternal role (just as Queen Elizabeth took over an orphaned England).

Without wishing to overstress the autobiographical implications of these parallels, I do wish to point to the very prominent emphasis given to father-son relationships in *The Prince and the Pauper* and to the bearing which these relationships have on the idea of inheritance. The transmission of the story itself is attributed to storytelling from father to son, as indicated in the prefatory note:

I will set down a tale as it was told to me by one who had it of his father, which latter had it of *his* father, this last having in like manner had it of *his* father—and so on, back

and still back, three hundred years and more, the fathers
transmitting it to the sons and so preserving it. (45)

The emphasis Twain places on a masculine tradition is a deliberate contravention of a maternal, female oral storytelling tradition such as he experienced in his own family and in the culture
at large, where women writers largely dominated the literary
marketplace. It also represents an invention of a father-son
legacy reaching back in history and conferring and conserving a
sense of identity.

If the story itself represents a legacy handed down from father
to son for many generations in a stylized fashion that is reminiscent of the oral transmission of fairytales, it is a mythic rather
than an actual tradition Twain is invoking. It is appropriate,
however, that the tale is described in terms that link it to the
folktale, for the story needs to be read on one level as a fairytale
of good, evil, and Manichaean good and evil father figures. The
mythic import of the story is that each son has a configuration
of three father figures, ranging from good to evil; each son is
thrust into a society which denies his identity as his physical
father's son; and each must regain that identity but do it largely
out of his own resources. For example, Tom Canty has three
symbolic fathers. His physical father, John Canty, a version of
pap Finn, is ignorant, brutish, and cruel. He beats his son and
exploits him in every way he can. He is a drunkard and a representative of the dregs of society. Tom's spiritual father in more
than the religious sense, his good father, is the kindly, elderly
priest Father Andrew, who has been forced into retirement on
a scant pension by a harsh edict of Henry VIII's. The priest
teaches the boy Latin and introduces him to the romance of
folktales and the world of old books. By doing so, he provides
the boy with means of escape from the ugly, narrow confines of
his day-to-day life of begging, starvation, and physical abuse.
Once he is at court, Tom meets another of his father figures: the
aged King Henry, an awesome personage to little Tom Canty

but someone who treats him with kindness and indulgence, despite the real prince's statement that his father did not always
spare him with his tongue and that he had "not a doll's temper"
(61). Henry soon dies, and John Canty, significantly, kills the
one man in Offal Court who pleads for Tom/Edward when the
boy appears to have lost his mind: Father Andrew. Thus, symbolically, the cruel father kills the kind father and Edward is
left to fend for himself. Tom has to act out of his own resources
and impulses at court. As in the ordeal formula common to the
genteel fiction of the period, his innate gifts prove largely adequate to the challenge of the circumstances he must face (Kelly,
Mother Was a Lady 39–43). However, Twain's narrative is distinct from typical ordeal formula fiction in that no permanent
return to the safety of adult protection is possible.

Edward has a similar configuration of father figures. He also
has to rely on his own resources despite the fact that he is aided
by Miles, a kind, courageous, and protective father figure.
Henry, his real father, is a harsh ruler but an understanding
father, despite occasional outbursts of rage, though he is no
longer of practical importance to Edward after the boy is kicked
out into the street by the disrespectful guard at the palace gate.
From that point on, and especially after his death, Henry becomes instead the looming symbolic presence of the kingship.
Tom, Edward's alter ego, stands in an Oedipal relation to this
kingly father, whom he symbolically destroys by rejecting the
cruel aristocratic ethos Henry lived by, but he is seduced by
Henry's courtly privileges into betrayal of his mother.

His mother belongs to the constellation of saintly and martyred females in Twain's fiction. She is, at least on the surface, utterly benevolent, while her husband, John Canty, is
utterly malevolent. As if to prove that John Canty's villainy
is not limited to males, his mother—Tom's grandmother—is
equally vicious (which may illustrate Twain's faith in the all-
determining significance of "training," an idea that he culled
from W. E. H. Lecky's *History of European Morals* and applied

with growing enthusiasm in *A Connecticut Yankee*). The saintly
mother is hardly realized as a character except through her
self-sacrificing actions toward her son. Thus the main lines of
relation between mother and son are gratitude and guilt, for
the son does not demonstrate the same nurturant responsibility
toward his mother as she shows to him (or as Miles shows toward
Edward). The danger of the good mother lies in her powerlessness, which almost amounts to complicity in her husband's
violent tyranny. Similarly, the danger and deficiency of Miles's
fiancée lie in her inability to defy or overrule the villainous
Hugh Hendon. (Interestingly, her denial of Miles is the thing
that comes closest to making Miles despair of human nature.)
But the weakness of the good female characters is not a source
of complication to Twain, merely of pity and outrage (as in
the burning of the Baptist women). What truly terrifies Twain
is the deceptive presence of "feminine" traits of gentleness in
violent men, exemplified at their worst in the mad hermit.

It is this mad hermit whom Edward encounters as a third,
this time a chilling, evil father figure. In a sequence which
could have been taken directly from folklore or fairytale, innocent Edward falls into the clutches of the insane old priest,
who, disappointed at not having been made pope by Edward's
father, Henry, regrets bitterly his low status as archangel. In
revenge for his fancied outrage at the hands of Henry, he plots
to kill Henry's son. In scenes worthy of the penny dreadfuls,
the grizzled hermit whets his knife, chuckling over his task at
the thought of the vengeance to come. First he threatens to kill
Edward in his sleep, but then Mark Twain raises the stakes: he
has the hermit bind Edward hand and foot and brandish his
sharpened knife over the now wakened, terror-stricken boy.

This demonic father figure is clearly mythic. He too, like
John Canty, is akin to Huck's pap, who in the grip of delirium tremens attempts to kill his son. They are all nightmare
images of the demented, murderous father. Joseph Campbell
has pointed out that in myth "the ogre aspect of the father

is a reflex of the victim's [the child's] own ego" and that the
father is "the archetypal enemy" throughout life (129, 155). Yet
what is perhaps most frightening about the mad hermit as a
father figure is his deceptive gentleness. In his seemingly sane
moments, he displays a nurturing tenderness: "The old devotee
moved the boy nearer to the fire and made him comfortable;
doctored his small bruises and abrasions with a deft and tender
hand; and then set about preparing and cooking a supper—
chatting pleasantly all the time, and occasionally stroking the
lad's cheek or patting his head, in a gently caressing way" (228).
The "womanly" qualities of the hermit are emphasized especially when the narrator describes him "tucking [the boy] in as
snugly and lovingly as a mother might" (229); but his "feminine" gentleness is not to be trusted, for as soon as the boy
is asleep, the old man becomes a demonic killer. The duality
within the hermit mirrors the larger dichotomy represented in
the conflict between good and evil father figures in the story.

The pattern that emerges in the connections between the
father figures is that of competition and conflict between the
good and the evil father figures. The evil fathers struggle to
control their sons, while the good fathers are repeatedly powerless to protect the boys. John Canty kills Father Andrew; Hugh
Hendon jails Miles; the protective father Henry dies, leaving
both sons to their fates. If one looks for similar patterns in *Huck
Finn,* the striking fact is that none of the potential father figures (except Jim) is ultimately benevolent: certainly not pap,
nor Colonel Grangerford, Sherburn, or even Silas Phelps, who
contributes to setting an armed mob at the heels of the fleeing
heroes. As Keith Opdahl has pointed out, "all of the (male)
adults . . . are a single character: the father" (618). Both
books convey the nightmarish aura of threat that emanates
from powerful adult males. In *The Prince and the Pauper,* though,
that threat is sometimes mitigated by the good father figures,
who are, however, temporarily deprived of social legitimation.
Edward's most significant relationship to a father figure—for

example, resembling Huck's with Jim—is with Miles Hendon, the boyish, good-hearted soldier who is himself in a predicament parallel to Edward's.

Both Miles and Jim are figures who share the qualities of the nurturing female; Jim is the nurturing presence, sometimes dressed as a female, who is solicitous of his own deaf child in the moving story in which he shifts from the punitive father to the nurturant parent. Miles does not make Jim's mistake of not taking account of the child's perceptions: whereas Jim does not realize that his daughter is deaf, Miles assumes that, though his "son" is insane, his reality nonetheless deserves to be respected. However, positive as Miles's and Jim's compassionate qualities are, they are both disenfranchised. Twain displays to us the reality that concern for power overrides nurturance in his culture. Miles must suffer before he is able to reclaim his rightful inheritance. He has to cope with an evil father substitute: his wicked younger brother Hugh, who has usurped their good father's—and Miles's—rightful position after their father's death. Hugh has claimed the estate as his own and married Miles's fiancée by force. Hugh, as the false paterfamilias, denies knowing Miles and has him thrown in jail. The utopian quality of Twain's story inheres in the fact that Miles's compassion opens the way to the restoration of his rights: only through the power of the boy who has been his symbolic son and becomes his symbolic father, Edward, does Miles regain his estate. As king, Edward is Miles's sovereign and lord. Edward's power to repay Miles's loyalty and love in real coin is an expression of Twain's faith in the redeeming power of the child. Edward embodies the very American idea that the child can become the "father" of *his* father.

Metaphorically, one might argue, the central question of *The Prince and the Pauper* is the one which Tom Canty cannot repress when he hears that his "father," King Henry VIII, will not be buried right away but instead in several days: "Will he keep?" (159).[11] What the question implies, metaphorically, is a central theme of the book and an enduring American concern: what qualities, good or bad, will sons inherit from their fathers? What of their fathers will keep? Will their fathers keep? The literal meaning of the question echoes the concern of fairytale characters to preserve dead bodies until they can be transformed or laid to rest (See "Snow White" or "The Juniper Tree," for example). Yet the mythic dimension is rooted in the author's life. The well-known circumstance of young Sam Clemens witnessing his father's postmortem through a keyhole sheds further light on the significance to Mark Twain of the painful question of the physical destruction of the father's body after death (Wecter 116–17).

The symbolic transformation of Twain's own profoundly disturbing experience of a distant, judgmental father into a mythic trinity of fathers can perhaps help us to understand one of the signal failures of Twain's fiction: his inability to imagine convincing, complex women characters. With very few exceptions, Roxana in *Pudd'nhead Wilson* and Judith Loftus in *Huck Finn* being the prime examples, Mark Twain's women are flat and one-dimensional. The women in *The Prince and the Pauper* are not exceptional: they are figures rather than characters. Tom Canty's mother is angelically good and kind, while John Canty's mother is wicked and witchlike. The angelic women of Twain's fiction represent a higher moral standard than the average man can achieve, and they are frequently martyred for it. Joan of Arc in Twain's worshipful hagiography, the Baptist women burned at the stake, and Tom Canty's mother spurned by her son fall into this category. Except for Laura Hawkins in *The Gilded Age,* women who serve their own interests appear in Twain's fiction as thoroughly evil, again as in the fairytales.[12] Mark Twain was locked into the struggle with the domineering father too obsessively to variegate his portrayals of women.

The masculine code of domination of self and of others that Twain could not escape he nonetheless persistently criticized through the authentic representation of his boy characters' self-realization: Huck's struggle of heart against conscience and Edward's education through experience that leads him to tell unsympathetic courtiers, "What dost *thou* know of suffering and oppression? I and my people know, but not thou" (335). But the father is seen schematically and externally, as I have shown in *The Prince and the Pauper,* unless and until he becomes a boy like the hero, powerless in some way, as Jim is when he is humiliated by Huck's practical joke or when he is lonely and yearning for his family, or as Miles is when he finds himself excluded from his family and inheritance. Twain's moral indignation, the source of his satire, is softened only by identification with the parent as child, and for more than the obvious reasons Mark Twain can imagine the boy self more readily as father than as mother. It is true that his boys can incorporate "maternal" qualities, but mothers are not empowered to act forcefully in the realm beyond the home, so the good father remains the complex ideal worth striving for. Twain's women remain schematic, just as Europe remains schematic (the two are represented in Twain's writings at their extremes in Queen Elizabeth's bawdy profanity in *1601* and in Joan of Arc's otherwordly purity). The masculine trinity of his Protestant heritage, not the androgynous divinities of an alien Catholicism, stands at the source of Twain's images of fear and hope.

It is doubly paradoxical, then, that the story with which he delighted his daughters and the girls of the Saturday Morning Club at his sumptuous home in Hartford was set in the remoteness of sixteenth-century England, but an England that served him as a stimulant for writing about father-son inheritance and the problematic nature of succession in a characteristically American way. Mark Twain's boyish heroes must largely fend for themselves, and their innate qualities are better than their society's values. To use Georg Lukacs's terms, Twain affirms a dissonance between the hero and the world (70–83, 128). He conceives the European past in *The Prince and the Pauper* as a mythic world of cruelty, injustice, and artificiality but also a world of grandeur and hope. Boys whose hearts are still natural find themselves confronted with a stratified society that denies their social identity, their parentage. In seeking to reclaim that identity, they develop instead an authentic one, for which they require the aid of substitute fathers. Their physical fathers fail them, socially and personally. Their only genuine legacy, as in *Huck Finn,* lies in their own resources: character and the companionship they offer one another. Even in the sixteenth-century England Mark Twain imagined, fathers will not keep. For Twain, as for Americans of every generation, new fathers must be found. Samuel Clemens not only created Mark Twain, he invented his own version of the myth of the boy who creates and selects his own father. His invention of new fathers in *The Prince and the Pauper* is close to the deepest impulses of his art and of the literary aims of nineteenth-century American culture.

Chapter four
~✶~

SEXUAL POLITICS IN
A CONNECTICUT YANKEE

In *A Connecticut Yankee in King Arthur's Court* (1889), Mark Twain again addresses the filial-paternal themes of *The Prince and the Pauper* in the context of a fictionalized European past, but this time he chooses to address them mainly from the parental perspective, with a more explicit political agenda. *A Connecticut Yankee* is a further expression of his anxieties concerning gender and cultural continuity, yet it also reveals how Twain's preoccupations in these areas developed in the preceding decade. Hank Morgan, the brash Yankee, represents some of Twain's projections of the desire to assume the paternal role, both in the family and in the nation, yet Hank is curiously unsuccessful in his efforts in this direction. This seemingly most confident, aggressive male is defeated in his attempts to assume a lasting place in a family constellation of his own invention as well as in the political structure he creates. Hank's efforts to become a satisfactory surrogate father and surrogate son in both political and personal terms are doomed to defeat by forces envisioned and represented as female.[1] The psychological subtext of this often explicitly political tale demonstrates how significant the language of European culture, in particular of class, was, not only to Twain's attacks on feudalism and superstition but to his quest for a definition of masculine identity that would lend credence and force to his advocacy of American culture.

Trapped in the sentimental and moralistic dualism of stereotypical views of women, Mark Twain is able to imagine neither a satisfactory resolution of the social contradictions he is concerned with nor a lasting form of family relations. Fear of female domination, the disintegration of primary emotional ties, and the defeat of Hank Morgan's social ideals are all connected. Whereas *The Prince and the Pauper* presented a somewhat hopeful (if temporary) solution to these difficulties, though one in which the child functioned as an adult and the female was largely excluded, *A Connecticut Yankee* ends in a poignant if sometimes sentimental despair at the failure to achieve a resolution of these issues, though the resolution aimed at in *A Connecticut Yankee* is a more mature one, involving both adult sexuality and parenthood. Just as the mass slaughter of the sand-belt prophetically foreshadows the mechanized butchery of World War I, the abyss that opens up between Hello-Central's parents testifies to the essential bankruptcy of Victorian gender divisions and the approaching disintegration of the image of the idyllic conventional family.

What writers such as Theodore Dreiser, William Dean Howells, and Kate Chopin were soon to establish through realistic fiction, namely the inadequacy of romanticized images of the family as a refuge from the divisive forces of human nature and society, Twain adumbrates through satiric fantasy into which he incorporates sentimental elements of romantic fiction. Howard Fulweiler establishes the context in which the sentimentality of *A Connecticut Yankee* gains larger cultural significance:

> The special emphasis on the nuclear family, with its all-powerful father, its compliantly sweet mother and obedient children, isolated from the organic connections that united the older extended family, is a Victorian creation, an example of the intellectualized insistence on participation that is at the root of sentimentality. It is this emphasis which began to insist, formally and consciously, on specialized roles for family members. Children's litera-

ture and newly devised pursuits suitable for females are peculiarly Victorian. All of this may be seen as an effort, a desperate effort, to define the nuclear family as a defense against final isolation and alienation in a mechanized world. (245)

One can also see the function of *A Connecticut Yankee* in the transition from popular fiction to the realism of Howells, Chopin, and Dreiser in the light of Alfred Habegger's argument:

Women's novels offered a heroine who the reader could playfully and temporarily become. Popular fiction of all kinds—the sensation novels, Beadle's dime novels, working girl fiction of the 1880s and 90s, the historical romances of the latter decade—all spotlighted a single leading character, who was of greater intrinsic interest than anyone around her or him. Fiction worked by offering the reader an alternative ego. Thus, the pleasure the reader experienced at the end was an ego-pleasure—a happy embrace, a successful coup, a completed journey, a threat finally averted. This satisfaction, and the fantasies containing it, reflected to some extent the atomization of society, the individual's growing isolation, and the well-publicized success of a few great achievers. The surge of industrial activity in nineteenth-century America puffed up the ego with dreams of stunning personal success, of inevitably triumphant personal nobility. Realism was a critical response to the simultaneously inflated and privatized ego that was made hungry by contemporary society and fed by the fantasies in popular fiction. That is one of the reasons realism was often "pessimistic"—it insisted that the self was limited and conditioned and not capable of the apotheosis promised by mass fantasy. (108–09)[2]

A Connecticut Yankee illustrates the conflict between the desire for romantic glorification of the (male) ego and an opposing sense of the limitations imposed by reality. Thus it contains many elements of popular fiction, but it does not offer the "ego-pleasure" of a happy ending.

As a brash young American male confronting and challenging the authority of European culture, Hank Morgan bears a great deal of resemblance to the hero of *The Innocents Abroad:* a self-confident, ambitious young man, proud of his self-taught skills in a competitive profession.[3] Mark Twain is at some pains to emphasize, even exaggerate, some of the less attractive characteristics of his hero, such as his vulgar taste in art, yet this is entirely consistent with the self-representation sometimes bordering on self-caricature in *The Innocents Abroad.*

If Mark Twain's forte is, to paraphrase Wordsworth, innocence recollected in maturity, *A Connecticut Yankee* presents us with a significant new variation in the pattern. For now the central character, unlike his previous boy-heroes who at most attain a stage of adolescence, experiences courtship, marriage, and paternity, though the latter two are significantly cut short. Whereas Miles Hendon's progress through the stages of life culminated in a long-delayed marriage, Hank Morgan's ends with the disintegration of his young family. It is true, as James M. Cox asserts, that the "Yankee is in many ways Tom Sawyer grown up—but Tom Sawyer grown up is, alas, somehow grown down" (220).[4] Hank remains unconsciously conventional and yet is driven helplessly toward an unwitting exposure of the bankruptcy of his unexamined morality in the shadow play of Twain's gender fantasies, which Hank symbolically enacts. Henry Nash Smith noted that "Hank's yearning for his Lost World is expressed in conventional terms, but it is nevertheless erotic. Since the Lost World is also identified with memories of childhood, one might conjecture that Mark Twain's latent hostility to industrialism is related to the psychological conflict between Eros and civilization that Herbert Marcuse has explored. But the prelogical fantasies of this sort are buried too deeply to be more than glimpsed" (106). My argument is that these fantasies are visible enough to be analyzed.

The Brave Sir Mark: A Yankee Writer at King Arthur's Court,
Life, 1903. Illustration by Lovis Rhead. Library of Congress.

The masculine figures in *A Connecticut Yankee* display a range of traits incorporating many conventionally "feminine" characteristics; yet the same is not true in reverse in any positive sense for the female figures. The ending of the novel seems to express a yearning for a synthesis of "masculine" and "feminine" qualities, yet it fails, not least because of the distortion of female virtues and vices.

As is the case with so many of Mark Twain's boy heroes, Hank Morgan's unacknowledged desire is to become both surrogate son and—more explicitly here than in Twain's earlier works—surrogate father, a desire that is temporarily fulfilled but ultimately frustrated. The roles of mother, wife, and daughter mirror the futility of that desire, an issue that will be explored more fully later. The urge to find a surrogate father, so evident in *Huck Finn* and *The Prince and the Pauper,* is here reversed in the primacy of Hank Morgan's urge to become both a general father to the nation ("The Boss") and a particular father to his own child. The roots of this reversal are visible in the earlier works in the efforts of the boys to assume the paternal role in relation to their "fathers"—for example, Huck's shielding Jim and Edward's conferring privileges on Miles Hendon. But in *A Connecticut Yankee* Twain seems to have lost faith in the potentialities of boyhood innocence.

Clarence, the page ("Go 'long . . . you ain't more than a paragraph," 61), who is the first human being in Arthur's England with whom Hank establishes friendship, is a curious departure from Mark Twain's earlier boy figures. Instead of being, like Huck, a boy who sees the adult world from a limited adolescent perspective, Clarence is a boy who is seen from an adult man's perspective. His innocence is evidenced by his harmless self-satisfaction and by his girlishness, which like Jo's boyishness in *Little Women* suggests a stage of freedom from gender expectations, preceding maturity. Yet his is a very knowing kind of innocence: quite the reverse of Huck, who is apprehensive about himself and in awe of everyone higher on the social scale than he, Clarence is blissfully confident of himself and mockingly sarcastic about his elders and superiors. Hank calls Clarence "the Scoffer" (77). Twain presents Arthurian society as a collection of immature adults, and Clarence operates as a foil. Hank comments about the prevalence of challenges to dueling between strangers, "I had always imagined, until now, that that sort of thing belonged to children only, and was a sign and mark of childhood; but here were these big boobies sticking to it and taking pride in it clear up into full age and beyond" (68).[5] Despite Twain's hostile feelings about their simplicity ("There did not seem to be brains enough in the entire nursery, so to speak, to bait a fish-hook with"), he finds them appealing (he refers to their having "something attractive and lovable"). There is something intentionally grotesque about Arthurian society as Twain portrays it, namely that it is a society, to phrase it in Freudian terms, in which the forces of the id are not restrained by a superego of public opinion: Queen Guenever "flings furtive glances at Sir Launcelot that would have got him shot, in Arkansas" (370), Merlin tells an intolerably dull story for the thousandth time, and "many of the terms used in the most matter-of-fact way by this great assemblage of the first ladies and gentlemen in the land would have made a Comanche blush" (78).

In such a society of naive and coarse self-indulgence, it is significant that the knowing insider, a boy, forms an instantaneous, instinctive alliance with the knowing outsider, the grown man. This is a different version of the bond between Huck and Tom or Edward and Miles. Clarence does not merely assume the task of helping to save the man (the son rescues the father, a pattern that is rooted in the dynamics of Sam Clemens's loss of his father), but the man accepts the responsibility of shaping the character and career of the boy. When Clarence cowers in fear of Merlin's power (Merlin being an echo of the hermit in *The Prince and the Pauper*), Hank urges him to "come, come, be brave, be a man" (83). Clarence is still a child who faints at Hank's threat to darken the earth and who innocently changes the date of Hank's execution, not knowing what danger he is exposing his friend to (though ironically the change saves Hank, a contrivance of the plot that validates the boy's "good-hearted foolishness").

If Hank is at some level a version of Mark Twain, Clarence is also a version of Sam Clemens that verges on the autobiographical:

> Clarence was twenty-two, now, and was my head executive, my right hand. He was a darling; he was equal to anything; there wasn't anything he couldn't turn his hand to. Of late I had been training him for journalism, for the time seemed about right for a start in the newspaper line. . . . He took to it like a duck; there was an editor concealed in him sure. Already he had doubled himself in one way: he talked sixth century, and wrote nineteenth. (129–30)

Furthermore, he displays the sense of humor that Hank increasingly lacks. Mark Twain puts into Clarence's mouth the proposal that Europe should be governed by cats: "They would be as useful as any other royal family, they would know as much, they would have the same virtues and the same vices, the same fidelities, and the same treacheries, the same disposition to get up shindies with other royal cats" (445); and it is not until he concludes his utopian projection of a "reign of universal peace" with "Me-e-e-yow-ow-ow-ow—FZT! -WOW!" that Hank catches on to the joke.[6] Clarence emerges from nowhere: he has no family or friends worth mentioning. Perhaps this accounts in part for his appearing to have no existence apart from Hank. Yet he does have a personality distinct from his mentor's. He is, curiously enough, the more sceptical and pragmatic of the two, as demonstrated when Hank has qualms about destroying the knights of England and proposes to convey a message of truce to his enemies. Clarence effectively ridicules Hank's naïveté by enacting the scene he assumes will happen when the messenger conveys the truce proposal to their opponents. Clarence comes to act as a slightly cynical foil to Hank's naïveté. If Clarence is in some sense the inheritor of the consequences of Hank's idealistic vision of a democratic England, he is also a pragmatic survivor who endures (though presumably not for long) to write the story of the Boss's end, a task completed by "M.T." himself. Thus Hank's final fate is conveyed to the reader by two postscripts, the first of which begins, "I, Clarence, must write it for him."

Yet as a separate character Clarence lacks substance. Without the Boss he is insignificant. This is reinforced by the nature and fate of the fifty-two boys who uncannily resemble Clarence as a boy (Hank describes them as "a darling fifty-two! As pretty as girls, too," 476) and whom Clarence selects for special training just as Hank selected him. The uniformity of these boys springs from the abstraction of the ideas Twain seeks to convey: namely that "training" is all-important in the formation of character. The boys are abstract human material, without individuality, and the effort to create a new civilization through them can aptly be described in William Dean Howells's judgment about a play he wrote with Twain: "The thing will fail, and it would be a disgrace to have it succeed" (*Mark Twain-Howells Letters* 557). The effort to raise a new generation according to the Liberal reformist ideas of the Yankee Boss results (perhaps unwittingly) in imposing a new conformity and a new tyranny. The imagined failure of the new civilization is by no means due entirely to the obstinacy of the old: it is due also to an imaginative failure in conceiving the new. The attempt to establish a tradition is doomed in part by Hank's (and Twain's) inability to acknowledge the necessity of tradition.

This inability is accompanied by an odd reluctance to relinquish the old tradition. How to account for Hank's and Twain's remarkably gingerly treatment of Arthur? Considering that monarchy is one of his main targets and that Twain spares no ridicule in his presentation of the members of the Round Table, it is incongruous that Arthur is treated with so much sympathy, mixed with condescension though it is. Clemens had written to Mary Mason Fairbanks, "Of course in my story I shall leave unsmirched & unbelittled the great & beautiful *characters* drawn by the master hand of old Malory. . . . I shall hope that under my hand . . . Arthur [will] keep his sweetness & his purity" (*Mark Twain to Mrs. Fairbanks* 258). Clearly, Mark Twain deferred to the enormous prestige the mythic figure of Arthur enjoyed in his culture; yet this does not seem an entirely adequate explanation. The reason for Arthur's gentle treatment must lie at least in part in the fact that Arthur stands in a fatherly relation to Hank, or perhaps more accurately, that Hank accepts and cultivates a filial relationship to Arthur. Like so many father-son relations in Mark Twain's fiction, this one also involves the son's care for and protection of the father. When Arthur, disguised as a commoner, ventures out among his people with Hank, Hank says of him, "If you have ever seen an active, heedless, enterprising child going diligently out of one mischief and into another all day long, and an anxious mother at its heels all the while, and just saving it by a hair from drowning itself or breaking its neck with each new experiment, you've seen the king and me" (312). Hank assumes the protective parental role of a mother to Arthur, whose position of privilege has kept him childlike. "I persuaded him to throw the dirk away; and it was as easy as persuading a child to give up some bright fresh new way of killing itself" (313). The dirk has inescapable sexual significance, especially since Morgan le Fay uses a dirk to kill her page. Possession of the dirk lends the queen the power of killing; the king's possession of a dirk merely illustrates how childlike he is and that he does not know how to use it properly.

This is in keeping with Mark Twain's intent of showing us ancient Britons who were "a childlike and innocent lot" of a "most gentle and winning naivety" (66), yet from the beginning Twain is reluctant to belittle the masculinity of the Arthurian knights. Whereas the ladies of the court are perfunctorily de-

scribed as decorative, "that massed flower-bed of feminine show
and finery" (69), the description of the lords bespeaks an uncon-
quered romantic impulse about masculine dignity: "There was
a fine manliness observable in almost every face; and in some
a certain loftiness and sweetness that rebuked your belittling
criticisms. . . . A most noble benignity and purity reposed in
the countenance of him they called Sir Galahad; and likewise
in the king's, also; and there was majesty and greatness in the
giant frame and high bearing of Sir Launcelot of the Lake" (69).[7]
  The incongruity of Hank's insistence on the manly dignity
of Arthur and of the best of Arthur's knights and his exposure of their childlike simplicities and foolishness suggests an
unresolved or even unrecognized conflict (as does the dualistic
portrait of Henry VIII in *The Prince and the Pauper*): not merely
between respect and iconoclasm (Clemens could always display
plenty of reverence for the past and its cultural icons when he
chose to) but between alienation and identification. For though
A Connecticut Yankee is a critique of the ideology and institutions
of aristocracy, it is not an unequivocal one. As the book pro-
gresses, attacks on the ruling class increasingly yield to attacks
on the subordinate classes, and Hank Morgan begins to recognize within himself similarities to Arthur and other monarchs.
Beneath the explicit satire and parody of chivalry, there is a disturbing subtext of self-recognition. Despite the king's stupidity
and unconscious cruelty (bred into him by his privileged position), he has an ineradicable pride in himself that makes him
innately superior, in Hank's eyes, to the mass of subservient-
minded folk. The efforts of the slave driver to reduce the king's
"style" dramatize the fact: "Even that dull clod of a slave-driver
was able to see that there can be such a thing as a slave who
will remain a man till he dies; whose bones you can break, but
whose manhood you can't. . . . The fact is, the king was a good
deal more than a king, he was a man; and when a man is a
man, you can't knock it out of him" (398). Though Mark Twain
tries to distinguish between Arthur's innate and his artificial

nobility, the implication clearly emerges that royalty is closer to full humanity than the peasantry is. Adversity is required to bring out the full stature of a member of the privileged class such as Arthur is, but prosperity does not increase the humane instincts of the poor, as the episode with Dowley, the "self-made man," demonstrates (despite its obvious democratic political didacticism). Faced with the prospect of an age when "a man will be his own property, not the property of magistrate and master," Dowley shouts, "Perdition catch such an age! . . . An age of dogs, an age barren of reverence for superiors and respect for authority! The pillory—" (377). Furthermore, Hank essentially aspires to become king himself. Hank embodies a yearning widely felt by American men in the late nineteenth century. As Alfred Habegger has written, "The new way of proving one's masculinity was to fight one's way to the top so that the whole world could see that you were number one. Kingship became the number one male American fantasy in the Gilded Age" (221).

A *Connecticut Yankee* can be seen as an extended moral debate between egalitarianism and elitism, but the terms of the debate are limited by the view of human nature that underlies it. An incipient misanthropy is visible in sentiments such as Hank's when he exclaims, "Well, there are times when one would like to hang the whole human race and finish the farce" (348) or when he makes his contemptuous reference to "human muck" (473). As Judith Fetterley has written about Hank, "Despite his frequent democratic pronouncements, his occasional 'a man is a man, at bottom,' or his perception that a king can be a man, Hank has a basic contempt for people" ("Yankee Showman and Reformer" 670). The dominant traits of human nature as Mark Twain portrays it in this book are greed, pride, entrenched habit, and cowardice—traits Hank Morgan is not exempt from.[8] On the positive side are "manhood"—defined as self-respect—and compassion, but these virtues are narrowly conceived and sentimentalized. The explicit evils of institutions and traditions that Twain attacks are indicative of fears and obsessions at a less visible level, which is not to devalue the conscious political and social arguments made by Twain and ably analyzed by critics such as Henry Nash Smith, Louis Budd, and Roger Salomon. Specifically, Hank's failure to reform the mythical Arthurian England is due at least in part to Twain's failure to reconcile in Hank Morgan the "sentimental," idealistic, compassionate yearning for the "feminine" and relational with the "hard-headed," competitive, practical masculinity of stock exchange, mechanical skill, showmanship, and warfare.[9]

Mark Twain gives his protagonists, Clarence and Hank, some "feminine" traits: Clarence's girlish prettiness and decorative clothing, Hank's motherly concern for Arthur. The childlike Arthur at his best is a figure who displays traits that are not exclusively masculine or feminine but might be described as androgynous: courage, compassion, and sympathetic suffering. In the smallpox hut, Arthur gently bears the dying girl downstairs in his arms, an act which Hank eulogizes as "heroism"; and as Arthur watches the woman fondling her dying child, Hank "saw tears well from the king's eyes, and trickle down his face" (332).

Yet these positive signs of androgyny are rare and are overshadowed by complex forms of love and fear of the feminine as Other. As in his earlier works, such as *1601* and "A Memorable Midnight Experience," Twain represents female power at its best as a kind of blundering innocence, at its worst as unmitigated evil. In his preface, Twain moots the question of the divine right of kings. The example he uses to contradict the idea that the "executive head of a nation" must be "a person of lofty character and extraordinary ability" (45) are "the Pompadour" and Lady Castlemaine, both mistresses who governed through their influence on kings, both women well known for their strong sexual appetites and powerful wills. Clemens wrote in his notebook of February to September 1879:

> In countries where wives hold the first place in the husbands' hearts, the men govern the country—they govern

it, receiving wise & unselfish counsel from the wives. The
wives do not *govern* the country, for they do not govern its
men. But concubines do govern the men, & in the very
nature of things they govern them with selfish ends in
view. A nation governed in all its big & little details by
foul & selfish & trivial-minded prostitutes is not likely to
have much largeness or dignity of character. As for purity,
& real refinement, they are impossible under such a system—plenty of sham refinement, though. (*Mark Twain's
Notebooks and Journals* 2:322–23) [10]

Whereas on the symbolic, psychological level Mark Twain in
A Connecticut Yankee seems to suggest that in men the mitiga-
tion of pride and cruelty—the will to rule—by compassion is
positive, he also suggests that the only alternatives to women's
victimization are domesticity or heartless female cruelty, a cari-
cature if not a worse version of male tyranny. What is explicitly not imagined, as most nineteenth-century writers did not
imagine, is that women are legitimate players in the public
game of power. Hank sets up his ambition to "boss the asylum," if it was an asylum, or to "boss the whole country inside
of three months" explicitly as a game. "One thing at a time,
is my motto—and just play that thing for all it is worth, even
if it's only two pair and a jack" (63). While the notion of the
exercise of male ambition as a game serves to legitimize Hank's
manipulations and is connected with his theatrical flair (Hank,
watching Sir Kay in a tight spot, says admiringly that "he was
equal to the occasion. He got up and played his hand like a
major—and took every trick," 69), there is also a sense in which
this vision reduces men to boys. When Hank has his way with
the knights of the Round Table, he refers to them as boys and
has them playing baseball and the stock market. It is no accident that Hank's allies in his last stand against the forces of
tradition are an army of boys, not men. Boyhood predicates a
certain innocence, lending an aura of humor and of play to male
activities, including even the Battle of the Sand-belt.

Female innocence is another matter. Mark Twain's portrayal of women in Arthur's England implies, paradoxically, that their innocence is their guilt. Or, to put it somewhat differently, their guilt is their lack of shame, particularly about sexual matters. In chapter one, in which an idyllic tone still predominates, Hank's first encounter exemplifies in a piquant way the paradox that tantalized Twain about female innocence in his version of Arthurian England: "Presently a fair slip of a girl, about ten years old, with a cataract of golden hair streaming down over her shoulders, came along. Around her head she wore a hoop of flame-red poppies. It was as sweet an outfit as ever I saw, what there was of it. She walked indolently along with a mind at rest, its peace reflected in her innocent face" (56). Her shock when she discovers Hank is ironic to Hank (and Twain) because her nakedness violates not merely the taboos against nudity but the imperative of shame: "That she should seem to consider me a spectacle, and totally overlook her own merits in that respect, was another puzzling thing, and a display of magnanimity, too, that was surprising in one so young" (57). Whereas this early introduction to a lack of consciousness about the need to hide the body is a sign of primitive civilization (in a town that incidentally remarkably resembles Sam Clemens's Hannibal, Missouri, and suggests a primitive Eden), Hank's later encounters of a similar kind imply more than naïveté. At Arthur's court, Merlin gives the command to have Hank stripped, so that soon he was "naked as a pair of tongs!" Hank's response is: "And dear, dear, to think of it: I was the only embarrassed person there. Everybody discussed me; and did it as unconcernedly as if I had been a cabbage. Queen Guenever was as naively interested as the rest, and said she had never seen anybody with legs just like mine before" (80). A sense of shame about the body is thus the litmus test of civilization versus primitivism ("white Indians," Hank calls the Arthurian circle), while Hank insists that a sense of pride is the litmus test of manhood.

Shame and pride define the limits of Hank's sense of self and of his conception of civilization. Women lacked the proper

sense of shame and men the proper sense of pride in Arthur's
England, Mark Twain charges. However, Hank's conscious
judgments are complicated by ironies of his character and
stance. For example, despite the exaggerated sense of propriety
he exhibits in his reluctance to take off his armor in the presence of Sandy "because it would have seemed so like undressing
before folk" (153), he chooses an exhibitionistic outfit that displays his body theatrically when he goes into battle against
the knights: "flesh-colored tights from neck to heel, with blue
silk puffings about my loins" (431), an outfit which causes the
queen to ask, "Wilt fight naked?" (432). Nakedness is associated with situations of life and death in this novel rather than
with sexuality. More specifically, nakedness is often associated
with scenes of torture and execution: Hank at the stake, the
slave woman who is whipped by the slave master, or the poacher
who is tortured on the rack in Morgan le Fay's dungeons. These
scenes suggest that the shame of nakedness is connected with
vulnerability and powerlessness. This is true even in Hank's
"fighting naked," for his apparent vulnerability compared to
the lumbering colossi in armor merely dramatizes his superior
practical skill. Hank combines the specious innocence of simu-
lated nakedness with the pride of superior technical ability.
Despite his occasional diatribes about conscience and his prim
insistence on propriety, he is essentially shameless.

   Jungian psychology can help to illuminate some of the significant contradictions of Hank Morgan's masculinity. C. G.
Jung has defined the anima as the "other side" of the masculine
character, "the woman in a man" (19), and the animus similarly
as "the man in a woman." Despite the clear-cut distribution of
shame as appropriate particularly to the psychological economy
of women and pride as definitive of manhood in *A Connecticut
Yankee,* Mark Twain is concerned with the inversions implicit in
anima and animus, or what James Hillman refers to as "contra-
sexuality" (5–15). Hank's inner conflict—often glossed by critics as philosophical contradiction—between compassion for the

sufferings of the human race and contempt for its docility and submissiveness is also a conflict between contradictory parts of the masculine psyche. His feeling for the oppressed issues in a passion for justice and a new order ("a new deal"), but his recognition that humanity loves the existing order simply because it exists causes him to dismiss the human race as subhuman: pigs, dogs, cats, and other beasts serve Twain as means of dramatizing that, from Hank Morgan's perspective, the mass of unreflective human beings are not worthy of compassion—they deserve their doom. However, the ultimate revelation which Hank Morgan never fully admits about himself is that he is like the aristocrats he condemns: he shares the oppressor's instincts.[11] He too is the architect and sustainer of an order which oppresses and exploits because it ultimately disdains the value of human identity. The conflict between the passion for control so evident in Hank Morgan and his equally important movement of compassion and identification through vulnerability to suffering can be described as, though it should perhaps not be reduced to, the drama of the conflict between the persona, or public self, and the anima, or the inner self, encompassing the unconscious "pre-gendered" impulses of the psyche.

Since the anima is a projection of the masculine psyche, we can see evidence of Hank's anima in the women who are significant to him. Hank Morgan's anima is visible in the two female figures dearest to him: Alisande la Courteloise, Sandy for short, and "Puss" Flanagan, usually referred to as "Hello-Central."[12] Both are characterized by their voices. Sandy's is the antiquated speech of Malory. "Puss" Flanagan is hardly more than a disembodied voice over a telephone wire; her nickname "Hello-Central" itself is the dehumanized designation of a utilitarian function and a conceptual location. It is entirely appropriate that Hank thinks of her with a mixture of sentimental idealization and practical valuation of her worth in capital: "To hear her dear voice come melting back to me . . . was music of the spheres to my enchanted ear. She got three dollars a week, but she was worth it" (181). She performs, like the telephone itself, a function of instrumentality for Hank. The problem with Sandy is, from Hank's point of view, that she does not. Her ceaseless conversation is to Hank a "mill"; her tongue and jaws are "her works," with the fatal flaw that she "finished without a result" (173). To Hank, Sandy's endless talk is circular and digressive, enveloping him in a fog of words in which he cannot find an issue. Hank's mode of thought is linear and purposive, while Sandy's, insofar as she is more than a convenient mouthpiece for the satiric use of Malory's prose, is a comic representation of an opposite, female mode of expression. This point is driven home by a comparison Hank makes between Sandy and "a damsel named Maledisant" (188), who traveled with Sir Cote Male Taile on "an excursion like this one of mine" (188), as Hank refers to it. Maledisant, though "as handy with her tongue as was Sandy," is a less attractive character: "Her tongue churned forth only railings and insult, whereas Sandy's music was of a kindlier sort" (188). Male Taile's experience with Maledisant allows him to assume that Hank is having a similarly difficult time of it with Sandy, which causes him to feel sympathy for Hank. Hank says, "I knew how to interpret the compassion that was in his face when he bade me farewell. He supposed I was having a bitter hard time of it" (188). Hank's recognition of Male Taile's sympathy is a male bond based on the Otherness of the female.

Yet Sandy and Hank are not so unlike each other in some respects. Like Hank, Sandy manipulates gullible courtiers through their superstitions. By invoking the name of The Boss she intimidates Morgan le Fay, and by threatening the destruction of the castle she keeps Hank's enemies at bay, much as Hank threatened destruction of the sun to control his enemies. For both, the power of words controls and defines reality. Both use language for dramatic effect, and both employ the power of a complex, opaque language: the Germanic. At the climax of his plot to restore the fountain in the Valley of Holiness,

Hank spews out awesome German portmanteau words. Hank's "mysterious and shuddery reverence" for Sandy is based on his feeling that, before her, he stood "in the awful presence of the Mother of the German Language" (259). He describes his attitude toward her as unconscious reverence, and the timing of his realization suggests that his growing "reverence" for her, linked to his sense of guilt at chiding her for not understanding his idiom, is one of the reasons he ultimately marries her. Sandy's turgid eloquence has its counterpart in Hank's tendency to discourse at length upon the social evils of Arthurian England and upon his own achievements. Ultimately, however, Sandy represents Hank's anima not because of their similarities, which he does not recognize, but because of the Otherness she represents in his dialogue with himself. The intense yearning with which he addresses Sandy as the embodiment of all his hopes in the moments before he dies testifies to the significance she has acquired for him: wholeness, peace, rootedness in time and place, happiness, "all that is dear to me, all that could make life worth living!" (493). Susan K. Harris argues convincingly that Hank finds in the love of Sandy, a "good woman," the escape from time he seeks (*Mark Twain's Escape From Time* 56–57).

The cyclical, irrational, attachment-oriented elements of being that Sandy represents to him become increasingly necessary to him, as his final cataclysm reveals. But the effort to be united with his female counterpart, his anima, fails in part because he is defeated by forces that may be described in Jungian terms as his shadow. The shadow, in Jung's conception, "the character that summarizes a person's uncontrolled emotional manifestations . . . his inferior qualities or peculiarities" (20), can be a dream or imaginative projection, or it can be, like the anima, a character external to the individual, embodying the qualities in question. Hank's shadow is, first of all, Morgan le Fay. The similarities between Hank Morgan and Morgan le Fay are hinted at in the name they share. Hank condemns Morgan le Fay with an unequivocal directness that he never uses concerning Arthur or even Merlin: "All her ways were wicked, all her instincts devilish. She was loaded to the eye-lids with crime; and among her crimes murder was common" (188). Yet in the same breath he acknowledges that her power stems from a source identical to his: "She was held in awe by the whole realm, for she had made everybody believe she was a great sorceress" (188). Morgan is the demonic woman, beautiful and cruel. Hank is in fact at pains to point out her attractiveness as a woman: "To my surprise, she was beautiful; black thoughts had failed to make her expression repulsive, age had failed to wrinkle her satin skin or mar its bloomy freshness" (189). At first he is convinced that she must have been "misrepresented" when she asks him questions "with all manner of pretty graces and graciousness" (190). "Dear me, it was like a bird, or a flute, or something, talking." Anima and shadow, Sandy and Morgan, can be regarded as a pair.[13]

Yet Morgan is, like Queen Elizabeth, a thoroughly evil and threatening figure not merely because she is a cold-blooded murderer but because she is so completely in charge. Her power as a woman, her sexual attractiveness, and her wickedness are inseparable. Hank feels the same sort of instant male bond with Morgan's husband, Brer Uriens, as La Cote Male Taile felt with Hank. Uriens is a cowering victim, "a kind-faced old man with a subdued look" (190), "always on the ragged edge of apprehension" (191). Morgan le Fay has the "masculine" role of being in control; she is the female in whom the animus dominates.[14] As such, she is characterized by Twain as the epitome of cruelty: not only does she knife her errant servant in cold blood and relish the torture inflicted on her captives, such as the young man suspected of poaching, but she designs a form of psychological torture especially for a prisoner who is the object of her particular hatred. She causes five funerals to be staged where they are visible from his cell, knowing that he has left behind five children and his wife, so that he is tormented by the question of who is still alive in his family. His crime: calling Morgan le Fay's hair red. The extravagance of the punishment in relation to the crime is intended partly as a joke ("That was no way to speak of it [her hair]. When red headed people are above a certain social grade, their hair is auburn," 215), but it is merely one more heightening of a portrait of feminine cruelty that is fundamentally serious.

What Hank cannot recognize or acknowledge is the disturbing similarity between himself and Morgan le Fay. Though it is clear that elements of burlesque enter into the portrayal of Hank's encounter with the queen, the humorously treated similarities hint at the darker congruities between her callous brutality and his contempt for human nature. Both Hank and Morgan le Fay are executioners.

> In a gallery a band, with cymbals, horns, harps, and other horrors, opened the proceedings with what seemed to be the crude first-draft or original agony of the wail known to later centuries as "In the Sweet By and By." It was new, and ought to have been rehearsed a little more. For some reason or other the queen had the composer hanged, after dinner. (196)

After Sandy intimidates the queen with the threat that Hank will cause the castle to dissolve, she

> was so scared and humbled that she was even afraid to hang the composer without first consulting me. I was very sorry for her—indeed any one would have been, for she was really suffering; so I was willing to do anything that was reasonable, and had no desire to carry things to wanton extremities. I therefore considered the matter thoughtfully, and ended by having the musicians ordered into our presence to play that Sweet By and By again, which they did. Then I saw that she was right, and gave her permission to hang the whole band. (198)

While this anecdote is of the same burlesque cloth as the running joke about the "petrified" humor of Sir Dinadan, it illuminates the supremely self-satisfied nature of Hank, who will ultimately take satisfaction in blowing up hundreds of Arthur's knights in the Battle of the Sand-Belt.[15] The desire for domination and revenge is as strong in Hank as in Morgan. While she enjoys inflicting suffering, Hank takes a similar if somewhat less harmful pleasure in intimidating his audiences (as when he relishes the sight of "a thousand acres of human beings groveling on the ground in a general collapse of consternation," 105). Just as Sandy comes to represent Hank's idealistic yearnings to escape from the social circumstances he seeks to create and is increasingly unable to control, Morgan le Fay represents the base impulses in Hank that are increasingly evoked by the difficulty of shaping human nature and society to his will.

The episode at the conclusion of Hank and Sandy's visit to Morgan's castle cryptically conveys this message. When Hank absentmindedly expresses a wish that he could photograph the pitiful procession of survivors of her dungeons (the underworld of the queen's domination, also symbolic of the unconscious), Morgan attempts to do it with an axe. Hank the observer and Morgan the executioner are linked in a symbiotic union of moral outrage and cruelty, the one wishing to fix in visible representation, the other in annihilation, the suffering human being. "I have seen a good many kinds of women in my time, but she laid over them all, for variety," Hank says, echoing in negative form Huck's eulogy of Mary Jane Wilks. The variety she represents is the shadow side of himself, all the more frightening to Twain because she is female.[16]

If Morgan le Fay represents an unacknowledged side of the Yankee himself, his ultimate foe, the force that defeats him, is represented by an entity with uncanny resemblances to Morgan the queen. This is the towering female figure of the Church.

Before the day of the Church's supremacy in the world, men were men, and held their heads up, and had a man's pride, and spirit, and independence. . . . But then the Church came to the front, with an axe to grind; and she was wise, subtle, and knew more than one way to skin a cat—or a nation: she invented "divine right of kings," and propped it all around, brick by brick, with the Beatitudes—wrenching them from their good purpose to make them fortify an evil one; she preached (to the commoner,) humility, obedience to superiors, the beauty of self-sacrifice; she preached (to the commoner,) meekness under insult; preached (still to the commoner, always to the commoner,) patience, meanness of spirit, nonresistance under oppression; and she introduced heritable ranks and aristocracies, and taught all the Christian populations of the earth to bow down to them and worship them. (113)

Interestingly, Henry C. Lea, whose *History of the Inquisition of the Middle Ages* (1887) confirmed Twain's anti-Catholic prejudices and provided him with material to use in *A Connecticut Yankee*, consistently refers to the Church as "it." W. E. H. Lecky, whom Twain follows even more closely than Lea, avoids, in his *History of European Morals*, personifying the Church and employs the pronoun "it" also. The passage quoted above is a simplified and distorted reproduction of the idea presented by Lecky (2: 266–274).[17] Twain himself elsewhere frequently uses "it" to refer to the Church in *A Connecticut Yankee*, but his revealing use of the female pronoun here illuminates a significant psychological subtext.

The imagery of the axe and the skinned cat not only provides a subtle link with the portrait of Morgan le Fay but, appearing as it does in connection with fears of loss of manhood, suggests a particular kind of terror of emasculation. Hank Morgan's most vivid images of oppression are rooted in female sources—the Church and Morgan le Fay—in comparison with which monarchy and its male representatives, such as Arthur and Launcelot, seem harmless bumblers. The extremes of virtue and vice are represented by female beings; even virtue in males is associated

with temporary or partial accession to standards and types of behavior represented primarily by females, for example Arthur's
demonstration of selflessness in the smallpox hut or Hank's
domestic attachments to Sandy and Hello-Central, which provide a brief respite from the chaos of intrigue and war toward
the end of the novel.

The insistent repetition of images of female virtue victimized provides a revealing index to the nature of the conceptions
of gender underlying this novel. There are no fewer than nine
episodes involving innocent women victims, several of which
are developed at considerable length. Several of these episodes
emphasize the mother-child bond as the primary defining characteristic of the woman (in one case, the woman is a grandmother). The vulnerability of the virtuous woman, portrayed
in sentimental scenes of separation and loss, lies in her maternal love. The first of these scenes, significantly, pits a grieving
grandmother against Morgan le Fay, who has killed her grand-
son, in a tableau of virtue condemning vice:

> There appeared under the arch of the far-off door at the
> bottom of the hall, an old and bent and white-haired lady,
> leaning upon a crutch-stick; and she lifted the stick and
> pointed it toward the queen and cried out—"The wrath
> and curse of God fall upon you, woman without pity, who
> have slain mine innocent grandchild and made desolate
> this old heart that had nor chick nor friend nor stay nor
> comfort in all this world but him!" (197)

It is Sandy, the anima figure, who invokes Hank's destructive
power and who protects the old woman from being sent to
the stake by Morgan, just as the old woman herself invokes
the wrath of God in her condemnation of the "woman without pity."

The appearance of the wronged woman follows immediately
after Hank's outraged description of "the worst spectacle" at the
wild banquet, where bawdy stories are told "that would almost
have made Queen Margaret of Navarre or even the great Eliza-

beth of England hide behind a handkerchief" (Twain clearly had *1601* in mind here):

> a lovely young duchess, whose wedding-eve this was; and indeed she was a spectacle, sure enough; just as she was, she could have sat in advance for the portrait of the young daughter of the Regent d' Orleans, at the famous dinner whence she was carried, foul-mouthed, intoxicated and helpless, to her bed, in the lost and lamented days of the Ancient Regime. (197)

Thus the appearance of the virtuous, suffering woman is framed by the presence of two types of female evil: sensuality and dissoluteness on the one hand and cruelty and pitiless power on the other. The old woman's protest against the arbitrary dominion of the evil queen is legitimated by her loss of a grandchild and her outraged maternal instincts and enhanced by its contrast with the image of female degeneracy.

Similarly, one of the strongest condemnations of Church and king is made by the woman in the smallpox hut as she caresses her dying daughter. Like the bereaved grandmother, she is granted the privilege of righteous cursing, for in her grief and despair at the injustice committed against her family and herself, she "uttered a deep blasphemy—oh! a thousand of them! against the Church and the Church's ways" (334). Though the immediate agents of her family's destruction are the patriarchal aristocratic law and the male priest, who "carried my trespass to his betters" (334), it is the lurking omnipotent, cryptofemale agency of the Church that the woman recognizes as her primal enemy. She utters her "blasphemy" when she is "out of my mind with hunger and loss of my boys, and grief to see my husband and my little maids in rags and misery and despair" (334). Thus it is her suffering on behalf of her husband and children that drives her to denounce the forces ranged against them. The rightness of her cause is guaranteed by her selflessness as a woman.

The most extended, melodramatic, and sentimental of the

scenes of female virtue persecuted in *A Connecticut Yankee* is that
of the woman who is hanged for stealing "a piece of linen cloth
of the value of a fourth part of a cent" (402). Her story, significantly, is mediated not by her own telling but by the voice of a
sympathetic priest, whose narration stirs Hank Morgan's compassion. Hank hears "pity in his voice—how seldom a sound
that was in that ignorant and savage land! I remember every
detail of what he said, except the words he said it in, and so
I change it into my own words" (401).[18] The young woman
is described, both by Hank and by the priest, in sentimental
language. Hank sees her thus:

> a comely young girl of about eighteen, suckling a baby,
> which she squeezed to her breast in a passion of love every
> little while, and every little while wiped from its face the
> tears which her eyes rained down upon it; and always the
> foolish little thing smiled up at her, happy and content,
> kneading her breast with its dimpled fat hand, which she
> patted and fondled right over her breaking heart. (400–1)

The priest says,

> A little while ago this young thing, this child of eighteen
> years was as happy a wife and mother as any in England;
> and her lips were blithe with song, which is the native
> speech of glad and innocent hearts. (401)

These images equate motherhood with childhood, innocence,
and feeling. In opposition to this idealized maternity stands
"the law": the law that robs her of her husband by his being
impressed into the navy and the law that condemns her to death
for stealing a trifling object to keep from starving.

    The sight of maternal innocence wronged, as in the case of
the woman in the smallpox hut, moves some men to compassion. When the owner of the stolen linen realizes that the young
woman will be executed for her crime, he loses his reason and
commits suicide. The priest eulogizes him as "a kindly man; a

man whose heart was right, at bottom" (403) and describes him as a victim of murder by the law. The priest himself is a mediator between the opposing systems of value established in this episode. He both defends law ("A law sends this poor young thing to death—and it is right") and attacks law ("Another law had placed her where she must commit her crime or starve, with her child—and before God that law is responsible for both her crime and her ignominious death!" 401). He unites within himself, as so rarely happens in Mark Twain's fiction, compassion and legalism, attitudes which are generally characterized by Twain as feminine and masculine respectively. He becomes in fact an androgynous figure, for when the mother laments her child's abandonment, saying, "Oh, my child, my darling, it will die! It has no home, it has no father, no friend, no mother—" the priest replies, "It has them all! . . . All these will I be to it till I die" (403).

Thus the innocence of the childlike mother becomes a redemptive catalyst to some men. Though she takes her look of gratitude, which Hank describes as "fire," away "to the treasury of heaven, where all things that are divine belong" (403), she serves as an object lesson to the men who remain on earth. Similarly, the wife of the poacher, who preferred to starve to death rather than allow her husband to be tortured, is praised by Hank as "true wife and true woman that you are . . . it humbles a body to think what your sex can do when it comes to self-sacrifice" (203). Self-sacrificial females are represented as unattainable ideals for men, yet ideals nonetheless.

Those women who seek to defend themselves fare no better than those who exhibit submissiveness and self-sacrifice; if anything, their fates are worse. Hank tells the story of the orphan girl who inherits an estate and marries a penniless young man. The bishop of her diocese claims the estate for his own because she has not granted him the droit du seigneur. She contests his claim, but the king upholds it, and she and her husband are sent "out into the world homeless, bedless, breadless; why, the very beggars by the roadsides were not so poor as they" (286). Much more severe is the fate of a woman, a "commoner," who has been imprisoned in Morgan's dungeons for nine years. She also refused the droit du seigneur to "a neighboring lord," Sir Breuse Sance Pité, "and, moreover, had opposed violence to violence and spilt half a gill of his almost sacred blood" (211). Her fate is particularly pitiful, for she and her husband were imprisoned "kerneled like toads in the same rock; they had passed nine pitch dark years within fifty feet of each other, yet neither knew whether the other was alive or not" (211). Hank invests the freeing of this couple with his intensely idealistic hopes:

> I said we would take him to her, and see—to the bride who was the fairest thing in the world to him, once— roses, pearls and dew made flesh for him; a wonder-work, the master work of Nature: with eyes like no other eyes, and a voice like no other voice, and a freshness, and lithe young grace, and beauty, that belonged properly to the creatures of dreams—as he thought—and to no other. The sight of her would set his stagnant blood leaping; the sight of her—
>
> But it was a disappointment. They sat together on the ground and looked dimly wondering into each other's faces a while, with a sort of weak animal curiosity; then forgot each other's presence, and dropped their eyes, and you saw that they were away again, and wandering in some far land of dreams and shadows that we know nothing about. (212)

Mark Twain evokes here the pathos of the loss of youth as well as of personal identity. The bridegroom's dream of female beauty is replaced by the dream of the spirit detached from the body. The agency enforcing this antihuman fate, Morgan le Fay, is shadow not only to Hank but to Sir Breuse Sance Pité. She objects to the release of the imprisoned couple; "not that she felt any personal interest in the matter, but she thought it disrespectful to Sir Breuse Sance Pité" (212). Hank's response implies anger and the threat of violence, but his language itself is that of the tinkering mechanic: "I assured her that if he found he couldn't stand it I would fix him so that he could" (212). Hank's response does not reach beyond "photographing" Sir Breuse Sance Pité with an axe, so to speak.

At a subliminal level, Hank represents a struggle to come to terms with the threats posed by primitive sexuality, male and female. "The women here do certainly act like all possessed," he tells Sandy. "Yes, and I mean your best, too, society's very choicest brands. The humblest hello-girl along ten thousand miles of wire could teach gentleness, patience, modesty, manners, to the highest duchess in Arthur's land" (174). The list of virtues Hank misses in courtly women is almost identical to the qualities he claimed the Church instilled in the commoner—male—to oppress him and keep him in his place. Rodney O. Rogers has observed that "Lecky asserts that 'humility, obedience, patience, resignation, are all cardinal or rudimentary virtues in the Christian character [which] can . . . expand and flourish in a servile position.' Twain's characteristic accord with such criticisms is reflected in his autograph response in the margin: 'Christianity, then, did not raise up the slave, but degraded all conditions of men to the slave's level' " (443). However, the degradation applied only to men. What is loss of manhood to Hank is acquisition of true womanhood to him also.

Sandy does not know what a "hello-girl" is, so Hank tries to explain: "It's a new kind of girl; they don't have them here; one often speaks sharply to them when they are not the least in fault, and he can't get over feeling sorry for it and ashamed of himself in thirteen hundred years, it's such shabby mean conduct and so unprovoked; fact is, no gentleman ever does it—though I—well, I myself, if I've got to confess—" (174). Hank not only comes close to admitting that he is not a gentleman, his implicit admission has interesting parallels in Sam Clemens's own joking statement that he would never marry a girl he was worthy of: "*She* wouldn't do. She wouldn't be respectable enough." [19] The completion of the cycle of Clemens's own sense of his aggression against women, his remorse and self-accusation, are surely reflected in Hank's confession. Can it be entirely accidental that Twain then has Sandy, after Hank deflects her from speculating about the hello-girl's part in this cycle, launch into a narrative about Sir Marhaus, "a passing good man of his hands, but he hateth all ladies and gentle-women" (174)? Sir Gawaine, in Malory's account, is a moral arbiter who assesses Marhaus's misogyny:

> I will say you, said Sir Gawaine, it beseemeth evil a good knight to despise all ladies and gentlewomen, and perad-venture he loveth in some other places ladies and gentle-women, and to be loved again, and he be such a man of prowess as ye speak of——." (174–75)

This line of thought causes Hank to break out with one of the most revealing speeches in the novel:

> Man of prowess—yes, that is the man to please them, Sandy. Man of brains—that is a thing they never think of. Tom Sayers—John Heenan—John L. Sullivan—pity but you could be here. You would have your legs under the Round Table and a "Sir" in front of your names within the twenty-four hours; and you could bring about a new distribution of the married princesses and duchesses of the court in another twenty-four. The fact is, it is just a sort of polished-up court of Comanches, and there isn't a squaw in it who doesn't stand ready at the dropping of a hat to desert to the buck with the biggest string of scalps at his belt (175).

Hank's outburst reveals a combination of fear of and fascina-tion with female fickleness and masculine prowess. There is a mixture of contempt and envy in Hank's evocation of the image of nineteenth-century boxing champions Sayers, Heenan, and Sullivan acquiring titles and women in a primitive state of society with trimmings. The idea that, in a primitive society, sexual attractiveness and sexual affiliations are based on masculine strength and combativeness alone is both attractive and repulsive to Hank.

The repulsive side of this notion is related to the implications of the imagery Mark Twain uses to dramatize his attacks on feudal society. Here the women of the court are "squaws," but in chapter nineteen they become hogs. "The troublesomest old sow of the lot had to be called my lady, and your Highness, like the rest" (232). The ostensible targets of Twain's burlesque are aristocracy and superstition, but there is something of the misogynist Sir Marhaus in Hank as well:

> There was one small countess, with an iron ring in her snout and hardly any hair on her back, that was the devil for perversity. She gave me a race of an hour, over all sorts of country, and then we were right where we had started from, having made not a rod of real progress. I seized her at last by the tail, and brought her along, squalling. When I overtook Sandy, she was horrified, and said it was in the last degree indelicate to drag a countess by her train. (233)

This "countess" leads Hank for a chase in a circle, just as Sandy's tales are circular—like a mill—and the quest she leads him on seems to Hank aimless and circular. "Not a rod of real progress," Hank complains, using the navigational language of Mark Twain's youth but in a fashion that suggests sexual undertones.[20] Earlier Hank thinks of his struggle against the backwardness of the sixth century as "a gigantic and unassailable fact" (128). At the point of overwhelming the "dark land" with his power of progress, he says, in the original manuscript, "I stood with my hand on the cock, so to speak, ready to turn it on and flood the midnight world with light at any moment" (637).[21] But he does not do so: "I was not going to do the thing in that sudden way. It was not my policy. The people could not have stood it; and moreover I should have had the Established Roman Catholic Church on my back in a minute" (129). Twain places Hank somewhere between the totally subjected Brer Uriens, who was "always on the ragged edge of apprehension" (191), and the rapacious Sayers, Heenan, Sullivan, and Sance Pité. Hank allows himself to be restrained by the female forces of Sandy and the Church. Yet his indignation at the fate of what Clemens called the "castrated peoples" of "far-reaching, historic Europe" (*Mark Twain's Notebooks and Journals* 3:409) concentrates on their necessary suppression of anger at the treatment they receive:

> They had to let him [their lord or their bishop] plant fruit trees in their fields, and then keep their indignation to themselves when his heedless fruit-gatherers trampled the grain around the trees; they had to smother their anger when his hunting parties galloped through their fields . . . when the swarms from my lord's dovecote settled on their crops, they must not lose their temper and kill a bird. (156)

The culmination of this list of indignities is, not surprisingly, the droit du seigneur. Of this practice, Clemens wrote in his notebooks in 1888,

> In some savage tribes it was an *honor* to the girl & her family. In modern times it is an *honor* to a subject to be reigned over (that is, <made a slave> have his liberty debauched—) by a family called royal—a family with no decenter right than the medicine man. The stupid loyalty of to-day is the same sentiment, unaltered, that made le Droit possible, & the degradation is the same in quality & quantity—the form of it is changed, that is all. (*Mark Twain's Notebooks and Journals* 3:414)

To read Mark Twain's historical inscription backwards, that "sentiment" which he equates with being taken advantage of by the medicine man or the seigneur is that submission of feeling which puts the man in the position of the woman. If men submit to "stupid loyalty," meekness, humility, and patience, they become willing victims of the moral equivalent of rape. But if women lack loyalty, meekness, humility, and patience, they become castrating witches or beasts: Morgan le Fay or the sow. Seen in this light, the ambivalence toward gender roles that Twain displays in *A Connecticut Yankee* acquires a new clarity. Qualities which men and women are allowed to share in different degrees, particularly gentleness and compassion, make men human but women angels. Qualities which, in the imaginative scheme of the novel, men and women are not supposed to share, such as power, pride, and ambition, are represented as natural to men but degenerate or inhuman in women. More clearly than any novel preceding or following it, *A Connecticut Yankee* shows us that the father can assimilate the qualities of the mother, but the mother dare not usurp the qualities of the father. This disparity makes sense of an apparent absurdity in Hank's proposal for universal suffrage:

> Upon Arthur's death unlimited suffrage should be introduced, and given to men and women alike—at any rate to all men, wise or unwise, and to all mothers who, at middle age, should be found to know nearly as much as their sons at twenty-one. (444)

The joke cuts both ways: at male pride and at female aspiration. The ambivalence strikes at the root of one of the novel's most passionately held convictions: the doctrine of equality. The same ambivalence is evident in an ostensible joke that contrasts two types of female eminence in the chapter "A Competitive Examination." The first candidate's ancestor, the "wife of the founder of [his] line," "came of the highest landed gentry, yet she was not noble, she was gracious, and pure, and charitable, of a blameless life and character, insomuch that in these regards was she peer of the best lady in the land" (294). The great-grandmother of the next competitor "was a king's leman, and did climb to that splendid eminence by her own unholpen

merit from the sewer where she was born" (294). The reply of
the examiner, "Ah, this indeed is true nobility," is intended
to be ironic, but it may now appear doubly so, for the king's
leman does indeed represent a kind of aspiration to equality
and power not unlike Hank's own. Like Morgan le Fay, she is
an unacknowledged shadow of the democratic self. It appears
that, in Hank's meritocracy, women may aspire to the virtues
that will inspire men, while men carry on a complex battle with
those virtues. Women are to provide the sentiment, while men
exercise the power.

Hank, who calls himself "the champion of hard, unsenti-
mental, common-sense and reason" (430), is not so free of sentiment nor so clear of reason as he supposes himself to be.
The common sense which he represents has become as transparent as Sir Sagramour's veil. The conflict between sentiment
and reason in Hank is not an incidental one: it lies at the core
of the dilemma the novel dramatizes. Chadwick Hansen has
made the controversial argument that Hank Morgan resembles
the fascist personality of the twentieth century. His argument
is based on an analysis of the sentimentality of the novel. He
sees Hank Morgan as a character whose feeling is dominated
by sentimentality, which Hansen calls "an emotional bath for
himself" (72). As Hank briefly recognizes when he honors the
attachment of his legion of boy warriors to their nation and
origin, the unreasoning foundations of our loyalties are at the
wellsprings of our values. His love of chromos and baseball,
labor-saving machinery and showmanship, is based not on reason but on "sentiment," or on what one might call a cultural
predisposition. Though he calls himself "barren of sentiment,"
this means merely that he does not consciously have much of
what he thinks of as sentiment.

In a brilliant touch which conveys more truth about Hank
than many of his statements about himself, Mark Twain gradually has his Yankee hero become a native of Arthurian England
who on his deathbed thinks of his Connecticut existence as

"delirium" and "hideous dreams." Stanley Brodwin interprets
the death scene of Hank Morgan as manifesting "the agonizing
tension between the magnetic attractions of the Old God and
the New" (73) and aptly points out that Hank's final "effect"
is his "calling out of the guard to greet King Arthur, the
noblest servant of the Old Order" (73–74). Judith Fetterley
notes, concerning the word "effect," that "what stands behind
this word, as far as Hank is concerned, is the desire for power
over others and the ability to *affect* them. Hank seeks to control
people as he controls a machine, by switches and buttons; perhaps this is the central implication behind the contradictions
of his plan to send 'automata' to a 'Man-factory' to turn them
into men" ("Yankee Showman and Reformer" 668). But what
Hank's deathbed experience also expresses is an internal conflict
of psychological pressures. Hank, the aggressive, domineering male, relinquishes his accustomed identity in favor of a
new one.

Though Hank has been able, for a while, to make the Old
England into a New England, complete with stock market manipulations and baseball teams, he is not able to form human
nature in his own image. This failure is due not least to the
fact that the ideal Hank represents is flawed. The ineradicable
tendencies in human nature toward intrigue, conflict, and exploitation surface in the events that lead to the downfall of the
new Round Table. The masculine code of the new manhood
fails to establish a durable order: Hank Morgan becomes yet
another Twainian father who dies, leaving his child with an
elusive legacy. Twain dramatically, if not consciously, acknowledges the inadequacy of Hank's masculine values by showing
him, finally, not merely longing to be reunited with his anima,
Sandy, and with his child whose name echoes the technological
alienation of a distant future, but assuming a role poignantly
uncharacteristic of him: that of the martyred mother losing
her child. Hank's political failure is rooted in a psychological
failure. His challenge to monarchy and the Church leads him

through the effort to replace the role of king with that of boss, but technology and the conventions of Victorian family life cannot compensate for a deeper sense of lack that underlies the impermanence of Hank's and Twain's dream of fulfillment. The transformation of society that Hank seeks is not achieved. Ironically, Twain's challenge to Old World traditions affirms their monolithic power and in the process reveals the unsatisfactory nature of his ostensibly democratic challenge to the customs he seeks to discredit. Thus Clemens's imaginative reinterpretation of Arthurian narrative confirms rather than subverts the terms he attacks.

Chapter Five

ESCAPE FROM SEXUALITY:
MARK TWAIN'S JOAN OF ARC

Joan's potential stature was reduced by the patriarchial
imagination into that of Virgin-Warrior who aids
men to fulfill men's goals.
—MARY DALY, *Beyond God the Father*

Samuel Clemens's romance with Europe followed a trajectory
from his first astonished discovery of Joan of Arc on the page
that blew across his path when he was a boy to his elaborate fic-
tionalization of her in a novel decades later. *Personal Recollections
of Joan of Arc* is a further development of Clemens's paradoxical search for the missing sides of masculinity already seen in
A Connecticut Yankee. That the Joan who emerges in his *Joan of
Arc* is a projection of the male imagination is beyond dispute.
However, I wish to suggest that, in addition to seeing the ways
in which Joan is distorted or absent in Mark Twain's text, it is
fruitful to examine the nature of the male narrator who functions as Twain's mediator of Joan. By looking at the images of
masculine identity in Twain's narrative in relation to the kind of
ideal of femininity—and of humanity—represented by Joan,
we can see Twain's representations of gender and sexuality in
a clearer light. Joan, as Twain presents her to us, ought to be
seen not in isolation but rather in relationship and in contrast
to the others whom Twain surrounds her with. Joan is defined
not merely by her actions and by the statements of others about

her but by whom she is compared with, or, more accurately, whom she serves to measure. Furthermore, de Conte and other characters in the novel serve not merely to reflect upon Joan but to reveal Samuel Clemens's gender-related anxieties and aspirations in and of themselves. De Conte is both a narrative device and a character whose predicaments and evolutions discover Clemens's projections of a problematic masculinity that corresponds to the warrior saint's emblematic femininity. If Clemens's sense of morality is to any extent rooted in his ideas about masculinity and femininity, *Joan of Arc* provides a clear text for reading the connections between his gender conceptions and his culturally-relative ethos. Joan is the figure in whom Clemens's American faith in political and sexual innocence is most completely embodied.

It is remarkable how extraordinarily divergent recent feminist interpretations of *Personal Recollections of Joan of Arc* have been. On the one hand, Joyce W. Warren in *The American Narcissus* names Joan as "the only female character in Mark Twain's work that he really seemed to care about" (154–55) and claims that "Joan is Mark Twain's principal female character, the only one that he treated in any detail" (155). As such, she is the epitome of Twain's stereotypic ideal of woman: "more selfless, more modest, purer, and more pious than any other one female character . . . the epitome of Mark Twain's genteel maidens" (156). Since Twain's ideal woman is "obviously a child . . . prepubescent and asexual," she serves as the ultimate symbol of Twain's willful, egocentric exclusion of the otherness of woman from his life as well as from his fiction. "For Mark Twain, woman existed only as imaged by and in relation to the male self. Even at his bitterest, Mark Twain held to his original view of woman as the pure, innocent ideal of preadolescence. *Joan of Arc,* which he wrote after his bankruptcy and the failure of the typesetter, is the ultimate expression of this ideal" (184–85).[1] Christina Zwarg, on the other hand, argues that "Mark Twain assumes a feminist attitude toward history that situates his work (*Joan of Arc*) at the center of the theoretical problem [of women and history] engaging feminists today" (59). Zwarg reads Twain's biography of Joan as a parody of Michelet and indeed of all male attempts to "textualize women" (62). Thus, though the novel does not provide an alternative narrative version of Joan of Arc, it focuses on "her continued effacement and diminution throughout the text" (62). The "incipient feminism of Mark Twain's project" and "his faith in the lived reality of Joan of Arc . . . [keep] the novel from collapsing completely around itself. A 'sense' of Joan of Arc manages to escape from the work despite the fact that it is designed to show her imprisonment in it" (62). Zwarg credits Twain with adopting "a narrative technique that destabilizes every structure of authority of the novel, including the reader's" (62). She distinguishes sharply between de Conte and Twain: "De Conte never acknowledges the full extent of Joan's control over her environment, while Mark Twain consistently credits Joan with a meta-authority over everything" (64). It is de Conte's "final resistance to the major force of Joan of Arc's reality . . . his distortion of it toward . . . a traditional end . . . which Mark Twain most satirizes in his novel" (68).

In between these apparently polar opposite feminist interpretations of Twain's *Joan of Arc* we find the French critic Rolande Ballorain, who regards Twain as a misogynist (148–51) but finds in *Joan* redemptive evidence to "temper this image" (151). "Mark Twain's work is an all-American male world, but it could not be otherwise in his time. That is a first unifying pattern of his whole opus. It is not because of a strong conscious antifeminism on his part: he hated men as much as he hated women; he loved women more" (155). Specifically, "it is in *Joan of Arc* that the debunking of the myth of the boys is accomplished" (154). Joan is shown by Mark Twain to be brave, "having 'military genius, leonine courage, incomparable fortitude, a prodigy of a mind'" (162), while the men around her are "curs (the King), rascals, low and debased ingrates (the English and the

French), and traitors (the Church)" (162). Joan is "mostly a girl in a man's world; and a much better man than any man" (162). Ballorain finds in Mark Twain's presentation of Joan's reasons for assuming male dress "a very modern way of seeing" and considers that Twain champions her for dressing like a man, which is a symbol of "her refusal to keep to the role assigned to her by her society, by men and religion" (162). Ballorain praises Twain for being an advocate of Joan and regrets that American readers and critics have neglected the book. "One may guess why. It is about History; about French and English History; about a woman, and a Frenchwoman; matters of no immediate concern to Americans" (163). In my view, on the contrary, the very distance of these matters from the immediacy of daily American life is part of what gave them such imaginative attraction for Twain and what forms an essential element of his experimentation with fictional representations of gender.

Are these assessments of the significance of Mark Twain's Joan irreconcilably contradictory, or can we set in motion a play of dialogue (or discourse) between them? Warren emphasizes the conventional Victorian qualities of femininity that Twain associates with Joan, whereas Zwarg argues, from a sophisticated reading of narrative technique, that Joan is not to be found in the male platitudes about her in Twain's text and that the absence of the genuine historical Joan is precisely Twain's point. Ballorain proposes that Twain's male characters are equally distortions and stereotypes and that Twain celebrates after all what are admirable and superior traits in Joan. Leaving aside the easy (and frequent) objection that Twain's Joan is not a plausible human being, much less a woman, can we discover a new way of examining the text that will take us beyond these contradictions without ignoring the validity of each of these perspectives? The multiplicity of interpretations here is evidence not only of differences in theoretical approaches and national perspectives but also of the importance of Twain's

JOAN of ARC
ALIAS
MARK TWAIN

Joan of Arc Alias Mark Twain, *Life,* May 28, 1896.

Joan of Arc to the issues of gender as we are currently redefining them.

Rolande Ballorain introduces one of the central contradictions of the novel when she asserts that, for Mark Twain, Joan is "a much better man than any man" (162). The "Translator's Preface," in which Twain introduces his readers to his vision of Joan, piles up the superlatives in portraying her as a human being whose excellence of character transcends historical relativity and, by implication, gender. For, we are told, "the character of Joan of Arc is unique. It can be measured by the standards of all times without misgiving or apprehension as to the result. Judged by any of them, judged by all of them, it is still flawless; it is still ideally perfect; it still occupies the loftiest place possible to human attainment, a loftier one than has been reached by any other mere mortal" (1:xi). Twain compares Joan's virtues with the vices and deficiencies of her age, to the "society" and "men" of her time. When she is compared to individuals, it is the French king, Caesar, and Napoleon whom she is favorably contrasted with. The question inevitably arises, if Joan was the embodiment of Samuel Clemens's ideal human being, how did it matter to him (if it did) that she was a woman? Was her identity as a woman in any sense crucial for Clemens to her virtues as a human being? What relationship was there, in Clemens's mind, between her transcendence and her femininity?

Part of the answer must lie in the fact that, for Mark Twain, as foreshadowed in the many female martyrs in *The Prince and the Pauper* and *A Connecticut Yankee,* Joan's character represented an implicit critique of male character. If the "real Joan" is missing at the center of de Conte's narrative, as Christina Zwarg asserts, there is nonetheless a clearly defined set of virtues at the core of Twain's portrayal of Joan that serves as a measure of the deficiencies of men in general and of the male characters represented in the story in particular. Those virtues are honesty, sexual and ethical purity, bravery, unselfishness, intelligence, and prophetic faith or vision. As narrowly defined and conceived as these Victorian virtues may appear to us, we must not be blinded to the reality that in Samuel Clemens's mind Joan truly had them. It is not difficult to see that the intensity of Clemens's idolization of Joan must have sprung in part from his guilty awareness that he himself often lacked the virtues he projected upon her. He clearly felt at times, like Huck Finn, that telling the truth was "most like setting down on a kag of powder and touching it off, just to see where you'll go to" (239). He was obsessively aware of his sexual "impurity," and he dramatized his guilty conscience with unforgettable vividness in "The Facts Concerning the Recent Carnival of Crime in Connecticut" (*Selected Shorter Writings of Mark Twain*).[2] His knowledge of his own lack of bravery in circumstances analogous to those surrounding Joan of Arc, when he was about her age, is thoroughly evident in his "Private History Of a Campaign that Failed" (*Selected Shorter Writings of Mark Twain*). The failure of his program of investment in the Paige typesetter shook his faith in his shrewdness on the field of economic battle, the nineteenth-century American equivalent of a noble war, and, as *A Connecticut Yankee* plainly showed, his faith in the amelioration of life through political and social progress was becoming increasingly ambivalent at best. All these considerations add up to reasons why Samuel Clemens can be said to have found in Joan a truly *alter* ego, a version of the self as *other* than the faulty, lacking, familiar one.

Joan of Arc provides us with an ideal human being, Joan, and her tragicomic antithesis in the form of more or less ordinary, flawed human beings: men whose deeds do not measure up to expectations. The weak, vacillating Dauphin, later the King, is a prime symbol of empty masculinity. He has the emolument of authority, but he fails to exercise it. He is incapacitated by self-doubt, manipulation, and inertia. Significantly, Mark Twain hinges the King's self-doubts on the issue of paternity: Joan's assurance that he is his father's legitimate son infuses him with confidence and strength, though he is not able to sustain his new sense of identity. "Telling him he was of lawful birth was what straightened him up and made a man of him for a moment, removing his doubts upon that head and convincing him of his royal right" (1:113). The central psychological theme of *The Prince and the Pauper,* the son's need for some form of fathering to achieve an identity, reappears here, as it does so often in Twain's works. On this level, it appears that Joan's function is to reinforce the patriarchy by dispelling doubts about patrilinear legitimacy. The inability of the King to sustain the strength Joan offers is, in Twain's vision, a tragic weakness. Thus, when the story is read on a psychological level, history enfolds within itself drastic doubts about the symbolic father whose surrogate daughter does more than any ordinary mortal could to reassure and bolster him. Joan shares the innocence and questing nature of the boys in *The Prince and the Pauper.* That Joan is a surrogate daughter is suggested by the fact that she recognizes the King even in disguise.

The psychological conflict between self-doubt and the assurance of authority (self-authorization as well as social authority) is played out symbolically especially in the episodes and characters invented by Mark Twain. The nature of his additions to the story is a powerful clue to the reasons for Samuel Clemens's fascination with this particular material. If in *The Prince and the Pauper* Clemens imaginatively spun out varieties of paternity, in *Joan of Arc* he spins out varieties of masculinity, of which de Conte's is the most complex and psychologically autobiographical. Joan is, in the first section of the book, the ground upon which figures of masculine folly disport themselves, while in the final section male cruelty and folly become the ground upon which the figure of Joan's frailty is displayed. In Book I, "In Domremy," Joan's virtues unfold, contrasted with the pretensions of "the boys." In the incident involving "crazy Benoist," Joan demonstrates real courage by facing the madman with the axe. The axe echoes the violence of pap Finn, the hermit in *The Prince and the Pauper,* Hank Morgan, and Morgan le Fay.

The other children first run away in terror, then (when it is safe) boast about the bravery they would show if faced with danger again. Though both boys and girls join in bragging about their martial spirit, the boys are the most outrageously self-aggrandizing, and their roles foreshadow their later roles as soldiers in Joan's camp. Nöel Rainguesson is the clever one, and Edmond Aubrey, less intellectually gifted and already nick-named the Paladin ("because of the armies he was always going to eat up some day," 1:38), is full of boasts. Nöel represents the sly manipulator, while the Paladin is a type of Falstaff. The typology of the cast of characters, reinforced by their nick-names, resembles that of fairy tales and is reflected in a symme-try between children and adults. Rainguesson and the Paladin are paralleled by the priest (referred to as "the good father," 1:18—de Conte's surrogate father, like Tom Canty's surrogate father priest in *The Prince and the Pauper*) and by the twin ora-tors, the maître and the stranger in the storm. The maître is Edmond Aubrey's father, and, like the priest, he fancies himself clever but is exposed by Joan's sophisticated simplicity as self-indulgent in his speech about the responsibility of the stomach. Like the Paladin, the adult orators are carried away by their own oratory. "Eloquence *is* a power, there is no question of that," de Conte states (1:32).

But what is the precise nature of that power as Mark Twain portrays it? First of all, it is repeatedly and insistently associated with storms, implying that it is a force of nature. De Conte rel-ishes the memory of the winter storm that is the natural setting for the maître's and the stranger's speeches: "It blew a gale out-side, and the screaming of the wind was a stirring sound, and I think I may say it was beautiful, for I think it *is* great and fine and beautiful to hear the wind rage and storm and blow its clari-ons like that, when you are inside and comfortable" (1:25). But the storm as an emblem of the passion of nature is also a sym-bol of human passion, the passion of an eloquence that verges on the sexual. The stranger's rhetorical celebration of patriotism culminates in a communal orgy of emotion when he sings the Song of Roland for Joan: "a heart-melting, soul-rousing surprise":

> How fine he looked, how stately, how inspired, as he stood there with that mighty chant welling from his lips and his heart, his whole body transfigured, and his rags along with it.
>
> Everybody rose and stood while he sang, and their faces glowed and their eyes burned; and the tears came and flowed down their cheeks, and their forms began to sway unconsciously to the swing of the song, and their bosoms to heave and pant; and moanings broke out, and deep ejaculations; and when the last verse was reached . . . all burst out in sobs and wailings. But when the final great note died out and the song was done, they all flung themselves in a body at the singer, stark mad with love of him and love of France and pride in her great deeds and old renown, and smothered him with their embracings; but Joan was there first, hugged close to his breast, and covering his face with idolatrous kisses.
>
> The storm raged on outside. (1:34–35)

This storm of passion is not tinged with irony, as the response to the mayor's logic-chopping speech is (though that speech also evokes adulation). France ("she") is the projected love-object here, and Joan is closely identified with that object of projection through her act of feeding the stranger, which defies patriarchal authority. Jacques d'Arc, Joan's father, thunders commands at her when she seeks to help the outsider whose status as an outcast casts doubt upon his manhood: "The embarrassed poor creature stood there and appealed to one face after the other with his eyes, and found no welcome in any, the smile on his own face flickering and fading and perishing, meanwhile; then he dropped his gaze, the muscles of his face began to twitch, and he put up his hand to cover this woman-

Samuel Clemens with his daughter Clara in his London home, circa
1897. Photograph by Major J. B. Pond. Mark Twain Collection
(#6314-T), Clifton Waller Barrett Library, Manuscripts Division,
Special Collections Department, University of Virginia Library.

ish sign of weakness" (1:28). This is the same stranger whose singing about the valiant death of Roland arouses the passionate love of the crowd. Art, in the form of song, has the power to transform an uncertain masculinity more effectively than the spurious eloquence of logic, but it is ultimately subservient to Joan's motherly defense of all creatures, including the evil ones, as creations of God. Joan mounts the same kind of defense in the previous chapter when she forces the priest to recognize that even "a devil's child" was created by God and deserves compassion. There, too, eloquence is associated with storm: "She had torn loose from Père Fronte, and was crying, with her knuckles in her eyes, and stamping her small feet in a fury; and now she burst out of the place and was gone before we could gather our senses together out of this storm of words and this whirlwind of passion" (1:24). What Joan and the singer share is a self-forgetful passion which, ironically, makes them fully themselves, unlike the maître or the Paladin, whose eloquence is too self-conscious and self-aggrandizing and therefore leaves them looking ridiculous. Warren's analysis of self in Mark Twain's fiction does not adequately acknowledge that Twain questions and criticizes much of male self-aggrandizement. Self-realization is a problematic goal for men in Twain's vision, as is, to a lesser degree, self-sacrifice for women.

The self-conscious rhetoric of the maître and of the Paladin reaches for social legitimation, much like the calculated public poses of Hank Morgan in *A Connecticut Yankee*, but Mark Twain makes these speakers expose their hollowness as he did not do for the Yankee. The Paladin in particular is a comic portrayal of the self-made man and displays Mark Twain's characteristic yearning for the legitimation of a father:

He made his enlargements without flourish, without emphasis, and so casually that often one failed to notice that a change had been made. He spoke of the governor of Vaucouleurs, the first night, simply as the governor of

Vaucouleurs; he spoke of him the second night as his uncle the governor of Vaucouleurs; the third night he was his father. He did not seem to know that he was making these extraordinary changes; they dropped from his lips in a quite natural and effortless way. By his first night's account the governor merely attached him to the Maid's military escort in a general and unofficial way; the second night his uncle the governor sent him with the Maid as lieutenant of his rear guard; the third night his father the governor put the whole command, Maid and all, in his especial charge. The first night the governor spoke of him as a youth without name or ancestry, but "destined to achieve both"; the second night his uncle the governor spoke of him as the latest and worthiest lineal descendant of the chiefest and noblest of the Twelve Paladins of Charlemagne; the third night he spoke of him as the lineal descendant of the whole dozen. In three nights he promoted the Count of Vendôme from a fresh acquaintance to schoolmate, and then brother-in-law. (1:152–53)

The Paladin is a humorous portrait of the writer himself, for he is the one who has "the narrative gift" that keeps the people spellbound; and his performance is marked by inventiveness and sincerity. "The lineal descendant of the whole dozen," a "youth without name or ancestry, but 'destined to achieve both' "—these logically absurd though emotionally appealing phrases about the invention of ancestry are signals of Mark Twain's conscious if satiric encapsulation of the creation of masculine identity within the process of storytelling, the passionate art. For the Paladin is a creation of Rainguesson, the clever manipulator, the artist behind the scenes:

If this vast structure of brawn and muscle and vanity and foolishness seemed to have a libellous tongue, what of it? There was no malice behind it; and besides, the defect was not of his own creation; it was the work of Nöel Rainguesson, who had nurtured it, fostered it, built it up and perfected it, for the entertainment he got out of it. His careless light heart had to have somebody to nag and chaff and make fun of, the Paladin had only needed development in order to meet its requirements, consequently the development was taken in hand and diligently attended to and looked after. (1:105)

The Paladin, to use the terms employed by Hank in *A Connecticut Yankee,* is a man of brawn who is being played the fool by a man of brains. Yet in a sense Rainguesson and the Paladin are both creations of Sieur Louis de Conte, the " 'young man of noble birth' with the convenient initials," as Albert E. Stone, Jr., aptly refers to him (210). De Conte is mediated to us by the fictional translator, Jean François Alden, who is in turn another creation of Mark Twain's, who was invented by Samuel Langhorne Clemens. If we count Aubrey himself, we have before us half a dozen visible "ancestors," all collaborators in engendering the Paladin, who is so hungry for ancestry.

The Paladin, with his genetic anxiety and triumphs, represents an imaginative orientation toward the past. He inflates and celebrates his ancestry and his heroic deeds in an imaginary narrative history. But Joan, as embedded in her history by Mark Twain, represents an imaginative orientation toward the future which is heroic as long as it is effective but becomes tragic and pathetic when it ceases to operate eschatologically. Joan does not merely create herself from unpromising origins, she creates and enacts history itself, without ever denying her origins: her parents, her village, Catholicism, France. She is, however, in conflict with all of these, unlike any of the men, who always represent or oppose only part of this social universe.

But Twain strains to root Joan in an entity that lies outside the social realm yet is not merely a psychological resource within Joan herself (as the Paladin's storytelling capacity may be said to be): the fairy tree. The fairy tree and the fairies are transparent symbols of pagan nature, the ostensible source of Joan's power and inspiration. The fairies, the fairy tree of Bourlemont, and Joan's voices are numinous signs, but they are not Christian. They invoke for Joan the same conflict between Christian social morality and the authentic, passionate morality of the heart as Jim's friendship does for Huck in the face of slaveholding Christianity. But they are weak bearers of the symbolic weight Mark Twain makes them bear, partly because they are desexualized. They are relatives of Peter Pan, not descendants of Dionysus or Artemis. They share with Joan the sorry fate of being described again and again in the diminutive. They represent so much that is intrinsically positive to Twain: childhood, innocence, nature, life apart from society, ritual, play, and art.[3] Yet they can inspire only superficial delight and pity, not terror, because Twain keeps them, and Joan, "clean" of the primal forces that are their complementary opposites. Joan, like Huck, is most interesting and lifelike when she is torn between the inescapable corruption of social life and the beauty of the forces represented by the fairies, but Twain permits that conflict to exist only very briefly, at the outset of his story. Then the fairy tale of ideal versus corrupt humanity takes over.

The essence of corruption, in Mark Twain's fabulist version of history, is self-interested cruelty, symbolized most egregiously by Cauchon, the bloated, sly, wicked Inquisitor. Cauchon is, for Twain, a cautionary male villain: sensual, intellectual, deceitful, identified with an oppressive social institution, and sadistic. De Conte calls him "that bastard of Satan," evoking illegitimacy as a source of Cauchon's panoply of evils. De Conte's pity for Joan is contrasted with Cauchon's lack of it: "It was piteous. It would have touched the heart of a brute. But Cauchon was more than that" (2:207). Thus the villain is the epitome of the man without compassion: not a beast in human form, but a being at once superior to and more degenerate than an ani-

Samuel Clemens, Clara Clemens, and Olivia Clemens,
July 18, 1895, aboard the S.S. *Northland*. Mark Twain Collection
(#6314-T), Clifton Waller Barrett Library, Manuscripts Division,
Special Collections Department, University of Virginia Library.

Aboard the U.S.S. *Mohican*, Seattle, Washington, August 13, 1895.
From left: Samuel Moffatt, Olivia Clemens, Clara Clemens, Samuel
Clemens, an unidentified woman, Mrs. J. B. Pond. Photograph by
Major J. B. Pond. Mark Twain Collection (#6314-T), Clifton
Waller Barrett Library, Manuscripts Division, Special Collections
Department, University of Virginia Library.

mal. For Twain, compassion for an innocent suffering being (the compassion Joan demonstrates repeatedly at the beginning of the story) is the essence of human nature at its best. Cauchon, who consistently lacks any such compassion, is thoroughly evil.

But *Joan of Arc* is a story about war and warriors, and there is an inevitable conflict between Mark Twain's elevation of the ideal of compassion and the moral drift of a story celebrating political revolt, uprising, battle, and the defeat of a hated enemy. Joan and the soldiers who fight on her side cannot act only out of compassion: the independence of France is not to be gained through nonviolence. The consequence is a curious moral dualism reflected in exaggerated gender divisions. Joan is portrayed as having no personal animosity against her enemies whatsoever. The cool autocrat of the enemy camp is faced with raging anger by the mob but with this from Joan: " 'I would I might see thy head struck from thy body!'—then, after a pause, and crossing herself—'if it were the will of God' " (1:51). De Conte calls this the "only harsh speech" in her life. Joan cradles the heads of dying enemy soldiers and comforts them in their last moments. She represents the *idea* of pure compassion, not accidentally in female form. The "real" Joan's absence from the text is due not to an ironic strategy but to the fact that Twain's version of her represents an idea of perfect human nature.

She makes alliances, however, with the most violent and ruthless of soldiers. Baudricourt, the "Dwarf," and La Hire are all versions of the man of action, the rough fighter; and Mark Twain insistently shows us how these gendered opposites are, to his mind, delightfully complementary.

> Joan and he were inseparable, and a quaint and pleasant contrast they made. He was so big, she so little; he was so gray and so far along in his pilgrimage of life, she so youthful; his face was so bronzed and scarred, hers so fair and pink; she was so pure, so innocent, he such a cyclopaedia of sin. In her eye was stored all charity and compassion,

in his lightnings; when her glance fell upon you it seemed to bring benediction and the peace of God, but with his it was different, generally. (1:190)

However, it is crucial to note that these martial he-men, whose few words are themselves acts of violence, are ambivalently seen and relayed to us by a man whose gendering traits and perspective are much more equivocal: de Conte, the artist, the man of words, a man as sympathetic to Joan's female traits as he is admiring of the soldiers' male ones. This does not mean that de Conte's masculinity is in doubt so much as that Mark Twain is imagining a third existential truce, to use psychologist Robert Kegan's phrase, for maleness caught between the comic impotence of Paladin-style braggadocio and the immoral violence of ruthless manhood.[4] What, after all, is the essential difference between Cauchon, "the bastard of Satan," and La Hire, nicknamed Satan? Mark Twain does not make de Conte diminish the rapacity of La Hire. De Conte calls him "that lurid conflagration of blasphemy, that Vesuvius of profanity, forever in eruption" (1:181) and says that he not only is the match of "a mob of roaring devils" but is "probably the father of most of them" (1:181). "He is the frankest man alive, and the naïvest. Once when he was rebuked for pillaging on his raids, he said it was nothing. Said he, 'If God the Father were a soldier, He would rob'" (1:181–82). The question Mark Twain dare not raise explicitly is, "Would He rape?"

The subjectivity of de Conte as a man in the middle is essential to the ways in which Joan's he-men allies are described. The governor, Baudricourt,

> was an ideal soldier of the time; tall, brawny, grayheaded, rough, full of strange oaths acquired here and there and yonder in the wars and treasured as if they were decorations. He had been used to the camp all his life, and to his notion war was God's best gift to man. He had his steel cuirass on, and wore boots that came above his knees,

and was equipped with a huge sword; and when I looked at this martial figure, and heard the marvellous oaths, and guessed how little of poetry and sentiment might be looked for in this quarter, I hoped the little peasant girl would not get the privilege of confronting this battery, but would have to content herself with the dictated letter. (1:78)

The governor is similar to Hank Morgan (who says of himself, "I am barren of sentiment . . . poetry"), but here his type is seen from the perspective of a male who has a share of "sentiment" and "poetry" and who is sympathetic to the female confronting him. However, de Conte diminishes Joan in his description ("the little peasant girl") and augments the military man, "this battery" (which is also reminiscent of Hank facing his last desperate battle with machine gun and electrical batteries), in a manner that implies both empathetic identification with Joan and condescension to her as a female.

Just as we find the male villain (Cauchon) and the male hero (La Hire, Baudricourt, and others), we find a female villain (Isabel) and her heroic counterpart (Yolande, Queen of Sicily, the King's mother-in-law, "wise and good") represented in equally simplistic terms. But the roles of de Conte and of Joan are, in different ways, more complicated and conflicted. The essential conflict is superficially inscribed in prophecy as a struggle between the demonic and the angelic woman:

A prophecy of Merlin's, more than eight hundred years old, was called to mind, which said that in a far future time France would be lost by a woman and restored by a woman. France was now, for the first time, lost—and by a woman, Isabel of Bavaria, her base Queen; doubtless this fair and pure young girl was commissioned of Heaven to complete the prophecy. (1:90)

But the more genuinely felt conflicts dramatized in Mark Twain's inscription of Joan are these: how can Joan maintain her ideal integrity in a world of men whose values she is in part compelled to live by; and how can de Conte envision wholeness and continuity for himself in a world so fractured between ideality, as represented by Joan's virtues, and masculinity, which requires compromise with the exploitative use of force?

Psychologically, de Conte is intricately invested in creating and preserving his version of Joan of Arc. Because Joan suffered an inescapable martyrdom and de Conte suffered the loss of Joan, the progression of her life demonstrates his helplessness vis-à-vis fate and society. De Conte is, unlike the soldiers who fight with Joan, a helpless observer, more detached from the possibility of action than even Huck Finn. Instead of acting in history, he vicariously experiences life through his association with Joan. His power, like Mark Twain's, lies in his selective, shaping construction of vicarious experience. Joan appears to be at the center of the stage of history, acting decisively and suffering her fate. But in fact, of course, Joan is always interpreted to us through the de Conte-Alden-Twain-Clemens chain of interpreters. Jean François Alden, the "translator," should not be ignored, for he draws attention to the metaphorical activity of translation as well as to the John Alden of Longfellow's "Courtship of Miles Standish." Longfellow was, after all, one of the patriarchal "greats" of American literature whom Mark Twain felt he had insulted with his frontier anecdote at the dinner in honor of Whittier's seventieth birthday in Boston, December 17, 1877.[5] *Personal Recollections of Joan of Arc* is also a form of courtship through an intermediary: courtship of respectability on the literary scene, but also courtship of something deeper. It was written, Clemens told Mrs. Fairbanks, "for love & not for lucre."[6] If it was written for love of Joan, we must recognize what a contradictory and problematic symbol Joan was for Clemens. As if to deflect the idea that de Conte courted Joan in any erotic sense, Twain has him fall hopelessly in love with Catherine, Joan's close friend and companion, whom he unsuccessfully woos.

Whenever de Conte's perceptions of Joan touch on Joan's

beauty or physical development in a way that could suggest her emerging sexuality, Twain has him sublimate these perceptions into the spiritual. On the one hand, Joan is frequently characterized as innocent and childlike, "that gentle little creature, that wouldn't hurt a fly, and couldn't bear the sight of blood, and was so girlish and shrinking in all ways" (1:42). On the other hand, de Conte glances at her puberty: "She was sixteen now, shapely and graceful, and of a beauty so extraordinary that I might allow myself any extravagance of language in describing it and yet have no fear of going beyond the truth." This evasive maneuver leads towards the etherealization that follows: "There was in her face a sweetness and serenity and purity that justly reflected her spiritual nature" (1:51–52). When Joan dresses in women's clothing that some men might find erotic, de Conte is enchanted—spiritually:

> So then the gracious Queen imagined and contrived that simple and witching costume which I have described to you so many times, and which I cannot think of even now in my dull age without being moved just as rhythmical and exquisite music moves one; for *that* was music, that dress—that is what it was—music that one saw with the eyes and felt in the heart. Yes, she was a poem, she was a dream, she was a spirit when she was clothed in that. (1:138)

De Conte can deal with Joan's emergent womanhood only through the distancing maneuvers of metaphor.

> She was such a vision of young bloom and beauty and grace, and such an incarnation of pluck and life and go! She was growing more and more ideally beautiful every day, as was plain to be seen—and these were days of development; for she was well past seventeen, now—in fact she was getting close upon seventeen and a half—indeed, just a little woman, as you may say. (1:290)

As the phrase "little woman" suggests, Mark Twain faced the same dilemmas as Louisa May Alcott did in writing what Alcott herself referred to as "moral pap for the young," and for some of the same reasons. Joan is in some respects not unlike, if not as vital as, Jo March, and the aged de Conte is in a position like Pa March's of suppressing or diminishing the young woman's sexual development in favor of her moral growth in order to maintain control over her.

De Conte is in love with Catherine and expresses erotic yearning for her (1:293). Late in life, he maintains an idealized image of her that he has preserved for sixty-three years. Yet what is oddest about de Conte's attraction to Catherine Boucher, daughter of Jaques Boucher, treasurer of the Duke of Orleans, "eighteen, and gentle and lovely in her ways, and very beautiful" (1:206), is the curiously triangular nature of his courtship of her. First of all, she seems to be calculated to be a kind of pale imitation of Joan. "I think she might have been as beautiful as Joan herself, if she had had Joan's eyes," de Conte remarks (1:206). Catherine appears to be the surrogate whom the narrator can dare to love in a human way to compensate for the impossibility of aspiring to love erotically a being so superior as Joan. Secondly, de Conte's feelings for Catherine are marked by his desire to comfort Catherine as Joan does. Catherine seeks to prevent Joan from going into battle when Joan knows that she will receive a wound. But when Joan forces Catherine to recognize such an action as cowardice, Catherine breaks down and weeps with shame. De Conte says,

> I did so want to take her in my arms and comfort her, but Joan did it, and of course I said nothing. Joan did it well, and most sweetly and tenderly, but I could have done it as well, though I knew it would be foolish and out of place to suggest such a thing . . . though I . . . was many times tortured with doubts afterwards as having perhaps let a chance pass which might have changed all my life. (1:258–59)

Joan's absolute dedication to her cause inflicts the pain of moral self-recognition on Catherine, which Joan is eminently qualified to comfort her for—while de Conte helplessly stands by and wishes he could be in Joan's place. Like Laurie in *Little Women*, he envies women their freedom of emotional expression, especially of affection. Not only might de Conte's life have been changed by marriage if he had been able to comfort Catherine as Joan does, his character might have been transformed through the union of compassion and courage. His idealization of Joan through narrative becomes a substitute for the passionate union he did not have the courage to seek actively and for the children he might have had with Catherine.

De Conte's love for Catherine is expressed through his sentimental poetry, which is an elaborate idealization of the female. The story of his poem and its failure is one of two parodies or undercuttings of sentiment: first the heroic, in the parody of the Paladin's lies; next the romantic, in the parody of feeling by the Paladin, when he weeps so melodramatically that he turns sentiment to laughter. The structure of this succession of parodies is identical to that of *1601*, Twain's bawdy historical sketch: destroying pretensions of two kinds. La Hire's laughter, which concludes the episode, is remarkably like Sir Walter Raleigh's fart in *1601*: "He stood there with his gauntlets on his hips and his head tilted back and his jaws spread to that degree to let out his hurricanes and his thunders that it amounted to indecent exposure, for you could see everything that was in him" (1:215–16). La Hire is a man whose laughter exposes him completely, literally and metaphorically. His crass male physicality devastates de Conte's emotional aspirations expressed through romantic/sentimental art. La Hire, the "Satan" who is "converted" by Joan, is a symbol of a brute masculinity by which de Conte instinctively measures himself. La Hire forces him to reject as shameful and ridiculous his more tender emotions, while Joan elicits his admiration for her compassion and evokes his desire to comfort as she does someone like herself, but weaker.

If we accept La Hire and Joan, Satan and Saint, as the incongruous but complementary pair that Mark Twain represents them as, we can see how torturously ambivalent their modes of being are to de Conte, who is attracted to but feels judged by both, even as he represents them to us through the filter of his consciousness.

Joan herself, as Mark Twain represents her, is an incongruous and implausible combination of sensitive delicacy and fearless authority, the "soft little shepherdess" (1:202), "that poor child" (1:121) with her "girlish little personality" (2:156) and the "warrior soul" and "lion heart" that speaks with "battle-voice" (2:219). Her main function, in psychological terms, is to enable men to be men. This confirms Joyce Warren's point that woman is represented only in relation to the male self in Twain's works, but Zwarg is also accurate in pointing to the destabilization of all forms of authority in the novel, especially male authority. Joan's pivotal role in the King's career is to enable him to believe in his own legitimacy, but the novel also raises doubts about the value and authority of that legitimacy. Though Joan's certainty about her mission is at times ascribed to God, as when we are told that "this new light in the eye and this new bearing were born of the authority and leadership which had this day been vested in her by the decree of God" (1:76), her alliances with men such as "Satan" and the Dwarf, "a devil and the son of a devil when he turned himself loose with his axe" (1:225; an echo of Morgan le Fay) suggest a more complex and problematic genealogy for her authority. Yolande, Queen of Sicily, the only powerful good woman in the novel, articulates Joan's legitimation thus:

And whether she comes of God or no, there is that in her heart that raises her above men—high above all men that breathe in France today—for in her is that mysterious something that puts heart into soldiers, and turns mobs of cowards into fighters that forget what fear is when they are

in that presence—fighters who go into battle with joy in
their eyes and songs on their lips, and sweep over the field
like a storm—that is the spirit that can save France, and
that alone, come it whence it may! (1:129)

It is no accident that Yolande echoes the quasi-sexual language
of passion and natural violence earlier expressed by the patriotic
singer and by Joan in her defense of the fairies. As Mark Twain
defines gender here, courage is the essence of manhood, and
Joan has the magical ability to inspire courage. She says to the
Paladin, "Of old you were a fantastic talker, but there is a man
in you, and I will bring it out" (1:177), and de Conte makes a
point of showing us how the formerly empty braggart actually
becomes self-forgetful and brave on the battlefield under Joan's
eyes. "Being right under Joan's exalting and transforming eye,
he forgot his native prudence" (1:237).

Joan is the catalyst for bravery in ordinary men and the muse
for the artist (proleptically the singer) and storyteller de Conte,
whose name signals his role as narrator and spinner of tales.
Joan is not a plausible, round character, but neither are any of
the other characters. Joan's virtues serve to mirror the faults of
the male characters, but with the single exception of the artist's, the moral conflicts and issues dramatized in this book are
simplistic and flat: the failure of the imagination that prevents
Joan from coming alive also prevents the male characters—
braggarts, cowards, patriots, or villains—from coming alive.
The ghost story concluding in the finding of the rusty sword and
rotten fan symbolizes the stereotypically gendered imagination
that dominates much of the narration. Mark Twain never dares
to imagine that La Hire or the Dwarf could struggle with a sense
of horror at violence done to the enemy or with compassion for
anyone except designated victims: women and children. Ultimately, Twain's failure to apprehend the otherness of women,
as Joyce Warren charges, is also a failure to apprehend the complexities of humanity, male and female. Zwarg gives Twain

too much credit, I believe, when she claims that he is parodying the exclusion of Joan through the narrative strategies of the text. But I think that she is right in insisting on Twain's consciousness of something missing at the center of the text.

De Conte, as inconsistent and implausible as he is at times, is a symbolic spiritual autobiographer for Mark Twain, the figure Sam Clemens created. De Conte, representing the Samuel Clemens who became Mark Twain, recognizes and admires certain kinds of gendered virtues: selfless honesty and bravery in Joan, selfless soldierliness in men. The relation of literary creation to martial virtue is dramatized in *Joan*. Self-aggrandizement through storytelling is a lovable vice in men, as Mark Twain represents it, though it clearly would be an impardonable offense in Joan. The Paladin's excursions in this direction are treated as comic and ultimately, in an odd way, sincere:

> It was plain that there was a charm about the performance that was apart from the mere interest which attaches to lying. It was presently discoverable that this charm lay in the Paladin's sincerity. He was not lying consciously; he believed what he was saying. . . . He put his heart into his extravagant narrative, just as a poet puts his heart into a heroic fiction, and his earnestness disarmed criticism— disarmed it as far as he was concerned. Nobody believed his narrative, but all believed that he believed it. (1:152)

This is an apt description of the role of the novelist as Mark Twain conceives it. We cannot doubt Mark Twain's sincerity in *Joan of Arc* (as Zwarg does), and his earnestness did indeed disarm criticism as far as he was concerned. But though we are not meant to doubt that Twain believed in Joan as he represents her through de Conte, we can recognize in his symbolic narrator Twain's self-doubts, torn as he is between faith in Joan's virtues and a sense of the world as one in which the callous powers of La Hire and Cauchon operate conclusively.

What does it mean for de Conte to be brave? Twain dramatizes for us de Conte's failure of nerve in wooing Catherine, and it is significant that he has no direct offspring himself—he is telling his story to his great grandnephews and grandnieces, not to his own grandchildren. The story he tells becomes his offspring—he "fathers" his own legitimacy through narration. But to de Conte, who struggles with the issue of bravery in the realm of emotional intimacy, Joan offers only the unattainable superiority of a unique, divine, symbolic child. It is true that she has a symmetrically comparable struggle in her struggle to defend her assumption of authority and her wearing of men's clothes—her ventures into masculine roles—but the struggle is represented as almost entirely external, between Joan and her opponents, rather than within herself. Only through the symbiotic fusion of Joan and de Conte through storytelling, Mark Twain's "heroic fiction," does a sense of the potential of full humanity emerge—and that is achieved finally only through de Conte's experience of loss. De Conte appropriates Joan's virtues imaginatively, but he cannot incorporate them into his life except through his anguished role as storyteller.

Joan of Arc represents a search in history and gender for what Mark Twain perceived as the unattainable: a realm in which authority and compassion are synonymous. At one level, the book represents a critique of masculine values, for men are shown either as weak (the King), foolishly self-centered (the Paladin), or remorselessly cruel (Cauchon). Even de Conte can assume the cruel cynicism of masculinity, as he does in the most explicitly violent episode in the novel when he observes the slashing of the throat of a prisoner of war and reports it in pointedly cold-blooded, sardonic language. However, the idealistic fusion of authority and compassion in Joan is not plausible because Joan is angelic rather than human (her sexuality is suppressed and denied) and because she is martyred. A final alternative remains: that of the male observer sympathetic to the values represented by Joan. De Conte represents such an observer-

narrator, who through his retelling of Joan's life both celebrates
its attractiveness and laments its loss and failure.

In the evolution of Mark Twain's quest for wholeness and
continuity through the materials of European history, *Joan of
Arc* represents the effort to envision the fusion, in one figure,
of virtues conventionally and selectively assigned to women
and men separately in Twain's era. Specifically, Joan as Twain
imagined her embodies a fusion of courage and compassion, authority and gentleness. She stands in contrast to the incomplete
virtues and vices of masculine figures, from the manipulable
King to the manipulating Cauchon. Yet she is not a persuasive
character, for Mark Twain feels the need to deny her sexuality
and thus ultimately her humanity. Patriotism and storytelling (through literature and song) are as close to sex as Mark
Twain gets in this book: passion, rapture, emotional fulfilment.
Finally, de Conte is a pathetic rather than tragic reflection of
Joan's (and Twain's) failure. A feminist reading of Twain's biography of Joan need not stop at showing us how his conception
of femininity was flawed but can fruitfully show us the corre-
sponding sense of lack in his representation of masculinity and
the yearning it disguises. In seeking an idealistic solution to the
eternal problems of cruelty, cowardice, and corruption, Twain
was also seeking for a better representative human being. By
denying the full stature of Joan's humanity as a woman, he was
also forced to deny tragic depth and complexity to his central
male character, though what he was seeking was indeed a fusion
of qualities he had previously assigned more comfortably and
familiarly to women and men separately.

Joan of Arc is a crucial step in Clemens's translation of European culture into American terms. It represents the tragic failure of politics, but since Twain has faith only in individuals and
not in institutions, he denies the complicity of his characters in
the institutions of their society, which means that his characters have an ahistorical unreality. His failure to comprehend or
accept the intricate ways in which human beings are, for better

and for worse, simultaneously social and individual leads to the cynicism and despair of his later years. While this failure is a shortcoming of imaginative comprehension of human nature, it reduces social conflict and issues of gender identity to issues of power. This reduction helps the reader to see clearly Twain's views of gender and power. Kingship has lost its attraction for Twain by this point, and female innocence may be saintly, but it is also, in his representation of it, otherworldly and pathetic when it is not heroic. The alternative left, an expression of Twain's perpetual drive toward self-realization, is the search for narrative self-actualization through a male storyteller's quest. De Conte's quest for a self-defining strategy rejects both brutality and victimization, the postures of warrior and saint. This strategy shifts issues of power and identity from the public arena to the arena of language and of the mind. Thus it is not surprising that the images of European culture become more attenuated in Twain's later writing and that the stage of imaginative conflict shifts increasingly into the mind of the narrator. This movement toward interiority is reflected in the "Mysterious Stranger" manuscripts.

Chapter Six

CULTURE, DESIRE, AND GENDER
IN THE "MYSTERIOUS STRANGER"
MANUSCRIPTS

There are profound insights in Mark Twain's work . . .
that constitute a significant chapter in the history of
the relations between modern psychology and literature.
—SHOLOM KAHN,
Mark Twain's Mysterious Stranger:
A Study of the Manuscript Texts

In extracting his version of Joan from his European sources, interpreting her social world in American terms, and representing the dilemmas of his American Puritan legacy through the gender representations he projected onto European history in *Joan of Arc,* Twain contributed to the glorification of female sexual innocence that was part of the denial of women's sexual nature in nineteenth-century American society. The dilemma of the male narrator, caught between cruelty and martyrdom, demonstrates that Clemens at least partially intuited the unsatisfactory nature of the gender ideology reflected in his worship of an asexual Joan. The "Mysterious Stranger" manuscripts explore the boundaries of this gender ideology. By acknowledging female sexuality sympathetically, Twain is forced to confront the social constraints on sexuality. The three stories about young Satan reflect a deeper imaginative comprehension of human nature than *Joan of Arc* does. Not only are Europe and America almost continuous and women and men regarded as equally representative of human nature here, the doubling of his characters through dream selves allows Twain to look at the borders between psychological and social realities in new ways. In these fragmentary, exploratory tales, the outlines and barriers of gender and culture differences blur and blend.

Satan in "The Chronicle of Young Satan" is a self-assured, cynical young man; Quarante-quatre or Forty-four in "Schoolhouse Hill" is a deferential boy; Number 44, New Series 864,962 in "No. 44, The Mysterious Stranger" is "a most forlorn looking youth, apparently sixteen or seventeen years old" (235) who conceals his magical powers from almost everyone but his friend August Feldner, also sixteen. Despite the fact that these three characters are distinctly different in numerous respects, including their functions within their respective stories, they can each be described accurately with Sholom Kahn's phrase "ambiguous angel" (39). Kahn's reference is mainly to Satan's moral nature in "The Chronicle of Young Satan," but the concept of ambiguity can fruitfully be enlarged in relation to all three of the satanic strangers. Considered together, they constitute the figure of an "ambiguous angel" also in terms of gender and sexuality. Not only that, but the boys who are Satan and Number 44's human counterparts and opposites, Theodor Fischer and August Feldner, extend Mark Twain's exploration of the ambiguous sex role positioning of Sieur Louis de Conte in *Joan of Arc,* and the relations between female and male characters in all three fragments further enlarge the varieties of ambiguity about gender and culture that Twain both playfully and seriously explored as he moved through the last years of his creative life.

Satan transcends his sex in "The Chronicle of Young Satan" just as Mark Twain transcends nationality in all three stories. Gender and nation (masculine and feminine, America and Europe), polarities Mark Twain earlier frequently presented as simple dichotomies, here become transparent—not insignifi-

cant, but conduits for more abstract and complex speculations.[1]
The charismatic young man who goes by the name of Satan
transcends his sex in a sense simply by being superior to it: he
exudes a spiritual force that is erotically attractive to all earthly
beings, male or female, animal or human. It is no wonder that
Marget, the young woman whom Theodor Fischer idolizes ("a
lovely girl of eighteen . . . she had the best head in the village, and the most in it"), falls in love with Satan. He is, after
all, handsome, clever, well-spoken, cultured, and generous.
He exerts an irresistible fascination: "the main part of her mind
[Marget's] was on Traum, anyway; she couldn't keep her eyes off
him, he was so beautiful" (68). But this fascination is not limited to women. The boys too are infatuated with Satan in ways
that suggest romantic love. When Satan reappears after an absence, "Seppi poured out his gladness like water. It was as if he
was a lover and had found his sweetheart which had been lost"
(74). Satan possesses an animal magnetism that even the cat responds to. The nature of his attractiveness is not polymorphous
perverse so much as it is a spiritual force with an erotic spark.
Theodor employs the same rapturous language and metaphors
to describe his feelings about Satan as does de Conte to tell how
he felt about Joan:

> And there he sat, looking just like anybody—so natural,
> and simple, and charming, and chatting along again the
> same as ever, and—well, words cannot make you under-
> stand what we felt. It was an ecstasy; and an ecstasy is a
> thing that will not go into words; it feels like music, and
> one cannot tell about music so that another person can get
> the feeling of it. (54)

Here are the same disclaimers about the inadequacy of language, the same comparison to music, as in de Conte's description of his feelings for Joan. But a noteworthy difference is the
implied impersonality of the feeling: "We," Theodor writes, not
the anxious "I" with which de Conte sought to define himself in

relation to Joan, though the fundamental yearning is the same. The futility of being jealous of this transcendent creature is lost on Wilhelm Meidling, Marget's suitor, and this is one of the subtleties of this story.

Twain intended to explore the ironies of a supernatural stranger's transcendence of sex from the reverse direction in the "Schoolhouse Hill" story. In his notes, he wrote,

> Has never seen a human girl or woman until now. *Except in heaven* X Hellfire Hotchkiss./*Annie Fleming*. He feels a strange & charming interest in her. By the books he gathers that this is "love"—the kind that sex arouses. There is no such thing among his brothers & sisters. He studies it in the books. It seems very beautiful in the books. Presently the passion for Hl grows—becomes absorbing—is mutual. Papa uneasy—he is the only person who knows 44's secret. 44 sees that the happiness of hell —which is purely intellectual—IS TAME COMPARED TO THIS LOVE. (*Mark Twain's Mysterious Stranger Manuscripts* 438)

Though Annie Fleming does fall in love with Forty-four in "Schoolhouse Hill," the potentially comic metaphysical idea of an angel discovering human sexual love outlined above is never explored: human beings remain in awe of Forty-four's occult powers, while he never experiences the epiphany of human love so emphatically encapsulated in Twain's notes.[2] The intriguing possibilities for sexual discovery and experience foreshadowed in these notes are left to be explored in "No. 44, the Mysterious Stranger," but through the doubling of a human personality, not through the amorous adventures of an angel. What Mark Twain seems to be reaching for here, in ways that are not present in his earlier works, is a kind of speculative fantasy about sexuality and gender that both explores human limitations and leaves them behind.

The ambiguous angel figures are the catalysts and the touchstones for this speculative fantasy. But they serve ultimately as complex reflections of human character and aspiration. So it makes sense to examine the range of human personalities represented in these stories to see how Twain contextualizes the angelic/satanic individuals he creates. What we find are restatements of familiar gender concepts present in many of Twain's earlier fictions but also some interesting departures. Familiar to us from *The Prince and the Pauper, A Connecticut Yankee,* and of course *Joan of Arc* are images of female martyrdom, especially women being burned at the stake. Familiar also is the male narrator's turning away from witnessing the finale, unable to bear the sight of the innocent victim's suffering. Women still frequently represent the moral standard by which men are measured. Frau Brandt becomes the most Christ-like figure in "The Chronicle of Young Satan" when she forgives her tormentors in the name of a lost childhood: "We played together once, in long-gone days when we were innocent little creatures. For the sake of that, I forgive you," she says from the stake (133). Twain extends his indictment of religious fanaticism and cruelty explicitly to include Protestants, not only Catholics, through the episode of the Scottish woman who is trampled to death under a barn door by a Protestant mob. Related to these pathetic episodes of women martyred is the recurrent image of the tortured mother suffering and grieving over a lost child. The image of suffering motherhood is extended in Katrina's grief at her loss of Number 44 in "The Mysterious Stranger" and in her quest for revenge. The *mater dolorosa* theme is summarized in an encounter August has with a bereaved mother in the Procession of the ages:

> But to think how long the pathos of a thing can last, and still carry its touching effect, the same as if it was new and happened yesterday! There was a slim skeleton of a young woman, and it went by with its head bowed and its bony hands to its eyes, crying, apparently. Well, it was a

young mother whose little child disappeared one day and
was never heard of again, and so her heart was broken,
and she cried her life away. It brought the tears to my eyes
and made my heart ache to see that poor thing's sorrow.
When I looked at her tab I saw it had happened five hundred thousand years ago! It seemed strange that it should
still affect me, but I suppose such things never grow old,
but remain always new. (402)

The incident clearly is meant to demonstrate the universality
and timelessness of the pathos of this vision of suffering motherhood, superficial and sentimental as it may appear to us.

But motherhood is not all victimization in these stories. It
is noteworthy that Theodor Fischer has two relatively individualized parents in "The Chronicle of Young Satan" and that
Theodor's mother is indisputably the more shrewd and decisive
parent. Some of Jane Lampton Clemens's wit and fire emerges
in Theodor's mother's assessment of the strange phenomenon
of Satan: " 'Well,' said mother at last, 'it strikes a body dumb,
I must say. He is a most singular creature, take him how you
will. Embroiders like an angel, and admires rattlesnakes; a
most unaccountable mixture in the matter of tastes' " (99), an
interesting assessment of a paradoxical combination of gender
traits. Theodor's mother has more sense than his father and a
keener sense of irony. In spite of what she says, she is notably
not struck dumb, and neither are a number of the women Mark
Twain created in the three "Stranger" stories. In particular,
Twain created in each of the three manuscripts a female figure
who is admirable and in many respects superior to other human
beings but also representative. Just as he used the Otherness
of Europe as a means of dramatizing what he considered universal social conditions (as evidenced by the interweaving of
European and American characters, customs, and settings in
the three "Stranger" versions), he now employed female figures
with a range of inclusive referentiality to represent humanity,
male and female.

Samuel Clemens with guests at a dinner given at Delmonico's in
New York City in honor of Clemens's seventieth birthday,
December 5, 1905. *From left:* Kate Douglas Riggs, Clemens, Joseph
Twichell, Bliss Carman, Ruth McEnery Stuart, Mary E. Wilkins
Freeman, Henry Mills Alden, Henry H. Rogers.
Library of Congress.

Each of the three female figures is a servant, a woman who acts intelligently, independently, and courageously: the bold and compassionate Ursula in "The Chronicle of Young Satan"; Aunt Rachel, who notices both obvious and subtle details that others miss in "Schoolhouse Hill"; and most strikingly of all the forceful Katrina in "No. 44, The Mysterious Stranger." All three probably owe a debt to Aunty Cord, the black servant of the Cranes in Elmira, New York, whose story Twain recorded in "A True Story, Repeated Word for Word as I Heard It," submitted to the *Atlantic* in 1874.[3] All three are admirable figures who may be idealized in some respects but who have realistic failings and strengths. In each case there is an element of familiar stereotypes but also a dimension of striking truthfulness that contradicts Mark Twain's conventional images of women and shows him willing, at least ambiguously, to explore beyond them.

Ursula is the familiar image of the loyal servant, but she is also a courageous, independent woman. Mark Twain notably pays attention to—and treats respectfully—women's sources of income in "The Chronicle of Young Satan." Always interested in the cash nexus, he treats sympathetically Marget's independence based on her ability to teach music and Ursula's capacity to earn money, when given the opportunity by her neighbors, through her own enterprise. "Old Ursula . . . cook, chambermaid, housekeeper, laundress and everything else . . . said God would provide . . . but she meant to help in the providing, to make sure" (63). When Ursula fearlessly confronts Satan (though she does not know of his powers), Theodor is put in the position of being torn between sympathy for both a woman and a man in conflict with each other, just as de Conte was in *Joan of Arc*. He attempts to mediate, but Satan ties his tongue, and Ursula herself is invigorated by Satan's influence. Most significantly, when Satan playfully encourages Ursula's vanity, Theodor is keenly embarrassed by her foolishness, but he identifies with her and takes her to be representative of the human race—not just of women:

He [Satan] accomplished one thing which I was glad of—
he got on the good side of Ursula. He praised her to
Marget, confidentially, but speaking just loud enough for
Ursula to hear. He said she was a fine woman, and he
hoped some day to bring her and his uncle together. Very
soon Ursula was mincing and simpering around in a ridiculous girly way, and smoothing out her gown and prinking
at herself like a foolish old hen, and all the time pretending she was not hearing what Satan was saying. I was
ashamed, for it showed us to be what Satan considered us,
a silly race and trivial. (71)

Theodor is grateful for Ursula's happiness but ashamed of
the faults which he reluctantly recognizes as simply human.
Women are also, more positively, representative of progress
in "The Chronicle of Young Satan." Literate, self-supporting
women such as the Hussite woman named Adler and Gre-
tel Marx, a dairyman's widow, are sources of resistance to the
Church's authority. They represent the Protestant impulses
toward universal literacy, individual self-reliance, and faith in
a more merciful God, opposed to the male priestly authority
(embodied in the lecherous, dissolute priest Father Adolf),
associated with greed, superstition, and bullying exploitation. Women are sympathetically portrayed (despite Theodor's
orthodox, superstitious denunciations) as practitioners of common sense and hygiene. One woman, "a born lady," is hanged
for "the habit of curing people by devilish arts, such as bath-
ing them, washing them and nourishing them, instead of
bleeding them and purging them through the ministrations of
a barber-surgeon in the proper way" (151). Gottfried Narr's
grandmother, who is burned at the stake because "she had cured
bad headaches by kneading the person's head and neck with
her fingers" (79), is a sympathetic figure also, a rational victim
who chooses death at the stake to avoid the extended torture
of starvation and abuse. If we compare these women with figures such as Hans Oppert (the village loafer who beats his dog),

Father Adolf, or the Portuguese imperialist in India, we see that males are the most obvious targets of Twain's moral outrage. All his characters are meant to be types, but the women tend to typify rationality and progress, while the men stand for cruelty, self-interest, and oppression.

Aunt Rachel, the "elderly slave woman" in "Schoolhouse Hill," is a fictional relative of Jim from *Huck Finn*. She articulates the same dignified appeal to feeling as does Jim in his most poignant moments.[4] Aunt Rachel says: "Does a po' nigger want to git laughed at any mo' d'n white folks? No, Miss Hannah, dey don't. We's got our feelin's, same as *you*-all" (196), but she is not naive in ways that Jim is made to be. She is rational, vigorous, and clever: a truthtelling woman whose good sense and sharp observation put the other townfolk to shame.

Perhaps most impressive of all is Katrina in "No. 44, The Mysterious Stranger." Clearly similar to Ursula and Aunt Rachel, she is distinctly and memorably an individual:

> Next was old Katrina. She was cook and housekeeper; her forebears had served the master's people and none else for three or four generations; she was sixty, and had served the master all his life, from the time when she was a little girl and he was a swaddled baby. She was erect, straight, six feet high, with the port and stride of a soldier; she was independent and masterful, and her fears were limited to the supernatural. She believed she could whip anybody on the place, and would have considered an invitation a favor. (233)

She also is a vigorous and attractive character, someone who combines forcefulness and compassion. She is set opposite to and in direct conflict with the conventionally villainous Frau Stein, who is described thus: "She was well along in life, and was long and lean and flat-breasted, and had an active and vicious tongue and a diligent and devilish spirit, and more religion than was good for her, considering the quality of it. She hungered

for money" (230). The object of their conflict is Number 44
himself, who arrives as a starving waif, in a situation strikingly
parallel to the arrival of a hungry stranger early in *Joan of Arc*.
Frau Stein wants to throw the ragged stranger out; Katrina and
Marget, like Joan, want to feed him. A struggle for authority
ensues between Frau Stein and Katrina. Heinrich Stein, titular
master, refuses to become involved, and Katrina triumphs. The
master, a benevolent father figure who does not lack authority
but who sometimes hesitates to exercise it because he recognizes its limits, makes an argument concerning the boy in need
that is remarkably similar to the one the naive maître makes in
Joan: "The boy is not necessarily *bad* because he is unfortunate.
And if he *is* bad, what of it? A bad person can be as hungry
as a good one, and hunger is always respectable" (236), though
Theodor has insinuated that Frau Stein's hunger for money is
not.[5] The portrait of Katrina falls back into stereotype, though
it is a powerful one, as her emotions concentrate in motherly
love for Number 44: "She had her reward, for he was a graceful and beautiful creature, with the most wonderful eyes, and
these facts all showed up, now, and filled her with pride. Daily
he grew in her favor. Her old hungry heart was fed, she was a
mother at last, with a child to love,—a child who returned her
love in full measure, and to whom she was the salt of the earth"
(244). *This* kind of hunger, Mark Twain implies, is legitimate
in a woman, unlike Frau Stein's. Twain misses a magnificent
opportunity in not allowing Katrina to play a more major part
in the story. Instead, her presence is defined almost exclusively
by her relationship to Number 44, whom she mothers with
devotion. Her devoted motherhood is outraged by what appear
to be the magician's acts of abuse of Number 44 and culminates in what amounts to an embarrassing display of juvenile
wish fulfillment when Number 44 reveals that he is not dead
after all but has merely been disguising himself in the shape
of the demented magician. It is the old *Tom Sawyer* theme of
a boy staging his own death and resurrection to harrow female

hearts. Katrina, who sought revenge "grim and towering and soldierly" (389), charges with death-defying bravery toward the presumed magician—only to find in his stead Number 44 "in his supernal beauty and his gracious youth" (390). "Katrina crept on her knees to him, and bent down her old head and kissed his feet" (390–91). Number 44's powers are displayed in forms of vulgar self-indulgence that rival Hank Morgan's. He first appears in an effeminate costume resembling Hank's combat clothes in *Connecticut Yankee:* "It suited his whim, now, to come out dressed as [a gentleman] . . . pink silk tights; pale blue satin trunks; cloth of gold doublet; short satin cape, of a blinding red; lace collar fit for a queen . . . . He had a lace handkerchief in his hand, and now and then he would give his nose a dainty little dab or two with it, the way a duchess does" (303). His "eclipse," in which he transforms himself into the condescending supernal boy, is a performance of which "he said himself it beat Barnum and Bailey hands down" (391), but what it amounts to psychologically is a demonstration of an adolescent boy's power to humble his powerful "mother"— a mother figure so forceful in her rage that she challenges the manliness of men: " '*Back! woman, back, I tell you—force her back, men, have you no strength? are you nothing but boys?*' . . . 'A hundred of you shan't stay me, woman though I be!' " (390) The boy humbles her, tames her castrating rage, through her love for him. Number 44's superiority to sexuality in "No. 44, The Mysterious Stranger" is a symptom of his essentially adolescent fantasy function of transcending social complexities through supernatural powers. Yet Katrina, despite her maternal servitude to Number 44, retains a fierce individuality and dignity, while Number 44's self-dramatization is shown up not only as vulgar and tawdry but as rooted in adolescent insecurity.

It fits with Number 44's desire to humble even the most powerful admirable woman that he himself is not unequivocally manly and that August, whose projection he ultimately turns out to be, is involved in an intensely ambivalent struggle with himself over sexuality. It also fits that in "The Chronicle of Young Satan" and "No. 44, The Mysterious Stranger," rapacious adult men are the primary villains, while the good men are almost uniformly weak: Father Peter, Wilhelm Meidling, and Gustav Fischer, who is physically strong but not very influential. The rejection of sexuality evident in *Joan of Arc* is developed further here both through the predatory nature of the adult villains and through the sexual perplexities of adolescent young men.

Mark Twain again creates adolescent male characters on the verge of sexual discovery and female characters whose sexuality is defined almost exclusively by motherhood. But the difference here is that the ambivalence of the central male character is revealed more explicitly than ever before through the use of doubling. The boy's struggle with the implications of sexuality is related to the predicament of the artist/storyteller torn between male authority and female compassion. The "Satan" stories, like other, earlier stories of Twain's, suggest a fear of female sexual initiative but also that Twain was coming to see women as representative of humanity and, in a hopeful sense, as potential bearers of progress. The central male character's efforts to reconcile his recognition of the failure of male authority and his fear of authorizing his own compassion lead towards a vision of the artist/storyteller as compassionate cynic, detached by the very force of his involvement, a self-deconstructing authority.

August's courtship of Marget Regen echoes Mark Twain's account of his lifelong, recurrent vision of "My Platonic Sweetheart." Her first appearance is in a descriptive passage that points forward in Twain's life to the Angel Fish Club of his last years and backward to the idealized, desexualized version of female adolescence he had created in *Joan of Arc*. [6]

> Marget Regen was Maria's age—seventeen. She was lithe and graceful and trim-built as a fish, and she was a blue-eyed blonde, and soft and sweet and innocent and shrink-

ing and winning and gentle and beautiful; just a vision
for the eyes, worshipful, adorable, enchanting; but that
wasn't the hive for her. She was a kitten in a menag-
erie. (232)

The reference to Marget as a kitten is significant in light of the
fact that her chambermaid is later turned into a cat in order
to prevent the spreading of a rumor concerning Marget's innocence—or lack of it. August is clearly in love with Marget
for her stereotypically feminine qualities. Through his Dream-
Self he discovers the delights of having his love returned. But
through his double, Emil, he also discovers the agonies of jealousy and, worse yet, the reality of female sexual appetite, which
is frightening to him. The ironies are multiple and complicated
in Twain's drama of two male selves jealous over two female
selves alternating identities in the same body. Sholom Kahn
has proposed a Freudian reading of the male selves involved, as
follows:

> Mark Twain's psychology of love seems . . . roughly par-
> allel—very roughly so—to the Freudian anatomy of the
> self. The Waking-Self is clearly the ego; the Dream-Self,
> with its great imaginative freedom and tendency to chaos,
> points in the direction of the id and libido; and the Dupli-
> cate, with its complex suggestions of sensuality and fleshli-
> ness (implying also their opposites), points in the direction
> of the superego. Or, with a change of emphasis, one might
> see Forty-four as a dramatization of the problem of the
> superego—or conscience, in Clemens' terminology. (159)

I think the Freudian model of the self does not fit the multiple
selves in "No. 44, The Mysterious Stranger," at least not in the
form Kahn proposes. Both the Dream-Self and the Duplicate
display varieties of sensuality, or libido, but neither Forty-Four
nor the Duplicate functions as a controlling conscience.[7] It is important to notice that both August's and Marget's Dream-Selves

Samuel Clemens with three women, Dollis Hill House, London, 1900. Clara Clemens is seated to the left of her father. Mark Twain Memorial, Hartford, Connecticut.

Martin von Giesbach and Elisabeth von Arnim, have aristocratic names, indicated by the German "von." Their names hint
that the Dream-Selves are noble or ideal, a subtle and significant use of European ideas of nobility for American psychological exploration, showing how Twain shifted concepts of class
in the direction of concepts of gender. The Dream-Self, in the
scheme of the story, is the refined portion of the self, the spirit.
Yet it is a spirit that can feel erotic attraction. Few passages
in Mark Twain's writing are so unequivocally erotic as Martin/
August's account of his love for Lisabet:

> My passion rose and overpowered me and I floated to her
> like a breath and put my arms about her and drew her to
> my breast and put my lips to hers, unrebuked, and drew
> intoxication from them! She closed her eyes, and with a
> sigh which seemed born of measureless content, she said
> dreamily, "I love you so—and have so longed for you!"
>
> Her body trembled with each kiss received and repaid,
> and by the power and volume of the emotions that surged
> through me I realized that the sensations I knew in my
> fleshly estate were cold and weak by contrast with those
> which a spirit feels. (338)

This, interestingly enough, is exactly the reverse of what Twain
proposed to explore with Quarante-quatre's falling in love in
"Schoolhouse Hill" with Hellfire Hotchkiss. August/Martin
discovers that spiritual love is much more intense than the
merely physical. But it is important to see that both August
and Martin experience physical as well as spiritual sensations,
though in different proportions. Though Martin refers to himself as "invisible, impalpable, substanceless" (338), he, like
Lisabet, is able to feel all the sensations a body can feel. Not
only that, but the range of emotions he feels is broad and by
no means limited to the conventionally angelic—for example,
he feels intense jealousy of his "rival" Emil and is not above

"fetch[ing] him an open-handed slat on the jaw" (341) with
considerable force. One might say that Twain conceives Martin
as the distilled embodiment of August's essential self. It is also
important to note that Lisabet reciprocates his erotic feelings,
which is true from their first encounter, when Marget/Lisabet
walks through the invisible August/Martin: "As she passed
through me the contact invaded my blood as with a delicious
fire! She stopped, with a startled look, the rich blood rose in
her face, her breath came quick and short through her parted
lips" (336). Lisabet's capacity for erotic emotion leads Martin
into a predicament: she proposes to marry him on the spot. The
idea thrills him, but he has qualms, thinking that he ought to
reveal to her that he is a spirit. His ultimate goal is to persuade
her Waking-Self to love *his* Waking-Self and marry him, thus
eliminating the rivalry of the Duplicate. What all this business implies is that reciprocity in love is possible only in the
realm of the spirit—the closer erotic love comes to everyday
life, the coarser it becomes and the more the man is obligated
to take charge. For in order to carry out her suggestion (made,
as August puts it, "with the dearest and sweetest naivety," 348)
that they be married at once, he feels compelled to project
suggestions into *her* head, namely that she dress as a bride,
kneel before an imaginary priest and altar, go through an entire imaginary marriage ceremony, and finally blush "as a new-
made wife should before people!" (349). This passage charts the
movement from private passion to public and conventional role-
playing—and it is the man who directs the proceedings and
pronounces his judgment on its propriety. The whole process
delicately skirts the issue of seduction, which, as Susan Gillman has shown, Twain was almost obsessively concerned with
in his versions of the Evelyn Nesbit Thaw case and especially in
the "Wapping Alice" manuscripts (1898, 1907).[8] The legal and
moral problem of seduction in the Victorian era was rooted in
the assumption that a woman would not take sexual initiative.

For Clemens, as for many Americans of his time, the man was virtually always the active aggressor, the woman the passive victim in a sexual relationship.[9]

Chapter 24 of "No. 44, The Mysterious Stranger" records a descent from erotic spiritual bliss to base jealousy and sensuality. The Duplicate is a twin image of August, but it is his waking self seen from the outside. Twain demonstrates August's disgust and revulsion at seeing his own sensuality from an external perspective. There is an ambivalence about sexuality here that takes two forms: one is disgust at its physical coarseness; the other is a feeling of repulsion at the idea that a woman derives active pleasure from sex:

> The astonished and happy bullfrog had her in his arms in a minute and was blistering her with kisses, which she paid back as fast as she could register them, and she not cold yet from her marriage-oath! A man—and such a man as that—hugging my wife before my eyes, and she getting a gross and voracious satisfaction out of it!—I could not endure the shameful sight. (350)

The man whom August refers to as "such a man as that" and a "bullfrog" is his own double. Thus August is in effect watching himself in the arms of his "wife" and registering his revulsion at the coarse physicality of sexual desire. The repulsiveness of physical sexuality is located in male *and* female nature.

His next step, interestingly enough, is to get drunk, with the aid of Doangivadam. In his inebriated state, he wanders into Marget's boudoir, forgetting to make himself invisible. He voyeuristically enjoys watching Marget in a scene with unmistakable erotic overtones: "She was sitting before a pier glass, snowily arrayed in her dainty nightie, with her left side toward me; and upon her delicate profile and her shining cataract of dark red hair streaming unvexed to the floor a strong light was falling" (351). As he contentedly contemplates this scene, he decides to let Marget and her maid see him—and by that act he inadvertently moves his previously hidden love affair into the social arena and immediately begins to suffer the consequences, for he is discovered by Marget's mother as well as the maid and Marget, who all react to him violently. Ironically, only Marget recognizes him as August Feldner, the lowly print shop apprentice; the others assume he is the Duplicate, Emil Schwartz, the version of August that is free of conscience and that represents, at least to August, gross sensuality. August's efforts to push the blame for his appearance in Marget's chamber onto Emil have an undesired result: the master determines that Emil shall marry Marget. By denying his own participation in the web of sensuality, August excludes himself from the prospect of marriage and legitimates the claims of his rival sensual self.

Part of the point of the episode, surely, is to dramatize the social barriers placed around sexual interest in nineteenth-century America, for the melodramatic response to the mere presence of a young man in a young woman's boudoir is one of the many details that do not ring historically true for Austria in 1490 but rather suggest Twain's America. Samuel Clemens himself had been in the situation of the master in the story: hearing evidence about a claim of seduction in 1877 in the case of a maid of the Clemens family who said that a workman employed in the house had made her pregnant.[10] Like the master, Clemens had pronounced a mistaken verdict of guilt and sentenced the supposed culprit to marry. Clemens could have taken the opportunity to satirize his own authority, that of the paterfamilias acting as judge in a case of sexual transgression, but he did not do so. The mistaken identification of the culprit rebounds on August, who, instead of resenting the master's highhandedness, merely blames himself for trying to "ruin the creature that stood between me and my worshipped little wife" (353). August/Martin, the young man with the spiritual dimension, is made to assume the burden and the guilt of sexual desire in its social parameters.

Furthermore, the master furnishes vivid evidence of the

sexual politics of Twain's time in the master's thoughts about the situation. When August points out that Marget's evidence is not being mentioned, the master says, "Oh, her unsupported opinion is of no consequence! . . . She says it was you—which is nonsense, in the face of the other evidence and your denial. She is only a child" (352). While Marget—"only a child"—is not even given the status of having a voice (evidently August's worship of his wife does not extend to supporting her credibility when it would involve exposing himself as a liar), Emil Schwarz's behavior is not castigated by the master after his initial anger has passed. The master says of him, "This one is a good enough fellow, there's no deliberate harm in him" (352). The master again displays sympathetic tolerance for hunger, this time for sexual appetite, but he is also determined to maintain appearances. Because his niece has been "compromised" by the mere presence of a male in her boudoir, the two young people are to be forced to marry. The question of whether Marget desires the marriage is not even touched on. Allowing Marget no voice in the matter is what truly compromises her. The compromise the master refers to is merely the violation of social *appearances:* the maintenance of male control over marriage, property, succession, "honor."

In this situation August is "miserable"—but not out of concern for Marget. He wishes desperately for Number 44 to appear, to give him "help and comfort." The problem, as the master had described it, hinged on the unreliability of the maid. She "can't keep the secret; poor thing, she's like all her kind—a secret, in a lady's maid, is water in a sieve" (352–53).[11] The seriousness of the situation seems to be mocked by what happens next: a slave from South Carolina, three hundred and fifty years in the future, appears and performs a burlesque minstrel-show routine. The "matter of Hannibal" intrudes itself into the "matter of Europe" with jarring effect. Then the slave turns into Forty-Four. It is as if the predicaments of this highly charged sexual-social situation drive Mark Twain's imagination straight back to comfortably absurd comic and sentimental childhood memories of the minstrel show. But those memories have a powerful symbolic subtext. If we read the story at this point as a fictionally encoded dual struggle over sexuality— on the one hand between a "higher," spiritual erotic love and a "lower," physical sensuality (Martin versus Emil); on the other hand between the private experience of Eros and its control by society—the appearance of the minstrel man gains symbolic significance. As Henry Louis Gates has discussed, there is a "curious relationship between the figures of Harlequin and the American Minstrel Man" (51), the Harlequin being a phalle-phore and an ancestor of the Minstrel Man. Quoting Ducharte, he points out that the "Harlequin's authentic mask . . . suggests 'a cat, a satyr, and the sort of negro that the Renaissance painter portrayed' " (51). The Minstrel Man's antic capers signify the sublimated subject which he appears to be a digression from: sex. One might say that he is a carnivalesque displacement of the subject through the darkness of absence. Number 44's sug-gested solutions to the dilemma of the impending marriage are as outrageous as the burlesque digression: he first proposes kill-ing both Schwarz and the maid; then, when August vetoes that option, he proposes to create so many Duplicates that no one will know which one to marry to Marget, and to turn the maid into a cat—both of which he does.

As I interpret "No. 44, The Mysterious Stranger," August, Martin, Emil Schwarz, the master, and Number 44 are all pro-jections of the Twainian male self. In their relations with Marget and the maid in particular, they exhibit a range of male re-sponses to females that provides an index not only to Samuel Clemens's ways of thinking and feeling about the sexes but to the attitudes of his culture and time. August and Martin are continuous selves. August never delineates a clear distinction between his consciousness and that of Martin, his Dream-Self.[12] Martin is contained within August, so to speak. As Martin, August constructs for himself an ideally responsive and recep-

tive version of Marget/Lisbet. Lisbet is August's dream image
of his most desirable young woman. She is also, significantly,
free from social constraints. Marget is under the power of "a
mamma to be pacified" (348), but Lisbet von Arnim "had no
such incumbrances"—she is "free and independent," and in the
realm of the spirit she can exercise initiative, such as suggesting
marriage on the spot. Emil Schwarz is his fleshly self but free
of conscience; he enacts with the physical Marget the desires
August can fulfill only in spirit through Martin. Number 44 is
the cynical male self endowed with the power to make imagination become real, and perhaps as a consequence, he is indifferent
to merely human sexual interest (like Philip Traum, he transcends sex). Heinrich Stein, the master, is the traditional adult
male authority in this social family constellation, and he pronounces judgments that will maintain the conventional sexual
forms and institutions. He appears to be the most mature male
character, but he is also the most conventional, and he is de-
ceived about the identity of the young man in question. But
the most forceful irony emerges from Emil Schwarz, the Duplicate. By observing his Duplicate sympathetically for the first
time, August discovers things about himself that he had not
known before: how his voice sounds, how he looks from the
back, his general appearance and bearing. Even more impor-
tantly, August learns from Emil that his self without conscience
is miserably imprisoned in his body. The same Emil who seemed
to August to be an "astonished and happy bullfrog" sensually
revelling in Marget's embrace has the next day forgotten that he
loved Marget, and he makes an eloquent and impassioned plea
to be freed from the "bonds of flesh," "this loathsome sack of
corruption in which my spirit is imprisoned, her white wings
bruised and soiled" (369). He articulates the same themes of
contempt for the pettiness and limitations of humanity as does
Traum in "The Chronicle of Young Satan" and claims the same
freedom from moral restraints. It is his extended and eloquent
speech at the conclusion of chapter twenty-seven expressing his

desire to escape from the body that makes August recognize and acknowledge Emil as his "friend and brother," and in a handclasp of intense emotion they share the feeling that unites them. Precisely at this moment the cat enters. Both the emotional fraternity between August and Emil and the entrance of the feline female symbolize the conflict between spirit and body, soul and social constraints.

The cat is Marget's maid, transformed by Number 44. She is the third major representative of female roles as delineated by Twain in his Satan stories, the first two being the strong, shrewd, motherly servant and the desirable, "feminine" young woman. The maid, like Marget, is young and sexual, and like Katrina she belongs to the servant class and is independent. But she is not committed to her employers' interests, the male authority she serves. The combination of her social status and her repudiation of loyalty to her "masters" determines in large part how the male self/selves respond to her, and the result is a comedy of suppression and conflict. Kahn has declared, in revealingly conventional language, that "Mary G. [the name August gives the cat] is one of Mark Twain's most delightfully effective tributes to the fair sex" (168) and refers to the "evocations of feminine felinity—cathood or cattiness, so to speak" as "well managed" (167). Some of the scenes with Mary G. are indeed funny, but they are also permeated by a rather cruel, vengeful humor. The notion of turning a talkative maid into a cat is reminiscent of Twain's turning aristocratic ladies into sows in *A Connecticut Yankee*. But the aggressive suppression of the maid's freedom to speak as a human being does not express entirely the same contempt as does the similar episode in the earlier novel. Instead, Mary G. is treated with ambivalence, namely with a mixture of affection and contempt. The name August gives her, "Mary Florence Fortescue Baker G. Nightingale," is itself significant: it alludes to Mary Baker Eddy and to Florence Nightingale, two of the most influential women in public life in Twain's time. Baker G., as August calls the maid for short, is a lively mixture of cat and woman. She seems designed to illustrate Mark Twain's aphorism that if one were to crossbreed a human being and a cat, it would improve the human being but deteriorate the cat. Some of Twain's vitriolic contempt for Mary Baker Eddy spills over into his treatment of Mary G., confirming Joyce Warren's diagnosis that for Twain Mary Baker Eddy "is the ultimate example of the woman who did not fit the image 'of selfless womanhood' " (185).[13] August's anger at Mary G.'s illogicality links his aggression toward her with animosity toward Mary Baker Eddy in an expression that virtually threatens rape: "Baker G., if you open your mouth again I'll jam the boot-jack down it! You're as random and irrelevant and incoherent and mentally impenetrable as the afflicted Founder herself" (394). Even the phrase "mentally impenetrable" suggests a symbolic sexual undercurrent. But, as in *A Connecticut Yankee,* male rage and desire for dominance are not granted unequivocal preeminence.

For one thing, Baker G. is a vigorous, appealing character. She may be illogical by August's lights, but she has a logic and a method of her own which are by no means portrayed unsympathetically in spite of August's rather humorless animosity. Furthermore, Twain grants Baker G. a vernacular freedom and liveliness of speech that characterize her as authentic and self-validating, just as Huck Finn is. Number 44 and August treat her with typical male condescension. August says, "It's a good night's work we've done for that poor little blonde-haired lady's-maid [by turning her into a cat], and I believe, as you do, that quite soon she is going to be contented and happy," to which Number 44 responds, "As soon as she has kittens . . . and it won't be long" (362), stereotypically locating female satisfaction in maternity. Some of the satire in the episodes involving the cat's squeamishness about going to bed in a room with a man present seems to be directed at the prurient sense of propriety of Twain's time and perhaps also at the power women were able to exercise through that sense of propriety.

But Baker G. has independence, a stubborn will, curiosity, a sense of delight, and a love of life that confound and contradict both August's and Number 44's demeaning estimates of her and the quasi-nihilistic pessimism so many critics have found in the concluding chapter. She is interesting and alive in ways that escape the males' attempts to define and control her.

Specifically, Baker G. is a storyteller and a determined interpreter of stories, those of others as well as her own. She is not merely filtered through August's consciousness; she speaks for herself. Thus she connects with the dilemma of the search for an adequate, unequivocal narrator that we have seen in the ambivalences of Theodor and August. Number 44 ultimately collapses and consummates that desire for absolute unity by proclaiming that everything in the universe is a projection of the male narrator's mind. Chapter thirty-four, the final chapter that A. B. Paine attached to his version of "The Chronicle of Young Satan," is at least in one respect the appropriate conclusion to "No. 44, The Mysterious Stranger," because Number 44's callous boyish desire to dominate everything and everyone through game-playing (much like Tom Sawyer) is more consonant with the solipsistic self-dissolution at the end than with Satan's mixture of cynicism about humanity in general and compassion for individuals in "The Chronicle of Young Satan." The conclusion of "No. 44" represents one solution to the dilemma of contradictory voices; but the presence—and most of all, the speech—of Mary G. represents another.

Though Twain wrestles implicitly with his fear of female sexual initiative, and the old pathetic images of female suffering remain powerful for him, women are also representative of humanity to his imagination in these late stories, and male authority is questioned if not rejected. With a few exceptions, notably the humble and generous schoolmaster in "Schoolhouse Hill," Mark Twain exposes male authority as hollow and self-serving in character after character: Father Adolf; Heinrich Stein; the magician; and less obviously, August and Number 44 himself. But most of all, some of his female characters contradict and subvert the reigning ideology of gender. Katrina and Baker G., like Ursula and Aunt Rachel, are neither symbols of despair nor merely male symbols of womanhood in Victorian America. In spite of the male narrators' efforts to contain and control them, they escape from the margins: they have voices of their own.

Conclusion
~∿≈∿~

Samuel Clemens's fascination with the exoticism and romance of foreign cultures drove him to explore and reexplore European culture throughout his career. Inevitably, his image of woman as Other expressed itself through these explorations. For Twain, the Otherness of European culture represented an opportune opening, a convenient staging ground for exploring his fears, desires, and ideas about women, men, and their relations with each other. The imaginative representation of difference in this process enacts a triple inscription: a representation of broader cultural difference through the narrower but deeper representation of gender difference, which also serves to define and locate Samuel Clemens the writer and Mark Twain, his persona.

Compared to other American authors who dealt imaginatively with Europe, Mark Twain seems in some respects to have remained on the surface. He did not create complex European characters, rooted in the traditions of their time and place, as Nathaniel Hawthorne attempted to do in *The Marble Faun*, for example. He did not explore the subtle effects of snobbery, European mores, and entrenched values through sophisticated psychological portraits of Americans abroad, as did Henry James. Furthermore, his portrayals of European women in particular often seem simplistic, as if they were caricatures. Though he came to believe in "training" as the most powerful determinant of character, and though he immersed himself in the reading of history and often worked hard to get the details right, he was not able to imagine with sympathetic thoroughness how another historical era viewed the world differently. His imagination was moral, social, and ultimately cultural, in the sense of exploring and shaping the outlines of a society's identity. In a way, Twain would have made a good sociologist: he was fascinated by patterns and theories of social behavior. At the same time, and in contrast to much sociological work, he was not striving for detached objectivity in his observations. Instead, he so fully invested himself in his storytelling that it is often difficult to separate the narrator from the observations he narrated. He had a reporter's eye and instinct and an inherently dramatic—and dramatizing—imagination.

This dramatizing imagination, in its very American representations of Europe and its very male representations of womanhood, has mutually interdependent psychological and cultural dimensions. That Clemens's autobiographical writings have a strong fictionalizing element, while his fiction frequently aspires toward historical authenticity, suggests the complex intertwining of shaping imagination and inherited perceptions.

In his European travel writing and fiction, Twain creates a kind of psychological drama of American male identity. By translating elements of European culture into American terms, he transforms his material into expressions of a new cultural identity based upon American concepts of gender instead of European ideas of class. The metaphors of class become figures of gender in Twain's American appropriation of them. He elevates "manhood," by which he means male pride and self-reliance, to a central position in his vision of a "new deal" democratic society. But his ideal of "manhood" is plagued by fears, yearnings, and inadequacies: the need for fathers who have social authority yet are kind and nurturing; the desire for male power and control accompanied by doubts about democracy, the means necessary to maintain dominance, and fears of impermanence and sexual submission; and, finally, a perplexed sense of the incompleteness and inner contradiction of the male self in the face of female modes of being, which are alternately idealized and demonized. European metaphors serve to exaggerate and intensify but also to disguise and conceal the psychological complexities beneath the social themes. The gender ideology Mark Twain articulates is not seamless; it reveals flaws and gaps, and it is a system of ideas in evolution. The flaws and gaps are perhaps the most promising for us as contemporary readers, because they show openings towards critique and revision.

When we read Mark Twain's characters and narratives simultaneously in a cultural and a psychological light, we can see in his work the dynamics of culture in general and gender in particular more clearly and accurately. What emerges is not merely a picture of evolution but a record of fluid and complicated explorations, discoveries, setbacks, and advances. The broad effect of this process of cultural interpretation is the transformation of European symbols (or symbols derived from European sources) into American myths and narratives. In this transformation, Twain's conflict with tradition comes to serve the expression of American gender ideology. Since class differences and fixed social boundaries based on birth were supposedly nonexistent or vanishing in America, other forms of difference come to the fore. Race, sex, and wealth are the new focal lines of difference in America, but the language to express these differences is not entirely new or invented. Instead, it is often improvised out of the cultural vocabulary of the Old World. In the process, the old terms change meaning. As interesting as any of the unequivocally expressed values, metaphors, or images that emerge are the contradictions and uncertainties— the projections of American anxieties onto European settings, for example, or of male fears onto female characters.

Samuel Clemens approached certain issues and questions that were deeply rooted in his American experience through the appropriation of European symbols, particularly his masculine experience in the appropriation of female characters and images. The same is undoubtedly true of me as scholar and critic—male, European-American, late twentieth-century—

in relation to Samuel Clemens/Mark Twain. I have been appro-
priating Clemens's texts and reading them in my own fashion,
in some cases against the grain of what appear to have been
Clemens's intentions. This appropriation is a necessary part of
my interpretation of the puns, gaps, and half-obscured desires
I see in his works. My purpose in interpreting these works as
I have done is to envision for myself what nineteenth-century
American culture looked like as expressed in the writings of
Samuel Clemens/Mark Twain. In particular, I have sought to
understand how Twain envisioned gender: masculinity, femininity, and the social and emotional currents between men
and women. I regard Twain's works as, in Derrida's terms,
tattooed columns with multiple inscriptions.[1] The inscriptions
have various meanings, depending on the angle from which
they are regarded. These meanings comment upon each other.
Twain's dramas of gender conflict and definition are representations of cultural differences and disagreements between Europe
and America, in which the symbols of class difference come to
represent American gender ideology. His political themes are
supported by psychological undercurrents, and the relative importance of each in relation to the other depends in part on
our judgments as readers. My theoretical assumption is that
the texts examined in this book can and do tell us things that
Samuel Clemens would not necessarily claim as his intention.

My own bent is to see symbolic autobiography in many of
Twain's historical fictions. I believe that Clemens did not escape
his cultural biases in writing about the European past, that, on
the contrary, his historical writing became a screen upon which
he projected his American vision. To vary the metaphor a bit,
his selective interpretation of European culture was a process
of finding and shaping images for his American consciousness.
This inevitably was a process of shifts, redefinitions, rotations,
translations, even deconstructions and reconstructions, if you
will. My own stake in examining this process and defining it
in my own terms is to begin to locate myself in relation to

American culture by locating Mark Twain in his envisioning of America through Europe. While I know well that there are many ways of knowing a culture, and each way individually has its limitations, I find Twain's involvement in and expression of American culture a particularly rich source of understanding. His writing makes certain claims that challenge us as readers to come to terms with them.

We tend, for example, to make moral demands of Mark Twain—or at least to ask moral questions about his writings—in part because the moral preoccupations of his works are so clear and so pervasive, in part because Twain sets himself up as a social prophet and critic. Certain features of Mark Twain, the public personality created by Samuel Clemens, promote this image: his witty and enduring gnomic sayings, for instance, or the cynicism and moralism of some of his best-known tales. Sam Clemens's extraordinary ability to cast himself as both an eccentric individual and a national spokesman, a character embodying the spirit of an age and of a culture, gives the figure of Mark Twain a kind of rare authority and fascination that permeates American popular culture as well as American literature. His authority and permanence rest ultimately not upon his moral stands or pronouncements, however, nor upon his humor or his forceful imagination, though all of these contribute, but on a dynamic tension between his writing and the issues that preoccupy our culture. The issue of whether *Huck Finn* is a racist novel continues to stir controversy, and we ask whether Mark Twain was free of racism in a way that we would not ask about William Faulkner or Flannery O'Connor, because Twain's novel is taken as a statement about race in American society, not just as a novel about the antebellum South. We regard Mark Twain not merely as a teller of tales but as a cultural authority. His anticapitalist and anti-imperialist radicalism in his last decades is often misunderstood as mere personal disillusionment and undervalued as political thought, but "The War Prayer" (*Mark Twain on the Damned Human Race* 64–67) and "The Man

That Corrupted Hadleyburg" (*Selected Shorter Writings* 245–89) remain topical, because he was able to expose the contradictions of pious patriotism, greed, and respectability in fictional forms that seem to be apolitical and ahistorical.[2] These facets of Twain's reception suggest a tendency in American culture to desire escape from historical conditioning, or rather from its recognition. That is why it is all the more important to examine these issues and the issues of culture and gender in Twain's writing in a manner that recognizes a symbiotic relationship among audience, text, author, and society.

One source of Mark Twain's disillusionment with "the damned human race" in his later years was his excessive investment in the solitary individual and the concomitant failure of community in its various forms. His vision of the isolated individual, not just the rebellious outsider but also the self-alienated "pillar of society," sprang from a Calvinist conviction of the loneliness of the soul in a fallen world but also from the consequences of an American individualism, bred in part by the frontier and by transcendentalist thought and intensified by the advance of technology. His faith in individualism, and the despair that grew from it, helped restrict his ability to see the subtle interfusion of social conditioning, historical circumstance, and individual character in a positive light. The forces of "training"—social conditioning—and character were difficult if not impossible for him to hold in balance, in part because he continually sought a vantage point outside of history from which to judge human personality and behavior. Either innate character won out, as happens temporarily in Huck or Joan, or social forces defeated the individual, as in the case of Hank Morgan or in the martyrdom of Joan. This conflict gives a tragic cast to his plots, even many of his comic ones.

The Americanness of this tragic or tragicomic vision lies in its taking to an extreme a pervasive conception of the individual as somehow separate from and in fundamental conflict with his society.[3] The obverse of this conception is a tremen-

Samuel Clemens at the House of Parliament, London, 1907.
Courtesy, The Mark Twain Project, The Bancroft Library.

dous pressure toward conformity, visible in the portrayals of social groups as faceless, often violent mobs ruled by passion, greed, and cowardice. Twain's tendency to see groups as driven by simple motives and his inability or unwillingness to differentiate social groups into personalities who are simultaneously social and individually complex (in the way in which, for example, George Eliot's or Tolstoy's characters are) participates in a form of simplification of reality that excludes certain kinds of recognitions but lends added force and emphasis to others. This process of simplification is inseparable from Twain's American cultural presuppositions about differences between Europe and America and from his envisioning of gender.

So, for example, his assumption that the representative American in *The Innocents Abroad* is the young, male American through whose eyes other Americans will see Europe afresh depends on a stance that sees the drama of cultural encounter as one of combat, conquest, and appropriation. Occasionally new cultural experience reveals a process of immersion and education, but this experience is largely an adversarial one. Mark Twain the narrator is always implicitly the subject and the center of the narrative. Hank Morgan, a different kind of tourist abroad, extends the male narrator's self-preoccupation in the face of an alien culture by first subjugating the whole of it and then perishing when he loses control over it. The increasing separation and alienation of Mark Twain's male narrators from particular times, places, and cultures is graphically illustrated in the multiple versions of Satan in the late "Mysterious Stranger" manuscripts that variously place the boyish central character in Austria or along the Mississippi and, through time travel and dream, isolate him in the boundless boundaries of the mind. The recurrent tendency in Twain's writings toward fable and allegory speaks of this male American individualism.

The ways in which female characters in Twain's European writings are defined in relation to male characters or to the male narrator further confirm the ontological individualism of

Samuel Clemens. The reduction of female characters to projections of male fears and desires goes far beyond stereotype into what Nina Baym has called "melodramas of beset manhood" and male myths.[4] These melodramas and myths can be read to a point in Lacanian fashion. So, for example, women and female presences are associated in Twain's writing with the preverbal experiential realm, as in the anthropomorphizing of Westminster Abbey into a giant primordial womb. The exclusion of the actual "Mother" Fairbanks from the *Quaker City* excursion in *The Innocents Abroad* and the narrator's implicit deferences to and rebellions against her opinions and her editorial influence make her the maternal presence through absence. Women in Twain's novels are frequently associated with death, not necessarily as murderers but often as maternal figures standing at the gates of death: Sandy in *A Connecticut Yankee;* Joan of Arc; and the many martyred virtuous women, usually mothers with children.

Fathers are associated with the realm of logos, the word —naming and defining. The logocentrism of fathers is related to their ability to define social identity, through naming, through command and judgment, through paternity, and through rhetoric. The matter of Europe supplied Twain with a vocabulary to express the desire for a loving father but also to explore his deep ambivalence about powerful, judgmental father figures. The rhetoric of command is also a rhetoric of oppression. The ambivalence about sexuality that recurs in his works is related to the son's ambivalence about the father, because the power and dominance of the "masculine" father is linked in Clemens's imagination to brutality and murderousness. The fear of the murderous father is often transferred symbolically in Twain's writing into fear of a murderous female figure. At one extreme, sanctioned domestic female sexuality is sublimated, in Twain's representation, into the image of the domestic angel, the woman whose purity guarantees selflessness and redemption. At the other extreme, public female sexuality is made demonic in Twain's imagination, for female power represents the triple threat of the Other in control: not merely the mystery of the unknown, but the projection of fears about the self and the possibility of ultimate loss of identity.

These psychological concerns are often expressed through the symbols and metaphors of European culture and history in Twain's works. The distancing maneuvers of metaphor and alienation inherent in the representation of American themes through European images clarify and intensify the distinctly American outlines of these themes. They reveal, finally, love of innocent youthfulness poised on the verge of sexual aware-ness but fearful of the consequences of experience; attraction to power and technological progress but increasing awareness of the destructive sides of these forces; and the desire for male autonomy drawn on to proud self-display, aided by female self-effacement but haunted by female self-assertion. One of the qualities that make Clemens's envisioning of these themes most American is that he saw them in terms of perpetual social conflict and change. In *The Innocents Abroad* he defines his iden-tity through the continual assumption of new and challenging roles: skeptic, cynic, gull, tormenter of tourist guides, victim of seductive European females, reverent admirer of culture, bad boy on the lam. Most of *The Prince and the Pauper* is taken up with the struggle to regain lost identities, and Edward's rule, when he is restored to the throne, is brief and precarious in its positive influence. In *A Connecticut Yankee* Hank's rule also ends soon, and violently; history is a series of upheavals. By the time of the "Mysterious Stranger" manuscripts, much of this sense of upheaval, though by no means all, has been internalized and is expressed through the inner conflicts and uncertainties about identity experienced by the main characters.

What Twain does not imagine is as revealing as what he does. Looking back in history, he does not imagine a stable, traditional society in a process of gradual evolution. Tradition for him signifies stasis, oppression, even the annihilation of the self. He does not imagine characters, in the European setting at least, who are the product of subtle interactions between social influences and personal character. And, though he does at times portray male characters who embody combinations of gentleness and courage, nurture and authority, he does not represent female characters who unite these qualities; perhaps most significantly of all, he does not envisage power-sharing and partnership between men and women or between the generations.

The vigor and appeal of the autonomous male selves that Twain imagined lie in their profoundly American search for self-realization. This energetic search is adventuresome and authentic. But the real or assumed innocence and autonomy of the Twainian male hero also conceal or reveal, depending on one's perspective, certain limitations, deceptions, and blindnesses of American culture. The limitations are hinted at or suggested by the contradictions, fears, and outcomes of the heroes' quests: the inability to imagine the relationship between the generations as a complex dialectic instead of either conformity or rebellion; the deceptive projection of male fears onto female characters; and the inability to resolve social and psychological tensions except through death, catastrophe, or solipsism. The choice between martyrdom and tyranny, so often played out in Twain's European writings, is a painful and ultimately unfruitful one.

Mark Twain's constructions of European culture and of gender were a significant part of his construction of American culture. In particular, his interpretations of gender in the European context are a rich source of revelation of the culturally conditioned ideas, anxieties, and desires of a powerfully imaginative nineteenth-century American male author. The limitations and distortions of the interpretations offered to us by his works and by the records we have of his life are properly subjects less for judgment than for our own efforts at comprehension, for we—and by "we" I name first of all myself—have our own cultural distortions and limitations. For me, finally, the effort to comprehend and critique Twain's cultural constructs is part of an effort to find and claim my own place and voice in the present dialogues about and between cultures and the sexes.

Notes

PREFACE

1. Hirsch goes on to say that "significance always implies a relationship, and one constant, unchanging pole of that relationship is what the text means" (8).

2. Carter seeks a "purist" reading of Twain, attempting to avoid the subjectivity of "significance."

3. Hirsch states that "symptomatic, involuntary meaning is part of a text's significance, just as its value or its present relevance is" (57).

INTRODUCTION

1. See de Beauvoir, Friedan, Daly, Chodorow, Lacan, Kristeva, Gilligan, and Miller.

2. I refer to Mark Twain as the public persona versus Samuel Clemens the private man, in the tradition of Justin Kaplan, though obviously there are ways in which the two are inseparable. This is acknowledged superbly in Kaplan's *Mr. Clemens and Mark Twain: A Biography.* For a popular account of Mark Twain's sojourns abroad, see Scott, *Mark Twain at Large.*

3. See especially Gillman. See also Rogin. For discussions of similar issues in the interpretation of other authors' lives and works, see Newberry, Steele, and Irwin.

4. See the chapter "Götterdämmerung" in Hill, *Mark Twain: God's Fool,* 91–177, concerning Clemens's strained relationships with his daughters, particularly Clara.

5. See the chapter "Impact of the American Male" in Fowler.

6. Compare Gribben's comments about Mark Twain's reactions to *Sense and Sensibility:* "Evidently his critical standards required the creation of at least one character with whom he might identify and sympathize; finding none, he lost patience with Austen's novel of manners" (1:34).

7. As Salomon drily noted concerning this remark, "Sexual promiscuity mingled with piety apparently was characteristic of an historical epoch that allegedly stretched from Constantine's toleration of Christianity to the French Revolution" (23). Twain's marginal comment is cited in Salomon 23.

8. *A Connecticut Yankee* reveals its author's fears of male *and* female savagery and sexuality, though the shapes of the fears are somewhat different for each sex. Hank is clearly both afraid of and attracted to the idea of male dominance through physical force. The male concern for female chastity is connected to anxieties about legitimacy, inheritance, and power. There is a link between Hank's entanglement in these concerns and the male search for fathers and for legitimacy in *The Prince and the Pauper.*

9. See Joyce W. Warren, Ballorain 143–70, and Zwarg 57–72.

10. "In the novel's first chapter de Conte exhibits the preconditions to comment on the conflicts of his society: he is a stranger to both parties with which he will eventually have to deal: the power structure of France . . . and the villagers of Domremy, none of whom share his rank or his literacy" ("Narrative Structure in Mark Twain's *Joan of Arc*" 49).

CHAPTER ONE
The Innocents Abroad

1. *The Innocents Abroad* is generally accorded prominence in the development of a distinctively American body of writing. Cox claims, "To read the book in relation to American literature is to be struck by the departure it signals" (38). If, as is clearly the case, Twain assimilated and transformed the genteel literary form of the travel narrative as thoroughly as he did the same for the tall tale of Southwestern humor, it is fitting to examine *The Innocents Abroad* with careful attention to authorial psychology and the construction of the self in the text. This is all the more the case since we have preserved for us two versions of the process of self-creation that is at the core of *The Innocents Abroad,* namely the *Alta California* letters that feature Twain and his unruly companion Mr. Brown in McKeithan, *Traveling with the Innocents Abroad,* and the volume that Twain fashioned from the earlier, cruder letters. The creation of a playful, contra-

dictory self against the backdrop of Europe and the Holy Lands reveals at times surprising glimpses of self-revelatory experience. See Steinbrink, "How Mark Twain Survived Sam Clemens' Reformation" 299–315.

2. Both *Innocents Abroad* and *Little Women* are related to John Bunyan's *Pilgrim's Progress* (Twain's ironically through his subtitle, *The New Pilgrims' Progress,* which points to his attacks on the "Pilgrims"; Alcott's more directly through her use of the moral pilgrimage of her characters). Comparisons between Alcott's and Twain's views of Europe are a subject worthy of another chapter. For example, Alcott wrote that in Rome, she and her sister May "indulge in our naughty criticism like a pair of Goths and Vandals as we are" (Saxton 341). One of Mark Twain's phrases for American tourists was the "Vandals Abroad."

3. The curious tendency of critics to interpret *The Innocents Abroad* as a work of fiction is rooted in the apparent mimetic freedom of the book. While some critics have approached Twain's travel narrative as a document of social history, others have taken an approach closer to that of Fiedler, who refers to the book as a novel. See Steinbrink, "Why the Innocents Went Abroad: Mark Twain and American Tourism in the Late Nineteenth Century" 278–86 and Fiedler, "An American Abroad" 77–91. Michelson, for example, has found in it the *paidia* ("play of the free and improvisatory sort" 386) of creative play (385–98), while Regan has examined the fundamental division between the "reprobate elect" and the pious pilgrims as an example of a pervasive theme of American literature ("The Reprobate Elect in *The Innocents Abroad*" 240–57). Henry Nash Smith places the book in the context of Mark Twain's development as a writer, pointing out his choice of diction, stance, and materials in relation to Twain's emergence as a master of the vernacular (*Mark Twain: The Development of a Writer*). Study of Twain's parody and imitation of literary models in the genre of travel literature has also occupied an important place in the constellation of commentary on the work.

4. See Fischer's claim that Twain may have been indebted to Sterne for the glove episode (17–21).

5. Twain was slyly addressing an issue that would soon erupt on a national scale with the movement that resulted in the founding of the Woman's Christian Temperance Union in 1873. His ironic insistence

on the respectability of Europeans' use of alcohol can be interpreted in several ways. It may be a rejoinder to those women who condemned drinking as an exclusive male pursuit. Or it may be—somewhat idealistically—seen as sincere praise of European domesticity and moderation. The mischievous intention is difficult to ignore, however. It is relevant to keep in mind that "temperance was clearly the cause women [in America] found most attractive in the late nineteenth century. The WCTU was the largest organization of women that had existed until that time" (Bordin 4). Clearly temperance was an issue in which the terms of conflict were drawn along gender lines.

6. The issue of nudity in art is one that concerns American authors from Hawthorne through Henry James. Hawthorne characteristically dealt with it in *The Marble Faun* by spiritualizing the physical. While Mark Twain denounced Titian's "Venus" in *A Tramp Abroad* (1880), Arthur L. Scott is mistaken when he sees in that denunciation merely a stronger "Victorianism" (*Mark Twain at Large* 100) than in *The Innocents Abroad*. Twain criticizes the censorship that permits explicit depiction in painting but castigates frankness in writing.

7. The allusion is to Robert Burns's poem "Tam o' Shanter. A Tale" (1790) (2:557–64). It is significant that Twain omits mention of the warlocks who dance with the witches in "*Alloway's* auld haunted kirk." In Burns's poetic tale, a witch named Nannie, in a "cutty sark" that is "in longitude tho' sorely scanty" (562) pursues and nearly captures the hapless Tam who has observed the wild dance.

8. Compare Marcus's comments (104–9, 140–46) about similar financial transactions in *My Secret Life,* a series of Victorian sexual memoirs. In both cases, the narrator exposes the assumptions of class and male privilege and their implications for sexual and financial relations. Marcus notes, "We can see how to use Marx's terms—the objectification of human relations which the circumstances of social class help to bring about combines with those sexual and pornographic fantasies in which all other human beings are only objects whose sole function is to satisfy our needs" (133). While Twain's anecdote is by no means pornographic, the linking of sex and economics in the encounter is inescapable.

9. According to Albert Bigelow Paine, Olivia Langdon helped Samuel Clemens make further revisions in *The Innocents Abroad* (Mc-Keithan xi). Clemens revised the *Alta California* letters between Janu-

ary and July 1868; "in the meantime he had met and fallen in love with Olivia Langdon" (McKeithan xi). The two first met on 27 December 1867 (See *Mark Twain's Letters*, II:145). *The Innocents Abroad* was published in July 1869.

10. "Dong" was a vulgar slang term for penis. Whether Twain intended the double entendre or not is impossible to determine. For a discussion of sexual intimations in *A Tramp Abroad,* see Bridgman, *Traveling in Mark Twain* 98–100. *A Tramp Abroad* attempts in several ways to recapture the attitude that made *Innocents Abroad* attractive to a broad American audience, but it strains and seldom succeeds.

11. Howells recalled that at their first meeting, Clemens "stamped his gratitude into my memory with a story wonderfully allegorizing the situation, which the mock modesty of print forbids my repeating here" (3). Scholars have since contested the accuracy of this memory, because the joke is to be found (again, I believe) in Mark Twain's note to Howells responding to Howells's review of *Roughing It*. Twain's fondness for a joke frequently led him to repeat it; I am among those who trust Howells's recollection and believe that Mark Twain could not resist resurrecting the joke that Howells could not forget.

12. Ganzel argues (272–75) that Mark Twain's expressions of gratitude to Mary Mason Fairbanks were largely "gentle flattery" and that her influence on his writing has been exaggerated and misconstrued. However, several critics have taken issue with this view, which was at least in part a reaction against Brooks's claim that Twain was dominated by the women close to him. See Leon T. Dickinson's review of Ganzel in *Modern Philology* 117–19. In any case, the fact remains that Twain excluded from his published work any mention of the woman whom he honored effusively in his private correspondence.

13. For a complex analysis of the patterns referred to here, see Chodorow.

CHAPTER TWO
Mark Twain and Female Power

I gratefully acknowledge the suggestions of U. C. Knoepflmacher, Fritz Oehlschlaeger, and Minrose Gwin, to whom I am indebted for ideas incorporated into this chapter.

1. *A Tramp Abroad* is a case in point: the narrator pretends to be a footloose young man without attachments, when in fact Samuel Clemens was traveling about Europe with Olivia, their daughters, and servants. Much formulaic writing results from his attempt to recapitulate the earlier success of *The Innocents Abroad*.

2. See Baetzhold 50. Baetzhold points out that *1601* and a list of "Middle Age phrases for a historical story" (*The Prince and the Pauper*) were results of Twain's researches in 1876.

3. "A Memorable Midnight Experience" is one of the few literary efforts from Mark Twain's 1873 trip to England that he decided to publish. The fact that he chose to place it first in the collection *Mark Twain's Sketches, Number One,* before the obvious drawing card of "The Notorious Jumping Frog of Calaveras County," may indicate something of his opinion of its attractiveness and/or quality. The cover shows a spectacled frog, sitting beneath a toadstool, smoking and perusing a copy of *Mark Twain's Sketches.* Three of the sketches are identified as being from "the Author's Unpublished English Notes." There has been remarkably little serious critical commentary on either *1601* or "A Memorable Midnight Experience." Salomon's analysis of the latter is one of the best.

4. Baetzhold notes that "the 'Memorable Midnight Experience' in Westminster Abbey mixes occasional humor with general reverence to show Mark Twain obviously captivated by the beauty, tradition, and literary associations of the Abbey" (20).

5. It is interesting to note that Twain anticipates her death as he projects the life of the Abbey into the future in this sketch.

6. It would be a mistake to identify the cupbearer to the queen too closely with Mark Twain himself, as A. H. Winkler did in an illustration for Franklin J. Meine's edition of *1601,* in which a venerable, white-haired Sam Clemens himself appears as cupbearer. This is additionally ironic because the Sam Clemens who wrote *1601* was a young man of thirty-one, not the white-maned sage of his later years. Clemens is no more "the Pepys of that day" (Meine's caption calls the figure in the illustration "the Mark Twain of that day") than he is Huckleberry Finn or the stranger who narrates "The Notorious Jumping Frog of Calaveras County" or the Sieur Louis de Conte who tells the story of Joan of Arc. The ironic distance achieved by having a narrator who is partly the butt of the joke should caution us to beware

of assuming that we can easily determine Twain's opinions about the events he describes.

7. The terms in which Brooks condemns this outlet of the "ferment" of Twain's blood echo the condemnations of masturbation in nineteenth-century moral tracts (227).

8. Shaxpur's soliloquy contains remote allusions to Prospero's speech from *The Tempest* (IV, i) which Baetzhold identifies as Twain's favorite among Shakespearean speeches. Baetzhold points out that the speech "came vividly to his attention during his tour of Westminster Abbey with Kingsley in 1873, for among the most vivid memories of his 'Memorable Midnight Experience' was the statue of Shakespeare with his finger pointing to a carved scroll bearing five of the lines" (231–32).

CHAPTER THREE
Fathers and Sons in *The Prince and the Pauper*

1. See chapter four in Baetzhold's invaluable *Mark Twain and John Bull*, 48–67.

2. See Towers's view that "*The Prince and the Pauper* remains a children's book . . . because it encourages the nostalgic denial of history, a dream which, even less than Tom's, admits of the sad truths of reality" (202). Coard sees its significance mainly in its relation to *Huck Finn* (437–46). For even more negative assessments, see Wiggins 72–77 and Baldanza.

3. Stone (120–23) discusses family relationships in *The Prince and the Pauper* in the context of the genteel historical romance tradition. Regan, in *Unpromising Heroes: Mark Twain and his Characters* 150–52, interprets the double father figures of all three heroes as a fable motif connecting the heroes to each other.

4. In that tradition his book in turn inspired a classic of genteel juvenile literature: Frances Hodgson Burnett's *Little Lord Fauntleroy* (or at least Mark Twain claimed so). See *Mark Twain's Letters* 2: 814. Stone, notes that Twain had copies of *The Prince and the Pauper* sent, "most appropriately, to Lilly Warner, Frances Hodgson Burnett, and (through Moncure D. Conway) to Charlotte M. Yonge" (111 note 26). See also Dickinson, "The Sources of *The Prince and the Pauper*" 103–6.

5. Blues sees parallels between *The Adventures of Tom Sawyer* and

The Prince and the Pauper in that in both books Mark Twain "arranges his boy-hero's triumph over the community without causing his alienation from it" (10). Blair provides the most extensive discussion of the parallels between *Adventures of Huckleberry Finn* and *The Prince and the Pauper* (chapter thirteen).

6. As Feuchtwanger points out, "the fable about the prince who trades clothing with the beggar boy is, of course, very old" (101).

7. Dodge 354. Many nineteenth-century women writers portrayed harsh facts of life in a realistic style (e.g., Rebecca Harding Davis's *Life in the Ironmills*, 1862).

8. Twain altered the physical attributes of his young prince from "pale" to "comely" in the revision of a draft of chapter three. Representing Edward as the sickly, sheltered boy of history would not have lent itself to the exchange of identities and to the credibility of Edward's survival of his later hardships, as Clemens must have recognized when he inserted "tanned and brown with sturdy out-door sports and exercises" in the revision of his manuscript (see "Alterations in the Manuscript," *The Prince and the Pauper* 462). The change makes Edward and Tom more alike, as did Twain's emphasis on Tom's studiousness in chapter one: "By and by Tom's reading and dreaming about princely life wrought such a strong effect upon him that he began to *act* the prince, unconsciously. His speech and manners became curiously ceremonious and courtly" (54).

9. Of course orphans are also frequently to be found in British literature, from Eliot and Hardy to Dickens, from *Tom Jones* to *Jude the Obscure*. While the orphan has always been an emblem for a disenfranchised identity, I would argue that orphanhood has a special resonance in the American consciousness because it so frequently corresponds to the cultural and familial experience of Americans.

10. Clemens to A. V. S. Anthony, 9 March 1881, Mark Twain Papers, Berkeley. Quoted in "Introduction," Salamo 11. By an odd coincidence, Henry VIII died just two months more than 300 years before John Clemens, Samuel Clemens's father, died. Henry VIII died 28 January 1547; John Clemens 25 March 1847.

11. There is some evidence that this question offended Edwin Pond Parker and Joseph Twichell, friends whom Mark Twain had asked to read the manuscript, and that they requested that he strike it out, but he refused. See "Introduction," Salamo 7.

12. See Susan Harris's argument concerning Laura Hawkins in "Mark Twain's Bad Women" (157–62).

CHAPTER FOUR
Sexual Politics in *A Connecticut Yankee*

1. I agree with Tom Towers, who argues, "Whether critics have made Twain the enemy of the middle ages or of the nineteenth century, whether they have understood Hank as the frustrated prophet of a higher civilization or as the egomaniacal destroyer of primitive innocence, most, I think, have concentrated too exclusively on the explicitly social and institutional materials of the book" ("Mark Twain's *Connecticut Yankee:* The Trouble in Camelot" 190).

2. The centrality of *A Connecticut Yankee* to this era of American history is well articulated by Gerald Allen, who has stated: "*A Connecticut Yankee* deserves the first attention of anyone interested in late nineteenth-century literature because of what it says about that literature. In its ragged but surprisingly complete way, the book expresses more consistently and engagingly than any other work the seminal attitude of American writers between 1870 and 1910" (437).

3. Hank Morgan is not Samuel Clemens or Mark Twain. The same caution about misreading fictional characters as self-portraits applies as in the case of Miles Hendon or of the cupbearer in *1601*. Yet Hank Morgan displays unmistakably autobiographical traits. Louis J. Budd states that Hank Morgan "comes the closest of his major characters to being Twain himself" (*Mark Twain: Social Philosopher* 112). Everett Carter comments, "From the opening of the tale to its end, Mark Twain treated his alter-ego sympathetically, weighting plot and characterization heavily in his favor" (423). David Ketterer presents an opposite view when he argues, "Hank, a narrowly pragmatic exhibitionist and something of a boor, is incredibly obtuse, unaware, and quite incapable of questioning his own attitudes. These limitations manifest themselves in a hackneyed and exaggerated speech which admirably serves the purposes of comedy and burlesque at the expense both of Arthur's England and of himself as a representative nineteenth-century 'Yankee' " (1104).

4. Cox acknowledges the complex autobiographical interrelations between Mark Twain and Hank Morgan and locates the ultimate

downfall of Morgan in Twain's confusion of slang for vernacular: whereas "in vernacular humor, the *form* indulgently inverts conventional values" (*Huck Finn*) . . . "in slang the *character* must attack them" (*Connecticut Yankee* 220). Gerald Allen states that "the voice of the Yankee is, throughout the book, that of the American Man epitomized" (437). Alfred Habegger explains that "male humor served to distance the laugher from an ideal gender role that had become impractical" (11).

5. It is worth noting that Twain had treated dueling admiringly in *A Tramp Abroad,* where he described Heidelberg fraternity life without irony.

6. In his notebooks, Clemens had jotted down the following: "In a constitutional—figurehead—monarchy, a royal family of Chimpanzees would answer every purpose, be <idolized> worshiped as abjectly by the nation, & be cheaper. I propose that, & send for a chimpanzee couple. Arthur has no children. Carry out the project. It is not <generally> known & is now revealed for the first time that this was the origin of the present royalty. It arrives at Wm through the tanner's daughter" (3: 419). The "I" of the note is presumably Hank. The notion of royal descent from chimpanzees "through the tanner's daughter" reveals a kind of reverse snobbery implicit in much of the attack on royalty in *A Connecticut Yankee.*

7. Compare this with the description of a group of ruling women in Charlotte Perkins Gilman's feminist utopia *Herland,* written early in the twentieth century: "They were not young. They were not old. I looked from face to face, calm, grave, wise, wholly unafraid, evidently assured and determined" (19). "We . . . were brought before a majestic gray-haired woman" (23). "They had the evenest tempers, the most perfect patience and good nature—one of the things most impressive about them all was the absence of irritability" (46). Twain's idealization of "purity" and "fine manliness" in the Arthurian knights is directly related to his idealization of Joan of Arc, the miraculous girl/woman who exposes the failure of ordinary men to be "true" men without female inspiration and who has the power of making men act courageously.

8. Fetterley further writes, "Armed with the gospels of democracy, Hank sets out to do battle with the evils of monarchy, aristocracy, and church, with all the tyranny of privilege that lives on egotism, self-

righteousness, hypocrisy, and aggression. But in the process of hating privilege and attacking its various forms, Hank takes on each of the qualities that it embodies" ("Yankee Showman and Reformer" 678).

9. Fetterley argues, "The source of Hank's self-betrayal lies essentially in . . . his aggression. It is no accident that Hank enters the world of King Arthur through a brawl; he is a violent man. Throughout the book Hank is filled with indignation, anger, outrage. He is himself much of the time a seething volcano just barely under control, always on the verge of exploding. This may explain why the imagery of explosion dominates the novel and why Hank is fascinated at once with the idea of a volcano and the thought of controlling it" ("Yankee Showman and Reformer" 672).

10. A decade later Clemens wrote, "If the master<s> of a kingdom is so important that God will not entrust his appointment to men but appoints him himself, it then follows that the master OF that master is a still more important officer, & so this one must *especially* be divinely appointed. Therefore one is logically compelled to say Nell Gwynne by the grace of God Monarch of Great Britain &c. Now name the other grace-of-God monarchs of European history" (*Mark Twain's Notebooks and Journals* 3:425).

11. Early on, Hank acknowledges his kinship with other powers behind the throne in English history when he says, "I could note the upspringing of *adventurers like myself* in the shelter of its long array of thrones: De Montforts, Gavestons, Mortimers, Villierses; the war-making, sceptre-wielding drabs" (109; italics mine). These "sceptre-wielding drabs" he had referred to in the original manuscript as "the revered mothers of English nobility" (Baetzhold 117).

12. Joyce Warren states that "the proper Twain female is an abstraction, a distant image of gentility—sweet, innocent, gentle, modest, selfless, preferably pretty, dependent, and a staunch preserver of society" (152). Sandy has some of these qualities, but it would be a mistake to see her as entirely distant, gentle, modest, or dependent, as my argument will show.

13. Jung notes, "Now a good fairy, now a witch; now a saint, now a whore . . . the anima also has occult connections with 'mysteries,' " and the "anima also has affinities with animals, which symbolize her characteristics. Thus she can appear as a snake or a tiger or a bird" (Hillman 56).

14. In this connection it is interesting to note that Alfred Habegger believes that "the essence of the tyrannical wife was her rigid and unquestioning self-righteousness" (155).

15. Fetterley writes, "Perhaps a more accurate way of looking at these passages" (jokes which reveal aggression) "is to see them as attempts on Hank's part to control his aggression. . . . This burlesque is an elaborate mockery of his indignation and as such is a form of control over it. By treating as a joke situations which have previously made him burn with anger, Hank manages, at least momentarily, to see the absurdity of his indignation and to divert its damaging and dangerous emotion into a kind of laughter" ("Yankee Showman and Reformer" 675). Here it is pertinent to cite Alfred Habegger's belief that "American humor has been the literature (and cinema) of bad boys defying a civilization seen as feminine" (119).

16. Edmund Reiss suggests that "Hank's surprise at Morgan le Fay's beauty is a means of indicating the ambiguity of good and evil but 'what appalls the Yankee in the character of Morgan le Fay are the same insensitivities Twain objects to in the Yankee's character' " (Ketterer 1110).

17. Rodney Rogers notes that "from Taine he borrowed primarily factual information, while his debt to Lecky was much more one of bias and perspective" (436). Gerald Allen accurately states that "the Church, which has no single representative, is the real culprit. Its religious character is almost irrelevant; only its vast temporal and psychological powers are to be feared" (441).

18. Hank's statement resembles Huck's disclaimer preceding his report of Colonel Sherburn's address to the mob, and the priest's oration resembles the Colonel's in that it represents an indictment of a governing social order; the mob itself, "men and women, boys and girls, who trotted along beside or after the cart containing the condemned woman and her baby, hooting, shouting profane and ribald remarks, singing snatches of foul song, skipping, dancing—a very holiday of hellions, a sickening sight" (401) also resembles the mob that pursues the Colonel. However, where in *Huck Finn* the rightness of the Colonel's actions is at the very least debatable, in this scene in *Connecticut Yankee* the innocence of the victim is complete and programmatic.

19. See Joyce Warren's discussion, 156–67. An interesting side-

light is the significance of Hank's putting his feet on the table, as depicted by Dan Beard in the illustration subtitled "Solid Comfort" (307). Alfred Habegger has stated, "Putting one's legs on the table was not merely a conspicuous way of taking one's ease. It was also a crude act of defiance" (123). An interesting contrast to Hank's near-confession that he is not a gentleman is to be found in his description of Earl Grip: "The owner of the voice bore all the marks of a gentleman: picturesque and costly raiment, the aspect of command, a hard countenance, with complexion and features marred by dissipation" (389). This portrait displays no traces of the childlike naïveté Hank ascribes to the Arthurian aristocracy, and its negative touches suggest an ambivalence in Twain about the kind of masculine character Earl Grip represents.

20. David Ketterer points to the aggression Hank expresses toward Sandy: "Meanwhile, in his despair at turning Sandy, his traveling companion, into a pragmatic nineteenth-century American woman, Hank can conceive the transformation only by blowing her up: 'It may be that this girl had a fact in her somewhere, but I don't believe you could have . . . got it with the earlier forms of blasting, even; it was a case for dynamite'" (1105). Also, note that Hank thinks of his industrial might as a smoldering volcano and calls his newspaper *Weekly Hosannah and Literary Volcano*—images that suggest suppressed sexuality. Similarly, the one *invention* of Hank's is the "gun-purse" that dispenses money—also sexually suggestive. The imagery that Ketterer interprets as apocalyptic seems sexual to me: "I was turning on my light one-candle-power at a time, and meant to continue doing so" and Hank's statement that he was as "snug as a candle in a candle-mould."

21. The editors of the California edition note that the *Century* replaced this sentence with the less suggestive "I stood with my finger on the button, so to speak, ready to press it and flood the midnight world. . . ." They point out that "the *Century* was especially sensitive about allowing anything off-color in its pages" and that "Mark Twain too had a horror of sexual innuendo in his writing and no doubt welcomed the change" (636). The imagery of the machine is revealing enough, whether the sexual double entendre is included or not. Fetterley argues: "Surely much of the satisfaction of this image [of Hank at the center of a great machine] lies in the disproportion be-

tween the effort he must expend—the merest impulse of a finger—and the result he can achieve; much of its delight resides in the ease with which he can produce vast changes in the world. This ease is the index of his control and the mark of his superiority. It is a most revealing image. . . . From the start, *A Connecticut Yankee* offered Mark Twain the opportunity for indulging in a fantasy of omnipotence" ("Yankee Showman and Reformer" 667). Alfred Habegger writes that Henry James, in *The Portrait of a Lady,* explored the heroine's "tragic doom." "And the most important agent in her doom was to be a displaced American with a secret and very American fantasy of absolute rule over others—a dream of kingship" (67). It is Hank's dream also, of course.

CHAPTER FIVE
Escape from Sexuality

1. Zwarg, Ballorain 143–70, and Joyce W. Warren provide three of the most important feminist readings of *Joan of Arc*. Warren contrasts Joan with Mary Baker Eddy, whom Mark Twain vilified: "What most incensed Mark Twain about Eddy was that she sought money and power *for herself.* The drive that governed his own life and that he admired in other men, he abhorred in women. The difference between Joan and Mary Baker Eddy is that Joan, although she acts independently, remains pure and modest and never acts for herself" (185). Various critics have made the comparison between Clemens's treatment of Joan and of Mary Baker Eddy. See Wilson, who connects Mark Twain's treatment of Mary Baker Eddy and of Joan of Arc and discusses the religious dimension of Twain's thought.

2. See Jones and Diel.

3. See in particular Susan K. Harris's discussion in chapter one of *Mark Twain's Escape from Time* 17–28.

4. "Every developmental stage . . . is an evolutionary truce. It sets terms on the fundamental issue as to how differentiated the organism is from its life-surround and how embedded. It would be as true to say that every evolutionary truce . . . is a temporary solution to the lifelong tension between the yearnings for inclusion and distinctness" (108). Kegan's term applies primarily to the psychology of ethical development; I am, however, using it here in more of a social-ethical

sense. Since the truce emerges in de Conte's psyche, however, it is also a psychological state. Twain's writings are a good illustration of Kegan's thesis that basic themes and conflicts of our lives recur, in altered form, in a kind of ascending spiral as we develop throughout our lives.

5. The anecdote Clemens recounted on that occasion played on the difference between the name and the substance of a man. In essence, Clemens had "translated" the image and prestige of three of the patriarchs of American literature into a frontier setting.

6. Mark Twain in a letter to Mary Mason Fairbanks, 18 January 1893, in Dixon Wecter, *Mark Twain to Mrs. Fairbanks* 269.

CHAPTER SIX
Culture, Desire, and Gender in the
"Mysterious Stranger" Manuscripts

1. David R. Sewell notes, in connection with the return to an Austrian setting, that "the print shop and its location function as symbols" (147). He argues that "like Poe's House of Usher, the castle represents a physical shell inhabited by a rational soul, a Self residing at the center of a labyrinth" (148). Walter Grünzweig makes the persuasive argument that Twain's essay "Stirring Times in Austria," describing the turmoil in the Viennese *Reichsrat,* is a commentary on democracy in general, not just on Austrian politics. As Grünzweig points out, "Austrian politics assumes a metaphorical quality by which Twain expresses his scepticism toward democratic institutions in general" (8). These observations confirm my thesis about the direction of Clemens's use of European material generally toward the end of the nineteenth and into the twentieth century. Grünzweig points to the similarities between Twain's account of the actual historical events in Vienna and the turbulent town meeting in "The Man That Corrupted Hadleyburg," a story which he wrote a significant part of in Vienna in June 1898 (8).

2. The fascination of this theme continues to be powerful. For example, the comedy of an angel discovering romance and sexuality and choosing to become human is also the premise of Wim Wenders's film *Himmel über Berlin* (*Wings of Desire*) 1987.

3. William M. Gibson, "Introduction," *Mark Twain's Mysterious*

Stranger Manuscripts 13. Katrina is undoubtedly based on "Rachel" Cord—actually Mary Ann Cord, the Quarry Farm servant whose story Twain told in "A True Story, Repeated Word for Word as I Heard It." Sherwood Cummings has discussed the parallels in "The Commanding Presence of Rachel Cord," a paper presented at the Modern Language Association conference, Chicago, 28 December 1990.

4. William R. Macnaughton thinks that "the writer's treatment of the black cook, Aunt Rachel, does threaten to become sentimental," but he finds that the threat disappears when the narrator remarks, "Her tongue was hung in the middle and was easier to start than to stop" (108).

5. Sholom Kahn notes the resemblance of Herr Stein's behavior toward Number 44 to Jervis Langdon's acceptance of Sam Clemens's courtship of his daughter, in effect holding Clemens blameless for his illegitimate appetites before marriage (152).

6. I am inclined to interpret Clemens's interest in school-age girls as the opposite of sexual fascination. The members of the Angel Fish Club reminded him of his daughters when they were preadolescents, and their vigor and innocence took him back in memory to the period in his life before he became actively aware of adult sexuality. Therefore I tend to see his cultivation of friendships with young girls as an effort to escape sexuality, not a disguise for perverse leanings, as some have surmised in the case of Charles Dodgson/Lewis Carroll, another fascinating Victorian double personality. See the excellent introduction by John Cooley to his *Mark Twain's Aquarium: The Samuel Clemens Angelfish Correspondence, 1905–1910* xvii–xxvi.

7. If I had to apply a Freudian scheme, I would argue that August is the ego (repressed by society), Martin is the superego, and Emil is the id or libido. But the Freudian apparatus is inadequate to explain Twain's characters.

8. The issue of seduction and Clemens's obsession with it is perceptively addressed in Gillman 112–35.

9. See Gillman's discussion of Mark Twain's polemics on the question of the "age of consent," 103–6.

10. See Gillman's commentary about the incident, 116–17.

11. One wonders whether Twain might not have been still venting his spleen in retaliation for having been tricked—the pregnancy his maid claimed in 1877 turned out later never to have existed. Turning

this fictional maid into a cat may have been a form of revenge through fantasy.

12. As Kahn points out, "though we have been given to understand that Lisbet loves only Martin, in all of this chapter (after the initial explanation) the name of Martin is not mentioned—it is as if the Waking-Self and Dream-Self have combined, or fused, in opposition to the Duplicate" (155).

13. Joyce Warren points out, as already cited, that "what most incensed Mark Twain about Eddy was that she sought money and power *for herself*. The drive that governed his own life and that he admired in other men, he abhorred in women" (185).

CONCLUSION

1. For a discussion of the concept of texts as tattooed columns, see Leavey 34.

2. For a view of Twain's political ideas in his later years that sees them in a Third World context and does not dismiss his bitterness and rage as despair, see Barrett 40–55.

3. Richard Poirier has observed that Mark Twain shared with Huck Finn "some larger distrust of social structures themselves" (148) and that Twain and other American writers do not possess Jane Austen's "positive vision of social experience" (153).

4. See Nina Baym's influential essay "Melodramas of Beset Manhood: How Theories of American Fiction Exclude Women Authors" 123–39.

Bibliography

PRIMARY WORKS

TWAIN, MARK. *Adventures of Huckleberry Finn.* Ed. Walter Blair and Victor Fischer. Berkeley: U of California P, 1985.

———. *The Adventures of Tom Sawyer. Tom Sawyer Abroad. Tom Sawyer Detective.* Ed. John C. Gerber, Paul Baender, and Terry Firkins. Berkeley: U of California P, 1980.

———. *The Autobiography of Mark Twain.* Ed. Charles Neider. New York: Washington Square P, 1961.

———. *A Connecticut Yankee in King Arthur's Court.* Ed. Bernard L. Stein. Berkeley: U of California P, 1979.

———. *Following the Equator; A Journey Around the World.* Hartford, Conn.: American Publishing, 1897.

———. *Huck Finn and Tom Sawyer Among the Indians and Other Unfinished Stories.* Ed. Dahlia Armon and Walter Blair. Berkeley: U of California P, 1989.

———. *The Innocents Abroad, or The New Pilgrims' Progress.* Hartford, Conn.: American Publishing, 1869.

———. *Letters from the Earth.* Ed. Bernard DeVoto. New York: Harper & Row, 1962.

———. *Mark Twain–Howells Letters.* 2 vols. Ed. Henry Nash Smith and William M. Gibson. Cambridge: Harvard UP, 1960.

———. *Mark Twain on the Damned Human Race.* Ed. Janet Smith. New York: Hill and Wang, 1962.

———. *Mark Twain to Mrs. Fairbanks.* Ed. Dixon Wecter. San Marino, Calif.: Huntington Library Publications, 1949.

———. *Mark Twain's {Date, 1601.} Conversation As it was by the Social Fireside in the Time of the Tudors.* Ed. Franklin J. Meine. New York: Lyle Stuart, 1938.

———. *Mark Twain's Fables of Man.* Ed. John S. Tuckey. Berkeley: U of California P, 1972.

————. *Mark Twain's Letters*. 2 vols. Ed. Albert Bigelow Paine. New York: Harper & Brothers, 1917.

————. *Mark Twain's Letters, Volume 1: 1853–1866*. Ed. Edgar Marquess Branch, Michael B. Frank, and Kenneth M. Sanderson. Berkeley: U of California P, 1988.

————. *Mark Twain's Letters, Volume 2: 1867–1868*. Ed. Harriet Elinor Smith and Richard Bucci. Berkeley: U of California P, 1990.

————. *Mark Twain's Mysterious Stranger Manuscripts*. Ed. William M. Gibson. Berkeley: U of California P, 1969.

————. *Mark Twain's Notebooks & Journals*. Vol. 1. Ed. Frederick Anderson, Michael B. Frank, and Kenneth M. Sanderson. Berkeley: U of California P, 1975.

————. *Mark Twain's Notebooks & Journals*. Vol. 2. Ed. Frederick Anderson, Lin Salamo, and Bernard L. Stein. Berkeley: U of California P, 1975.

————. *Mark Twain's Notebooks & Journals*. Vol. 3. Ed. Robert Pack Browning, Michael B. Frank, and Lin Salamo. Berkeley: U of California P, 1979.

————. *Mark Twain's Sketches. Number One*. New York: American News Company, 1874.

————. *Personal Recollections of Joan of Arc*. 2 vols. New York: Harper & Brothers, 1896. Vols. 21–22, *The Writings of Mark Twain*.

————. *The Prince and the Pauper*. Ed. Victor Fischer and Lin Salamo. Berkeley: U of California P, 1979.

————. *Pudd'nhead Wilson and Those Extraordinary Twins*. Ed. Sidney E. Berger. New York: Norton, 1980.

————. *Selected Shorter Writings of Mark Twain*. Ed. Walter Blair. Boston: Houghton Mifflin, 1962.

————. *A Tramp Abroad*. Ed. Charles Neider. New York: Harper & Row, 1977.

————. *Traveling with the Innocents Abroad*. Ed. D. M. McKeithan. Norman: U of Oklahoma P, 1958.

SELECTED SECONDARY WORKS

ALCOTT, LOUISA MAY. *Little Women*. Boston: Little, Brown, 1915.

ALLEN, GERALD. "Mark Twain's Yankee." *New England Quarterly* 39 (Dec. 1966): 435–46.

ANDREWS, KENNETH. *Nook Farm: Mark Twain's Hartford Circle.* Seattle: U of Washington P, 1950.

BAETZHOLD, HOWARD G. *Mark Twain and John Bull.* Bloomington: Indiana UP, 1970.

BALDANZA, FRANK. *Mark Twain: An Introduction and Interpretation.* New York: Barnes and Noble, 1961.

BALLORAIN, ROLANDE. "Mark Twain's Capers: A Chameleon in King Carnival's Court." *American Novelists Revisited: Essays in Feminist Criticism.* Ed. Fritz Fleischmann. Boston: G. K. Hall, 1982. 143–70.

BANTA, MARTHA. "They Shall Have Faces, Minds, and (One Day) Flesh: Women in Late Nineteenth-Century and Early Twentieth-Century American Literature." *What Manner of Woman: Essays on English and American Life and Literature.* Ed. Marlene Springer. New York: New York UP, 1977.

BEAUVOIR, SIMONE DE. *The Second Sex.* New York: Bantam, 1961.

BARRETT, CAROLYN M. "Mark Twain: Anticipator of Third-World Consciousness." *Philippine Journal of American Studies* 1.1 (1979): 40–55.

BAYM, NINA. "Melodramas of Beset Manhood: How Theories of American Fiction Exclude Women Authors." *American Quarterly* 33 (1981): 123–39.

———. "Portrayal of Women in American Literature 1790–1870." *What Manner of Woman: Essays on English and American Life and Literature.* Ed. Marlene Springer. New York: New York UP, 1977.

BEIDLER, PHILIP D. "Realistic Style and the Problem of Context in *The Innocents Abroad* and *Roughing It.*" *American Literature* 52 (1980): 33–49.

BERCOVITCH, SACVAN. "America as Canon and Context: Literary History in a Time of Dissensus." *American Literature* 58 (1986): 99–107.

BLAIR, WALTER. *Mark Twain and Huck Finn.* Berkeley: U of California P, 1960.

BLUES, THOMAS. *Mark Twain and the Community.* Lexington: U of Kentucky P, 1970.

BORDIN, RUTH. *Woman and Temperance: the Quest for Power and Liberty, 1873–1900.* Philadelphia: Temple UP, 1981.

BRADBURY, MALCOLM. "Mark Twain in the Gilded Age." *Critical Quarterly* 11 (1969): 65–73.

BRAY, ROBERT. "Mark Twain Biography: Entering a New Phase." *Midwest Quarterly* 15(1974): 286–301.

BRIDGMAN, RICHARD. *Traveling in Mark Twain.* Berkeley: U of California P, 1987.

BRODWIN, STANLEY. "Wandering Between Two Gods: Theological Realism in Mark Twain's *A Connecticut Yankee.*" *Studies in Literary Imagination* 16(1983): 57–82.

BROOKS, VAN WYCK. *The Ordeal of Mark Twain.* New York: Dutton, 1970.

BUDD, LOUIS J. *Mark Twain: Social Philosopher.* Bloomington: Indiana UP, 1962.

————. *Our Mark Twain: The Making of His Public Personality.* Philadelphia: U of Pennsylvania P, 1983.

BURNS, ROBERT. *The Poems and Songs of Robert Burns.* Vol. 2. Oxford: Clarendon, 1968.

CADY, EDWIN H. "Huckleberry Finn by Common Day." *The Light of Common Day: Realism in American Fiction.* Bloomington: Indiana UP, 1971.

CAMPBELL, JOSEPH. *The Hero with a Thousand Faces.* Princeton: Princeton UP, 1949.

CARTER, EVERETT. "The Meaning of *A Connecticut Yankee.*" *American Literature* 50(1978): 418–40.

CHAMBLISS, AMY. "The Friendship of Helen Keller and Mark Twain." *Georgia Review* 24 (1970): 305–10.

CHODOROW, NANCY. *The Reproduction of Mothering.* Berkeley: U of California P, 1978.

COARD, ROBERT J. "Huck Finn and Two Sixteenth Century Lads." *Midwest Quarterly* 23(1982): 437–46.

COOLEY, JOHN, ed. *Mark Twain's Aquarium: The Samuel Clemens Angelfish Correspondence, 1905–1910.* Athens: U of Georgia P, 1991.

COPLIN, KEITH. "John and Sam Clemens: A Father's Influence." *Mark Twain Journal* 15(1970): 1–6.

COX, JAMES M. *Mark Twain: the Fate of Humor.* Princeton: Princeton UP, 1966.

CUMMINGS, SHERWOOD. *Mark Twain and Science: Adventures of a Mind.* Baton Rouge: Louisiana State UP, 1988.

DALY, MARY. *Beyond God the Father.* Boston: Beacon, 1973.

DICKINSON, LEON T. "Mark Twain's Revisions in Writing *The Innocents Abroad.*" *American Literature* 19(1947): 139–57.

——— . Review of Dewey Ganzel, *Mark Twain Abroad*. *Modern Philology* 68 (1970): 117–19.

——— . "The Sources of *The Prince and the Pauper*." *Modern Language Notes* 64 (1949): 103–6.

DIEL, EMMANUEL. "Mark Twain's Failure: Sexual Women Characters." *San Jose Studies* 5 (1979): 46–59.

DODGE, MARY MAPES. "Children's Magazines." *Scribner's Monthly* 6 (July 1873): 354.

DOUGLAS, ANN. *The Feminization of American Culture*. New York: Knopf, 1977.

——— . "Art and Advertising in *A Connecticut Yankee*: The 'Robber Baron' Revisited." *Canadian Review of American Studies* 6 (1975): 182–95.

EARNEST, ERNEST. *The American Eve in Fact and Fiction, 1775–1914*. Urbana: U of Illinois P, 1974.

ELLIS, HELEN E. "Mark Twain: The Influence of Europe." *Mark Twain Journal* 14 (1968): 12–18.

EMERSON, EVERETT. *The Authentic Mark Twain: A Literary Biography of Samuel Clemens*. Philadelphia: U of Pennsylvania P, 1984.

FETTERLEY, JUDITH. "Disenchantment: Tom Sawyer in Huckleberry Finn." *PMLA* 87 (1972): 69–74.

——— . *The Resisting Reader: A Feminist Approach to American Fiction*. Bloomington: Indiana UP, 1978.

——— . "Yankee Showman and Reformer: The Character of Mark Twain's Hank Morgan." *Texas Studies in Literature and Language* 14 (1973): 667–79.

FEUCHTWANGER, LION. *The House of Desdemona, or, the Laurels and Limitations of Historical Fiction*. Detroit: Wayne State UP, 1963.

FIEDLER, LESLIE. "An American Abroad." *Partisan Review* 33 (1966): 77–91.

——— . *Love and Death in the American Novel*. New York: Criterion, 1960. Rev. ed. New York: Stein & Day, 1966.

FISCHER, JOHN IRWIN. "How to Tell a Story: Mark Twain's Gloves and the Moral Example of Mr. Lawrence Sterne." *Mark Twain Journal* 21 (1982): 17–21.

FOWLER, VIRGINIA C. *Henry James's American Girl: The Embroidery on the Canvas*. Madison: U of Wisconsin P, 1984.

FRIEDAN, BETTY. *The Feminine Mystique*. New York: Norton, 1963.

FULWEILER, HOWARD W. " 'Here a Captive Heart Busted': From

Victorian Sentimentality to Modern Sexuality." *Sexuality and Victorian Literature.* Ed. Don Richard Cox. Knoxville: U of Tennessee P, 1984. 234–50.

GANZEL, DEWEY. *Mark Twain Abroad: The Cruise of the Quaker City.* Chicago: U of Chicago P, 1968.

GARCIA, WILMA. *Mothers and Others: Myths of the Female in the Works of Melville, Twain, and Hemingway.* New York: Peter Lang, 1984.

GATES, HENRY LOUIS, JR. *Figures in Black: Words, Signs, and the 'Racial' Self.* New York: Oxford UP, 1987.

GEISMAR, MAXWELL. *Mark Twain: An American Prophet.* Boston: Houghton Mifflin, 1970.

GILLIGAN, CAROL. *In a Different Voice.* Cambridge: Harvard UP, 1982.

GILLMAN, SUSAN. *Dark Twins: Imposture and Identity in Mark Twain's America.* Chicago: U of Chicago P, 1989.

GILMAN, CHARLOTTE PERKINS. *Herland.* New York: Pantheon, 1979.

GOAD, MARY ELLEN. "The Image and the Woman in the Life of Mark Twain." *Emporia State Research Studies* 19 (1971): 5–70.

GREEN, GAYLE, AND COPPELIA KAHN. "Feminist Scholarship and the Social Construction of Woman." *Making a Difference: Feminist Literary Criticism.* Ed. Greene and Kahn. London: Methuen, 1985.

GRIBBEN, ALAN. *Mark Twain's Library: A Reconstruction.* 2 vols. Boston: G. K. Hall, 1980.

GRÜNZWEIG, WALTER. "Comanches in the Austrian Parliament: Austria as a Metaphor for Mark Twain's Disillusionment with Democracy." *Mark Twain Journal* 23.2 (Fall 1985): 3–9.

HABEGGER, ALFRED. *Gender, Fantasy, and Realism in American Literature.* New York: Columbia UP, 1982.

HANDLIN, OSCAR. *The Uprooted.* Boston: Little, Brown, 1951.

HANSEN, CHADWICK. "The Once and Future Boss: Mark Twain's Yankee." *Nineteenth Century Fiction* 28 (1973): 62–73.

HARNSBERGER, CAROLINE THOMAS. *Mark Twain: Family Man.* New York: Citadel, 1960.

HARRIS, SUSAN K. *Mark Twain's Escape from Time.* U of Missouri P, 1982.

———. "Mark Twain's Bad Women." *Studies in American Fiction* 13 (1985): 157–68.

————. "Narrative Structure in Mark Twain's *Joan of Arc.*" *Journal of Narrative Technique* 12 (1982): 48–56.

HILL, HAMLIN. *Mark Twain: God's Fool.* New York: Harper, 1973.

————. "Who Killed Mark Twain?" *American Literary Realism* 7 (1974): 119–24.

HILLMAN, JAMES. *Anima: An Anatomy of a Personified Notion.* Dallas: Spring Publications, 1985.

HIRSCH, E. D. *Validity in Interpretation.* New Haven: Yale UP, 1967.

HOWELLS, WILLIAM DEAN. *My Mark Twain.* New York: Harper, 1910.

IRIGARAY, LUCE. *Speculum of the Other Woman.* Trans. Gillian C. Gill. Ithaca, N.Y.: Cornell UP, 1985.

IRWIN, JOHN. *Doubling and Incest, Repetition and Revenge: A Speculative Reading of Faulkner.* Baltimore: Johns Hopkins UP, 1975.

JOHNSON, JAMES L. *Mark Twain and the Limits of Power: Emerson's God in Ruins.* Knoxville: U of Tennessee P, 1982.

JONES, ALEXANDER. "Mark Twain and Sexuality." *PMLA* 71 (Sept. 1956): 596–616.

JUNG, C. G. "The Integration of the Personality," *Aion.* Vol. 9, Part II. Princeton: Bollingen, 1959. Trans. Stanley Dell. New York: Farrar & Rinehart, 1939.

KAHN, SHOLOM. *Mark Twain's Mysterious Stranger: A Study of the Manuscript Texts.* Columbia: U of Missouri P, 1978.

KAPLAN, JUSTIN. *Mr. Clemens and Mark Twain: A Biography.* New York: Simon & Schuster, 1966.

KARPOWITZ, STEVEN. "Tom Sawyer and Mark Twain: Fictional Women and Real in the Play of Conscience with the Imagination." *Literature and Psychology* 23 (1973): 5–12.

KEGAN, ROBERT. *The Evolving Self: Problem and Process in Human Development.* Cambridge: Harvard UP, 1982.

KELLY, R. GORDON. *Mother Was a Lady.* Westport, Conn.: Greenwood, 1974.

KETTERER, DAVID. "Epoch-Eclipse and Apocalypse: Special 'Effects' in *A Connecticut Yankee.*" *PMLA* 88 (1973): 1104–14.

KHOURI, NADIA. "From Eden to the Dark Ages: Images of History in the Work of Mark Twain." *Canadian Review of American Studies* 11 (1980): 151–74.

KOLODNY, ANNETTE. "A Map for Rereading: Or, Gender and the

Interpretation of Literary Texts." *New Literary History* 11 (1980): 451–67.

KRAUTH, LELAND. "Mark Twain: At Home in the Gilded Age." *Georgia Review* 28 (1974): 105–13.

——— . "Mark Twain: The Victorian of Southwestern Humour." *American Literature* 54 (1982): 368–84.

KRISTEVA, JULIA. "Woman can never be defined." Trans. Marilyn A. August. Ed. Elaine Marks and Isabelle de Courtivron. *New French Feminisms*. Amherst: U of Massachusetts P, 1980.

LACAN, JACQUES. *Ecrits*. Paris: Editions du Seuil, 1966.

LAWSON, MARY. *A Lifetime with Mark Twain: The Memories of Katy Leary*. New York: Haskell House, 1972.

LEA, HENRY C. *History of the Inquisition of the Middle Ages*. 1887. Vol. 1. New York: Harbor, 1955. 3 vols.

LEAVEY, JOHN P., JR. *GLASsary*. Lincoln: U of Nebraska P, 1986.

LECKY, W. E. H. *History of European Morals*. 3rd ed. 2 vols. New York: Appleton, 1916.

LUKACS, GEORG. *The Theory of the Novel*. Boston: MIT P, 1971.

MACNAUGHTON, WILLIAM R. *Mark Twain's Last Years as a Writer*. Columbia: U of Missouri P, 1979.

MARCUS, STEVEN. *The Other Victorians*. New York: Basic Books, 1964.

MATTHEWS, BRANDER. *Essays on English*. New York: Scribner's, 1921.

MICHELSON, BRUCE. "Mark Twain the Tourist: the Form of *The Innocents Abroad*." *American Literature* 49 (1979): 385–98.

MILLER, NANCY K., ed. *The Poetics of Gender*. New York: Columbia UP, 1986.

MILLS, NICOLAUS C. "Social and Moral Vision in *Great Expectations* and *Huckleberry Finn*." *Journal of American Studies* 4 (1970): 61–72.

MONTEIRO, GEORGE. " 'Such as Mother Used to Make': An Addition to the Mark Twain Canon." *PBSA* 67 (1973): 450–52.

MOTT, BERTRAM, JR. "Twain's Joan: A Divine Anomaly." *Etudes Anglaises* 23 (1970): 246–55.

NEWBERRY, FREDERICK. *Hawthorne's Divided Loyalties: England and America in His Works*. Rutherford, N.J.: Fairleigh Dickinson UP, 1987.

OPDAHL, KEITH M. " 'You'll be Sorry When I'm Dead': Child-

Adult Relations in *Huck Finn.*" *Modern Fiction Studies* 25(1979–80): 613–24.

PARKER, GAIL. "Mary Baker Eddy and Sentimental Womanhood." *New England Quarterly* 43(1970): 3–18.

PELL, NANCY. "Resistance, Rebellion, and Marriage: The Economics of *Jane Eyre.*" *Nineteenth Century Fiction* 31 (1977): 397–420.

POIRIER, RICHARD. *A World Elsewhere: The Place of Style in American Literature.* New York: Oxford UP, 1966.

POUND, EZRA. "Hugh Selwyn Mauberly." *Personae.* 1926. New York: New Directions, 1971.

REGAN, ROBERT. "The Innocents Abroad: A Rough-hewn Monument." Ed. Robert G. Collmer and Jack W. Herring. *American Bypaths: Essays in Honor of E. Hudson Long.* Waco: Baylor UP, 1980. 187–211.

———. "The Reprobate Elect in *The Innocents Abroad.*" *American Literature* 54 (1982): 240–57.

———. *Unpromising Heroes: Mark Twain and His Characters.* Berkeley: U of California P, 1966.

REISS, EDMUND. "Afterword." Signet Edition of *A Connecticut Yankee.* New York: New American Library, 1963.

ROGERS, RODNEY O. "Twain, Taine, and Lecky: the Genesis of a Passage in *A Connecticut Yankee.*" *Modern Language Quarterly* 34 (1973): 436–47.

ROGIN, MICHAEL. "Francis Galton and Mark Twain." *Mark Twain's Pudd'nhead Wilson.* Ed. Susan Gillman and Forrest G. Robinson. Durham: Duke UP, 1990.

SALOMON, ROGER. *Twain and the Image of History.* New Haven: Yale UP, 1961.

SALSBURY, EDITH COLGATE, ed. *Susy and Mark Twain.* New York: Harper, 1965.

SAXTON, MARTHA. *Louisa May.* New York: Houghton Mifflin, 1977.

SCOTT, ARTHUR L., *Mark Twain at Large.* Chicago: Regnery, 1969.

———. "The *Century Magazine* edits *Huckleberry Finn.*" *American Literature* 27(1955–56): 356–62.

———. "*The Innocents Abroad* Revaluated." *Western Humanities Review* 7(1953): 215–17.

SEARLE, WILLIAM. *The Saint and the Skeptics: Joan of Arc in the Work of Mark Twain, Anatole France, and Bernard Shaw*. Detroit: Wayne State UP, 1976.

SEWELL, DAVID R. *Mark Twain's Languages: Discourse, Dialogue, and Linguistic Variety*. Berkeley: U of California P, 1987.

SHOWALTER, ELAINE. "Feminist Criticism in the Wilderness." *Writing and Sexual Difference*. Ed. Elizabeth Abel. Chicago: U of Chicago P, 1982.

SMITH, GARY CHARLES. "The Influence of Mark Twain's Journeys on His Work." *Mark Twain Journal* 20 (1980): 10–15.

SMITH, HENRY NASH. *Mark Twain's Fable of Progress: Political and Economic Ideas in A Connecticut Yankee*. New Brunswick, N.J.: Rutgers UP, 1964.

———. *Mark Twain: The Development of a Writer*. Cambridge: Harvard UP, 1962.

SMITH, J. HAROLD. *Women in Mark Twain's World*. New York: Carlton, 1973.

STAHL, JOHN DANIEL. "American Myth in European Disguise: Fathers and Sons in *The Prince and the Pauper*." *American Literature* 58 (1986): 203–16.

———. "Mark Twain and Female Power: Public and Private." *Studies in American Fiction* 16:1 (1988): 51–63.

STEELE, JEFFREY. *The Representation of the Self in the American Renaissance*. Chapel Hill: U of North Carolina P, 1987.

STEINBRINK, JEFFREY. *Getting to be Mark Twain*. Berkeley: U of California P, 1991.

———. "How Mark Twain Survived Sam Clemens' Reformation." *American Literature* 55 (1983): 299–315.

———. "Why the Innocents Went Abroad: Mark Twain and American Tourism in the Late Nineteenth Century." *American Literary Realism* 16 (1983): 278–86.

STONE, ALBERT E. JR. *The Innocent Eye: Childhood in Mark Twain's Imagination*. New Haven: Yale UP, 1961.

STRONG, LEAH A. *Joseph Hopkins Twichell: Mark Twain's Friend and Pastor*. Athens: U of Georgia P, 1966.

SYKES, MADELENE MCEVEN. "Mark Twain's Attitudes Toward Women as Revealed Through His Writings." *Missouri English Bulletin* 22 (1969): 1–9.

TOCQUEVILLE, ALEXIS DE. *Democracy in America*. New York: New American Library, 1956.

TOWERS, TOM H. "Mark Twain's *Connecticut Yankee:* The Trouble in Camelot." *Challenges in American Culture*. Ed. Ray B. Browne, Larry N. Landrum, and William K. Bottorff. Bowling Green, Ohio: Bowling Green U Popular P, 1970. 190–98.

——— . "*The Prince and the Pauper:* Mark Twain's Once and Future King." *Studies in American Fiction* 6 (1978): 194–202.

TROLLOPE, FRANCES. *Domestic Manners of the Americans*. New York: Vintage, 1960.

ULMER, GREGORY. "Sounding the Unconscious." In *GLASsary* by John P. Leavey, Jr. Lincoln: U of Nebraska P, 1986.

VARBLE, RACHEL M. *Jane Clemens: The Story of Mark Twain's Mother*. Garden City, N.Y.: Doubleday, 1964.

VOGELBACK, ARTHUR L. "*The Prince and the Pauper:* A Study in Critical Standards." *American Literature* 14 (1942): 48–54.

WALKER, FRANKLIN, AND EZRA G. DANE, eds. *Mark Twain's Travels with Mr. Brown*. New York: Russell & Russell, 1940.

WARREN, JOYCE W. *The American Narcissus: Individualism and Women in Nineteenth-Century American Fiction*. New Brunswick, N.J.: Rutgers UP, 1984.

WARREN, ROBERT PENN. "Mark Twain." *Southern Review* 8 (1972): 459–92.

WECTER, DIXON. *Samuel Clemens of Hannibal*. Boston: Houghton Mifflin, 1952.

——— , ed. *The Love Letters of Mark Twain*. New York: Harper, 1947.

WIGGINS, ROBERT A. *Mark Twain: Jackleg Novelist*. Seattle: U of Washington P, 1964.

WILSON, JAMES D. "In Quest of Redemptive Vision: Mark Twain's *Joan of Arc*." *Texas Studies in Literature and Language* 20 (1978): 181–98.

WOOLF, LEONARD. "Mark Twain." *Nation and Athenaeum* 36 (26 Sept. 1925): 765.

ZWARG, CHRISTINA. "Woman as Force in Twain's *Joan of Arc:* The Unwordable Fascination." *Criticism* 27 (Winter 1985): 57–72.

Index

Clemens, Samuel (*continued*)
2; "Schoolhouse Hill," 152, 154,
158, 160, 166, 175; "The Secret
History of Eddypus," 13; *1601:
Conversation As It was by the Social
Fireside in the Time of the Tudors,*
13, 15, 16, 48, 55–65, 66, 67,
83, 97, 109, 144, 194 (nn. 2, 3,
6), 197 (n. 3); "Stirring Times
in Austria," 203 (n. 1); *A Tramp
Abroad,* 192 (n. 6), 193 (n. 10),
194 (n. 1), 198 (n. 5); "A True
Story, Repeated Word for Word
as I Heard It," 158, 204 (n. 3);
"Villagers of 1840–3," 48; "Wap-
ping Alice" manuscripts, 167;
"The War Prayer," 181
Clemens, Susy, 59
Comanches, 91, 114. *See also* Native
American cultures
Comedy, 3, 32, 33, 34, 37, 38, 39,
41, 58, 71, 132, 154, 171, 173,
182, 197 (n. 3), 203 (n. 2); of
manners, 38. *See also* Bawdry;
Burlesque; Humor
Compassion, xiv, 21, 22, 67, 81,
96, 97, 98, 100, 101, 102, 110,
111, 117, 132, 135, 138, 144,
148, 149, 160, 163, 175
Competition, xiv, 80, 88, 96
Conformity, 20, 32, 93, 184, 187
Constantine, 190 (n. 7)
Conway, Moncure D., 195 (n. 4)
Cooper, James Fenimore, 3
Cord, Mary Ann, 204 (n. 3)
Cord, Rachel. *See* Cord, Mary Ann
Countess Granby. *See* Granby,
Countess
Courage, 18, 19, 24, 123, 126, 127,
128, 129, 144, 146–49, 158,
162, 187, 198 (n. 7)

Cranes, the, 158
Cruelty, 2, 14; female, 14, 15, 16,
66, 98, 104, 105, 106, 107; male,
16, 22, 24, 25, 67, 70, 72, 75,
77–79, 105, 106, 128, 135, 138,
147, 148, 150, 151, 160, 185, 190
(n. 8)
Culture: comparisons of, 1, 3, 5,
12, 30, 38, 178; differences in, 1,
8, 31, 152, 177, 179, 180, 184;
constructions of, 1–6, 8, 9, 12,
22, 26, 65, 72, 84, 85, 118, 178,
179, 184, 186, 187; European,
2, 9, 12, 53, 94; definitions of, 5;
popular, 5, 87, 88, 181; translation of, 7, 65, 141, 178, 180, 203
(n. 5); paradigm of, 32. *See also*
Europe, culture of

d'Arc, Jacques (father of Joan), 130
d'Arc, Joan. *See* Joan of Arc
Daughter(s), 83, 128, 189 (n. 4)
Dauphin (*Joan of Arc*), 123, 126,
127, 128, 145, 148, 149
Davis, Rebecca Harding, 196 (n. 7)
de Conte, Sieur Louis, 23, 24,
122, 123, 126, 128, 129, 134,
135, 138–50, 152, 153, 158, 190
(n. 10), 194 (n. 5), 203 (n. 4)
Democracy, 6, 8, 14, 20, 21, 56,
93, 96, 118, 120, 178, 198 (n. 8)
de Montfort, 199 (n. 11)
Derrida, Jacques, 180
de Tocqueville, Alexis, 3
Dickens, Charles, 196 (n. 9)
Dillberry, Lady Alice, 56, 62, 63
Dinadan, Sir, 105
Dionysus, 135
Doangivadam, 168
Dodge, Mary Mapes, 72